"This is a necessary and timely book. L̲   an open door into the heart and soul of women. Now more than ever the world needs to hear the stories and receive the wisdom of 'seasoned sistahs'— women whose lives speak of the power of the feminine."

Aeeshah Ababio-Clottey, author,
*Beyond Fear: Twelve Spiritual
Keys To Racial Healing*

Life's Spices makes me proud to be part of the bouquet of humanity that is "woman". The stories are a wonderful collection of colorful roses, painful thorns, and mighty oaks. Every woman can learn from, relate to, and feel the passion of these storytellers. Within their knowledge, wisdom, and character; lies lessons for us all.

Adrienne Traywick, Owner
MyAuntsPlants.com

"This book serves the most honorable purpose-encouraging women to *hold their space*. With sisterly support, women can achieve anything. The stories in this book allow other women to walk their paths with their heads held high knowing that their uniqueness serves them well!"

Sheri' McConnell,
President of the National Association
of Women Writers (www.NAWW.org)

This amazing volume of love, and of sharing takes everyday events in women's lives, exposing some of life's cruelties, but rather than just leaving you empty, they move forward, with details of how they grew from traumatic events and made positive changes with results they sometimes had never thought of. I am very glad we have this reference guide, and I will share it with my friends, and continue to refer to myself. These authors gave you a sense of familiarity as you walked along in their lives, endearing their experiences to us all.

Lynda Bell-Edner
Alcohol/Substance Counselor

In our growing and learning we seek wisdom. At times, we all live our lives feeling isolated in our trials, but this book delivers evidence of the fact that

WE are not alone. These stories from women who, through experience are now wiser in many aspects of life, are filled with inspiration. Through their joy and pain, they share their most cherished and challenging moments, that in reading, we all grow wiser.

Katherine "Kat" Smith
Writer,
www.awomanofwords.com

In our ever-changing, fast-paced culture, we need ways to bridge our cultural, and age differences, to strengthen our network for each other. Women need to be there to support other women through life's trials, sharing their goals, and plans, and to be there when life falls apart as it often does for all of us. The women in this book present strategies for this bonding, this sharing, ways that can be duplicated over and over again. I think we've found one of the treasures needed for survival.

Vera A. Franklin
Social Worker

The sisters who have allowed us into their lives through their stories are to be highly commended. I found several stories related here that could have been my own. The strategies they used to turn their lives around sometimes mirrored what I did, and they suggest others I hadn't thought of. They have once again shown us that we are all the same, and our experiences are to be shared, bringing us closer, and bonding us together as sisters.

Deborah Stephenson
Human Resources Specialist

In our ever-changing, fast-paced culture, we need ways to bridge our cultural, and age differences, to strengthen our network for each other. Women need to be there to support other women through life's trials, sharing their goals, and plans, and to be there when life falls apart as it often does for all of us. The women in this book present strategies for this bonding, this sharing, ways that can be duplicated over and over again. I think we've found one of the treasures needed for our survival.

Katherine Manning
Retired Seasoned Sistah

VICKI L. WARD

Vicki Ward has written poems essays, and short stories for most of her life, and directed her talents toward writing novels in her 40s. For several years she was a writer for *Roots Magazine*, where she interviewed R&B artists, wrote reviews for CDs by R&B, gospel, and jazz artists, and reviewed stage plays.

In 1999, as a member of a theater troupe she traveled to Russia, performing in the chorus of the Greek tragedy *Oedipus*. She published an article detailing her experiences as an African-American woman observing life and culture in the former Soviet Union. Vicki is the editor of *Life's Spices from Seasoned Sistahs: A Collection of Life Stories from Mature Women of Color*, an exciting and realistic anthology by women of color for all women of the world. The company she owns, Nubian Images Publishing, will publish this book.

She has presented a writers workshop at DeAnza College, and has presented writing and publishing workshops at the Empowering Women of Color Conference, University of California, Berkeley, and the Empowering Women of Color Conference, University of California, Santa Barbara. She is a member of two writers groups, the GG's and ZIKA Creative Arts and Literary Guild, Black Women Incorporated, The National Association Of Women Writers, NCBPMA, SPANN and is a founding member of the Black Publishers Association.

Life's Spices from Seasoned Sistahs

Life's Spices from Seasoned Sistahs

A Collection of Life Stories from Mature Women of Color

Vicki L. Ward

EDITOR

NUBIAN IMAGES PUBLISHING

Nubian Images Publishing
P.O. Box 1332
El Cerrito, Ca. 94530

ISBN 0-9755162-05

Library of Congress Cataloging-in-Publication Data
2005902338

The paper used in the publication of this book is acid free

Life's Spices from Seasoned Sistahs:
A Collection of Life Stories from Mature Women of Color

Epigraph

Despite the myth that women do not like each other, that we are in constant competition among ourselves for the attention of men, status, or the coveted window-view office, there are far too many examples to the contrary. I believe this fallacy is further defused, however, as women age and come into our sense, as we mellow, prepped and primed for that "seasoned time of our lives."

Perhaps the issues we encounter in our twenties and thirties—seeking career satisfaction, adjusting to marriage, bearing and raising children—are somewhat different from what women of forty-five years and older are facing. We are challenged by empty nests and aging parents, coping with widowhood, divorce, and health issues that tend to draw us into an innercircle of shared intimacies. Perhaps we have learned to sweat the small stuff less and to choose our battles more discriminately.

Women have always come together in the most trying of times, drawing strength from one another and celebrating our times of triumphs. Seasoned women know how to bring our younger sisters into the fold of the circle, bring the issues to the table and make things happen. Whether it is to plan an event for a non-profit agency, to better women's plight, to elect a public official, or to enjoy each other's company at a tea party, color barriers become nonexistent and class status becomes obsolete as we come to encourage and support each other.

Recently, at a church function where a group of women gathered to prepare food, we soon gravitated around the table in the dining area. I noticed that our circle soon expanded to span three generations. We laughed and talked, the younger women attentive and adding their flavor as they sat at the feet of their elders in the oral traditions of storytelling and call and response. The conversations centered on the "ways" of menfolk, the woes of raising children, wisdom and old wives' tales. To the table we also brought our joys and sorrows. I looked over at one of the elderly pillars of the church, a woman I have known since I was ten years old. When I was in high school, over thirty years ago, her only child, a son my age, was killed in a tragic car and train accident. She suffered the worst pain imaginable, yet by God's grace she is still here, faithful, steadfast on the job, dispensing advice to younger women and her peers, personifying a woman who has lived a well-seasoned life.

There is not always a physical table for us to gather around, but that is just an object. The table is symbolic of a shared place, a common ground to come together and bond. The mature, seasoned women can still pave the way for their daughters, nieces, and those they have adopted into the circle of unity and sisterhood, dispelling that myth, that old lie of discord among us.

Dera R. Williams

In the Company of Women: Coming to the Table

Foreword

We live in exciting times. Times our foresistahs could not have ever dreamt of. Our lifestyles are dramatically different. We are free to enjoy lives that include having husbands, attending school, raising children, and having careers. We can set goals and determine our own lifestyles, live where and with whom we choose. Women of past centuries would be envious of our progress and our liberation, but only to a point.

As modern women we may appear to be more in control of our lives, but in reality, we are less in control. While we should be enjoying the many accomplishments and improvements in our lives as we have become more fulfilled as women, we are not necessarily in the splendor we imagined. Today, as women we have gotten lost in the hectic pace of our busy lives, filled with working, mothering, being entrepreneurs, being wives, and more. The juggling of our lives leaves little time to form meaningful bonds with other women, and without the development of these important relationships women have become isolated from one another.

Life's Spices from Seasoned Sistahs: A Collection of Life Stories from Mature Women of Color is a wonderful step in the direction of sister bonding; an antidote for solitary thinking. This book is a heaping helping of love, of sharing and caring demonstrated by women who have experienced life in all its riches, heartaches, and rewards. These stories are sure to being comfort to women everywhere who will recognize some of their own experiences, and see how these women have triumphed!

There is joy knowing these vignettes will be shared again and again, and that the benefits that will be reaped by mature women, by women of all cultures, and by younger women is empowering. This simply continues the cycle of our lives. I invite you to curl up in a favorite chair, and get in touch with your sistahs, as they get in touch with you!

Enjoy.
Gail

Gail Perry-Mason
First Vice President of Investments
Oppenheimer & Co. Inc.
Co-Author of Girl, Make Your Money Grow

Acknowledgments

This book would not have been possible without the thoughts, prayers, and support of these people for whom I am truly thankful. My family including my mother, Mary Frances Brown, my son, Donnell L. Ward, Steve Manning, Drue Brown Jr. Darryl Brown, sisters Ellen Martin, Eleanor Taylor, Vera Franklin, and Arthelia "Cookie" Mosely. My skillful attorney, Ben Lyon, my writing group and editorial support, The GG's, Jean Sakahara, Felicia Ward, Danielle Unis, Michelle Mellon, and Dera Williams, editorial support members of the ZIKA Creative Arts & Literary Guild, Patricia E. Canterbury, Geri Spencer Hunter, Juanita Carr. I thank Gail Sukiyama for her support. I want to thank my pastor, Reverend Gordon A. Humphrey Jr., my typist, Joseph Magtibay, my praying 'sistah,' ReGina Bradford Tardy, Lauretta Bonds, Clarence Traywick, Dawn Griffey, Trina Crowell. Also, my Gibbs Girls, Deborah Stephenson, and Margaret Hurley. Thanks also to Vivian McCathrion, Anika Hamilton, Jim and Sharon Spain, Ondine Kilker, a talented typesetter, and Shannon Kokoska, a dynamic proofreader, and the members of The Black Publishers Association.

Contents

THEME VI.
Sistahs Survivin' and Workin' It Out

THEME VII.
Death Can Be an Awakening

THEME VIII.
The Spirit…Always Present

I CALL ME SEASONED

Found me a new life, yawl!
They call me sassy; some say I'm bold.
Like I turned that old seasonin' box
Upside down, and dusted me all over,
Cause, I call me Seasoned.
Fresh flakes fall, brown powder,
Mellow green bits, tiny yellow flakes
Firm brown leaves fell, too.
Yeah, I call me Seasoned.

Baked up from the scratch called life
Add fiery taste to stew, warm to the touch
May be pleasing to the eye!
My trials show sometimes.
My victories opened new worlds
Hurts left a deep trail,
Now closed, and mostly healed,
Yeah, I call me Seasoned!

Legs strong from the journey
Arms full from the love
New paths to walk, eyes staring ahead
Appetite strong for what's next;
Pride swelling to damn near bustin'
Thankful heart still beatin'
Yeah, I call me Seasoned!
Can you hear me callin'?
Saying bring it on, I'm ready.
For what? Some ask.
All of it, I call back, cause
I Call me Seasoned!

— *Vicki Ward*

Sistahs' Joys and Struggles with Family

Women have to summon up courage to
fulfill dormant dreams.
— Alice Walker

Of Gumbo and Avocados

PATRICIA E. CANTERBURY

I was born and reared in Sacramento with the threads of New Orleans in the form of gumbo, as well as sourdough bread, fresh salmon, avocados, and Japanese strawberries woven in California to make the fabric of a writer steeped in the joys of mysterious older women. I grew up with stories spoken by my great-grandmother Victoria Farrell, whom everyone called "Mama," and her daughters, my great-aunts, all of whom lived to be in their nineties. They used to sit in each other's homes, around the kitchen table, speaking of the times that something happened in the French Quarter, or saying to each other, "Remember the time that…?"

They'd reminisce about things that happened during World War I or the Indian Wars out west, or they would just make up things because the cousins and I were around. These stories were of magical times about magical ancestors that were captured by women who smoked unfiltered cigarettes, who spoke English with an accent, who spoke foreign languages, and who married dark men. I thought they were all so exotic.

My great-aunts all looked alike—they were short with coal-black hair, Asian eyes, firm handshakes, and iron wills. They were round, pale beings who wove tales while they cut okra, shelled peas, or peeled peaches for the cobbler. These women were the proud daughters and granddaughters of African merchants or traders, sisters to Buffalo Soldiers, and wives of doughboys.

I believe I was born a poet, then honed my writer's skills by listening to tales told over kitchen tables, in steam-filled rooms, and where the odor of wood-burning stoves filled the senses as much as the imagination.

I have a woman friend who writes letters to her dead grandmother, the one whom no one in her family will speak about. My friend is putting those discussions in a book. Me, I cannot imagine a family without a history.

Great-Aunt Mildred, the keeper of the family letters—some from great-great-grandfather Farrell, which he wrote while fleeing from Indians on the trail between Sacramento and San Francisco in 1839—died in October 2000. Though she was sightless in later years, Mildred's memory was clear, and she saw the events unfold before her as she remembered odors, a touch, or tastes that reminded her of New Orleans or Chicago.

To me, childhood was filled with half-remembered stories of my maternal grandmother, Celestine Farrell Ballon, nicknamed Padu, who died trying to give birth to her fifth child, when my mother was four. Yet, my great-aunts Ezell, Victoria Junior (nicknamed Coach), Myra, and Mildred kept grandmother's memory alive for all the hundred cousins. Great-aunts Bea and Ruth, who lived in Chicago, would visit New Orleans then Sacramento during their annual trips "home" to see Mama.

Perhaps the cell memory of common ancestors whispers stories of the 1920s, decades before I was born; then again, perhaps it's actual remembrances of bedtime stories when great-aunts shared secrets with each other. It was during those times, when all the great-aunts got together and talked, that the air was filled with stories of early twentieth-century city life, which waited like cotton candy to be stuck with black type and woven on blank pages for strangers to read.

Grandmother's Garden

JO ANN YOLANDA HERNÁNDEZ

In the South, the dirt is different than it is in most places. It not only feeds you; it nourishes you in ways folks not from the South don't understand. The dirt doesn't just hold bugs and rocks and roots; it can hold memories of the people who loved you.

The moist dirt packed tight in my fist, then crumbled easily back onto the ground. When I inhaled, filling with breath all the way to my gut, I could smell the mellow aromatic vapors of grass and freshly overturned earth. I walked barefoot. The soil would squeeze between my toes, and if I twisted my heels around, I could dig myself down an inch or two.

My grandmother's two daughters disapproved of her small garden that took up half her backyard. My mother and my aunt had worked hard to distance themselves from the poverty of having to raise food. They could afford to buy their fruits and vegetables at the big supermarket down the street.

However, it seemed to me the lettuce and tomatoes my mother brought home from the supermarket never quite matched the color, the texture, and especially the taste of the lettuce and tomatoes my grandmother grew in her garden.

I spent the summer of my fourteenth year helping my grandmother tend the garden.

Each morning, she would come out to the garden. The ground would sparkle with dew, as if the ground had been splashed with fairy dust overnight. She would take a fistful of soil, hold it up to the sky, mumble some words, then sprinkle the soil to the front of her, then to each side.

Once, when I sneaked up behind her to hear what she was praying, she threw the dirt over her shoulder, letting it fall on my head like miniature meteorites. I scrambled away as she chuckled all the way back to the house.

I was assigned the chore of setting up the hose each evening so in the morning, before breakfast, my grandmother would shower all the plants. I'd squat at the edge of the garden and count the rainbows that would appear as the early morning sun hit the fine spray from the hose.

Weeding was a morning chore I dreaded at first, especially when I pulled up a carrot by mistake. It looked puny, and the orange-yellow color was pale. My grandmother shook her head slowly and tossed it into the compost pile. For a long time, I stood there, staring at the carrot I had killed.

My grandmother may not have been able to say the words of educated people, but she knew the sounds that made you feel just as good. She tugged me away from the compost pile and knelt beside me in the bed of vegetables. She pointed at each plant and would talk to them. When one of the plants, heavy with vegetables, hung low like a bent-over old lady, she would smile and point for me to talk to it. Once I kissed a leaf, feeling the fuzzy protective layer, and she patted my shoulder. When she discovered a weed, her language would grow more rapid, scolding. She'd point to the offending plant, and with her hand on my shoulder, I'd pull the invading weed out. When we finally stood, behind us was a mountainous pile of weeds I had created. She smiled and nodded.

In the afternoon, because the Texas sun was too hot, we would sit under the cool shade of the pecan tree. The light, sneaking through the branches, created a jigsaw puzzle on the ground around us. She would have a bowl on her lap with something to keep her hands busy—peeling potatoes, shucking corn, or shelling pecans. I'd have my latest library adventure, and I'd read out loud to her. When I would look up, she would nod, following the tale I was reading.

Some afternoons she'd put her coarse, wide hand on the page. When I looked up, she'd put her finger to her lips. I'd silence my reading. She'd tap my ears and point to the tree.

I'd lean up against my grandmother's round and soft body and listen. At first, I'd hear my cousins in their front yard next door, squabbling and laughing. I heard the dogs barking from neighbors all around us; one woof would be answered by a howl from the dog in the next yard. Sometimes their barking would carry across the whole block like some ancient message service—a doggie Morse code. As I sagged against my grandmother, my ears would hear the concert closer to home.

The nosy birds scrambled for their daily bread. The woodpecker tapped with a diligence assigned saviors; he and his beak had many trees to reach. The LBJ's (Little Brown Jobs) flitted from one branch to another, always searching, always seeking, the morsel only one hop away. Their conversations would swing within seconds from doing their business to wild accusations. It was a privilege to be let in on their negotiations. Close by, the squirrels would investigate one branch then another, never satisfied, voicing criticism, complaining loudly, like a mother-in-law's visit.

When the wind would blow with river strength, each branch, fat with leaves, would rustle in annoyance. The branches would dip and sway like ballerinas, kicking high, bowing low.

With my head on her lap, I would look at the tree from underneath, the shades of green flashed dark and light with bunches of colors in between. The leaves strained, wrestling with their thin stem. I'd watch as with every puff of air the leaves would pull and twist to break away. Somehow, there close to my grandmother, the security of staying on the stem made more sense.

Yet, with each pat on my shoulder, with each stroke of my hair, my grandmother was shaking the hold of her stem on my life.

That summer I watched a seed I planted grow into the biggest tomato the whole world had ever seen, according to my grandmother. At Halloween, we had the largest pumpkin to carve and sit on our front porch because of me. My grandmother would touch my shoulder as softly as a leaf brushing up against my face, and I would feel the strength of century-old roots fill me up.

The next summer I was too busy with the idea of growing up, and I never spent another summer with my grandmother. Yet, now as an adult, when I take the moment I swear I don't have and stop in a shady spot, just for the relief, I can sense the peace swaying among the branches, and I imagine I can feel a strong wrinkled hand stroke my hair.

Enchiladas for Life

RENEE FAJARDO

My familia is from Colorado. It was rumored that we all came up from New Mexico about a hundred years ago and intermarried with the Europeans who had immigrated to the southern part of the state to work in the coal mines. The result was a colorful mixture of customs and cultures. Christmas usually was a celebration complete with tamales and Irish jigs. The most important ingredients, according to my paternal grandmother, were laughter and a love of life, and a good bowl of beans!

This new generation of mixed blood would one day be labeled as Chicanos. Growing up, my brothers and I knew only that we were extremely fortunate to have a larger-than-life family that worked hard and loved deeply. We did not realize we were, by most American standards, poor, or that the stigma of being half-breed Hispanics in an Anglo-run world had caused our ancestors much heartache.

Instead, we thrived in the glow of our family's commitment to making sure the next generation survived and bettered themselves. I was in my first year of college when I returned home for a family celebration. It was my grandparents' 50th wedding anniversary, and the whole Fajardo clan was busy with preparations for this auspicious occasion. While helping make what seemed like a million enchiladas, I stood at the kitchen counter and looked over at my great-aunt Lucia.

She was a beautiful woman, about 70 years old at the time. Being the youngest of eight siblings (born a decade after my grandmother), she usually took over the role of head cook for all family celebrations. Her reasoning was that she was younger and had more stamina. I suspect it was because she could roll enchiladas faster than any human being alive. It was a God-given gift.

I admired her greatly and was always amazed at her dedication to every detail of our fiestas. She baked all the bread from scratch, made tamales days ahead, cooked green chili to die for, and made enchilada sauce that to this day makes me weep with joy.

For the first time in my life, I really looked at her that day. She was always so busy with the comida or organizing the last details of preparing the food, she never had time to talk about herself. I smiled with puzzlement at her devout self-imposed exile to the kitchen stove. It occurred to me that my tia cooked for all of us and had been doing so for all of our lives. She had no grandchildren of her own. All three of her sons had died tragically, and her remaining daughter was childless.

I knew in my heart this must have been a terrible burden for her to bear, but I had never heard her complain. I never heard her once mention the hardships she had witnessed as a child growing up. Nor had I ever heard her speak of the humiliation she had endured because she was from a poor Chicano family. I knew from others in the family that my abuelos and my other old ones had seen great misfortune and pain.

I gathered my nerve and stared at her a long time before I asked her about her life. I recall stammering as I asked her how she always seemed so happy when she had lost so much. I think I even told her that most people would not have been able to go on after losing so many children.

What she said to me that day changed my whole outlook on life. She looked at me, wiped her hand on her apron, and smiled.

"Mija," she said softly, "I look at my life like making enchiladas."

I laughed when I heard her say this, but she went on.

"You see, my sweet, little niece, you start out with the corn tortilla, that is the foundation of the enchilada, and it is the family. Then you dip the tortilla in warm oil, which makes the tortilla soft and pliable to work with. I like to think of the oil as sacred, it is an annointing of the familia with all that is precious in life. It is similar to going to church and having the priest put sacred oil on your forehead. The family is being blessed.

"Next, you fill the corn tortilla with cheese and onions. The queso is sweet and rich, made from the milk of life. It is symbolic of the joy and richness of this world. But how can you appreciate the queso without the onion? The onion may make us weep; yet it also makes us realize that there is a reason the cheese tastes so sweet. That reason is because there is a contrast to the queso, there is a balance to the joy…Sorrow is not necessarily bad. It is an important part of learning to appreciate this life.

"Then, the enchiladas are covered with the most delicious sauce in the world. A sauce so red and rich in color, it reminds me of the blood of the Christo, a sacrifice of love. Still, to this day, my mouth waters when I smell enchilada sauce cooking on the stove. The most important ingredient in the sauce is agua.

"Water is the vital source of all we know. It feeds the rivers that make the great oceans. Water rains from the skies to nourish the fertile earth so the grains, grasses, flowers, and trees may grow. Water comforts us when we hear the sound of it flowing over mountain cliffs. Water quenches our thirst and bathes our tired bodies. We are baptized with water when we are born, and all the rest of our days spent on this earth are intertwined with water. Water is the spirit of the sauce.

"The enchilada sauce also has garlic, salt, chili powder, and oil. These are the things that add the spice and zest to the sauce. Making the sauce is a lot like making your own life; you get to choose the combination of ingredients, and you get to decide just how spicy and salty you like it.

"When everything is put together, you have the 'whole enchilada.' You must look at the enchiladas you have made and be happy with them. After all you are the one that has to eat them. No use whining about maybe this or maybe that. There is joy, sorrow, laughter, and tears. Every enchilada is a story in itself. Every time I dip, fill, roll, and pinch an enchilada, I think of some part of my life that has gone by or some part that is still to be.

"Mija, you have got to pinch a lot of enchiladas in this life! Make that experience a good one, and you will become la viejita like me."

I couldn't believe that my auntie, who had never spoken more than two words about her philosophy on life, had just explained the universe to me. I wiped my hands on my apron and laughed.

"Thank you," I said between tears and smiles. "I will never forget what you just told me!"

I never have.

The Cal Laythorne Affair:
Daughter of Infidelity

DEIDRA SUWANEE DEES

I don't know why they got married—maybe because they were from the same town, maybe because they were lonely, or maybe because my father was one of the few eligible Muscogee men in our predominantly white town. Perhaps my mother was seeking a father figure, since her father had been killed when she was a child. That would explain the 22-year age difference—Mother was 19 and Daddy was 41.

Was Mother attracted to him because he was a spiritual leader who practiced traditional Muscogee ways? Maybe she was attracted to his strong work ethic, or maybe it was his stability. Being a landowner was something very rare for many Native Americans in the first half of the 1900s. Perhaps she was attracted to his land.

Whatever the attraction, by all outward accounts they were in love, in the beginning. Mother and Daddy maintained two houses—one was near the city of Mobile, and the other, inherited from Grandpa Suwanee, was in the rural area just east of the Poarch Creek (Muscogee) reservation where my grandmothers and grandfathers lived.

They started a family right away; however, having children never interrupted their work. Daddy and us kids worked a small farm with a few acres of cotton, while Mother climbed the corporate ladder at AT&T. Their strong work ethic generated a respect for one another—a respect that my four sisters and I learned to emulate at an early age.

However, in the midst of all this respect, it became increasingly evident that my mother was not as attentive as Daddy. When I was in second grade, I remember that Mother began missing family outings when we went swimming in Dees Creek behind the reservation. She said she had to start working every holiday, including Christmas Day. But for important events like taking medicine and stomp-dancing around the sacred fire, she would somehow show up and take Daddy's arm. My family and I stood before the medicine pot, pretending our souls were in harmony with all living creatures.

While Daddy's love remained unchanged, my mother's actions vacillated from unpredictable, to confusing, to shamelessly hurtful. My mother said AT&T consumed all of her time, but she seemed to intentionally schedule her work hours at the precise time that all the family was at home.

Yet, there was one autumn afternoon when I got out of my third grade science class early and found her at home by herself. Excited to see her car in the yard, I exploded with greetings as I ran into the house. I showed her the exciting news of my picture being in the newspaper for the first time. I had been honored as a "Distinguished American Indian Artist" for outstanding watercolor paintings.

I thought she would be proud of me like Daddy always was, but instead, she peered through me and snarled, "So what? That's no big deal, Suwanee. You've done nothing great! Anybody can do that."

Poisoned with degrading pain, my body propelled itself into my bedroom closet, where I found a place to cry. I couldn't cry in front of her—Muscogees aren't allowed to cry.

Perhaps that shocking blow prepared me in an unknown way for the next one, which came the following summer. This blow rocked the entire foundation of my family and became known as the ominous "Cal Laythorne Affair."

For several summers, my father employed Cal Laythorne—a white man—to help us out on the farm, but his employment abruptly ended when the neighboring rancher Patterson came to visit one day.

I was 11 when my mother sat down all five of us kids—ages 2 to 11—for what appeared to be a disciplinary lecture. Instead, she shocked us with a story we could not comprehend: "Patterson came over to the farmhouse yesterday and he saw my car along with Cal's truck parked outside. He told your father that he knocked and banged on the door at length but no one answered. What he was doing was accusing me of being inside with Cal! Your father never took up for me, or said anything! How do you think that will make me look in front of the neighbors? Now I feel that if my back were to the wall, your father would never defend me—he would never fight for me—he would never take up for me ever again. It's over, kids! It's 100% over."

I've been told this same story more times than I care to remember. Nevertheless, it was the landmark event that brought about the destruction of my family. I sympathized with mother's version until I heard Daddy's. His version also emphasized what the neighbors might think. I listened intently as Daddy pulled me aside from my sisters and told me of Mother committing the ultimate taboo for a Muscogee woman by bringing suspicion upon herself and our family. Time after time, I found myself not knowing which side of the battle line to stand on.

Daddy and Mother arranged their breakup quietly, while we were forbidden to speak to anyone about it. My mother gave my sisters and me to Daddy, and they each took one of the houses. My sisters and I lived at the farmhouse with Daddy, while my mother lived at the house near the city. Although they lived separately, they were never divorced on paper—Muscogees aren't allowed to divorce.

Daddy and I grew closer from this sad turn of events in my family, while my relationship with my mother became more ambivalent than before. I tried to adjust to their separate lives, but I was constantly reminded that my mother had given me away. It always hurt to think that she didn't want me anymore. I wanted so badly for her to want me again. But instead, her venom toward my father spread to my sisters and me like a fire out of control.

Suddenly, I received the shocking news that Daddy had been killed in a suspicious automobile accident, and—if that weren't bad enough—his last will and testament had mysteriously disappeared. I was in utter shambles! I thought the Creator had required me to bear more than I could carry.

Daddy's death appeared to be harder to bear than the Cal Laythorne Affair until the fire was refueled. I encountered the most difficult trial that I would face. While my sisters and I were struggling to comprehend Daddy's death, the week after the funeral, I caught my mother and Cal in bed together at our farmhouse where they had first been accused. I couldn't believe what my eyes were seeing! Hurt, troubled, and ashamed—I was shocked to my foundation.

After collecting myself, my natural response was to confront my mother about the earlier affair, when Patterson had come knocking, but she never admitted to anything. I wish I could have found a suitable explanation to the question that no one knew the answer to: Why didn't you and Cal answer the door that day when Patterson had come knocking?

During the following autumn, the blazing Cal Laythorne Affair singed my soul as I watched my mother and Cal steal my father's land, dismantle his assets, and spend my sisters' and my inheritance. Later, a fight ensued between them, which ultimately led to their breakup.

I was only a young girl, forced to grow into an adult much earlier than I should have. Discarded, ruined, I tried to make sense of the Cal Laythorne Affair through the traditional Muscogee beliefs that Daddy had taught me.

No longer under pretense, I found myself returning to the medicine pot and dancing around the sacred fire without any of my family members…. The fire alone sustained me.

Many winters have passed, and no one speaks of the Cal Laythorne Affair anymore. My mother now finds herself aged and all alone except for a remnant of my inheritance. She makes miserable attempts to play the mother role, trying to salvage some form of respect from her children. Last Tuesday she dropped by my house unannounced to present me with a news-paper clipping perfectly mounted inside an expensive leather photo album.

It was a photograph of me in a recent article describing my Native American watercolor exhibit displayed at the Metropolitan Museum. I extended a sociable "thank you" as she awkwardly shuffled out the door. I thought back on the time when I first appeared in the paper and the painful words she wielded. As the winters have passed, my pain has been healed. I have learned to live my life without a mother or a father. I need-ed a mother back then when I was a young child—I don't need her now.

I smiled to myself, thinking about all of my artistic accomplishments, my triumph in the face of adversity—my strength that I inherited from Daddy. I thought about how far I have come on my own, as the trashcan swallowed a leather photo album.

Sister Solace

PAT MCLEAN-RASHINE

It's amazing how we sometimes underestimate the truly priceless people in our lives. I became vividly aware of some of the ones in mine during an incident that could have easily elevated into not only the loss of my life, but the loss of my children's lives as well. Several of my sisters (of whom there are six), Marlene, Yvonne, and Renee, would demonstrate to me the power of love, the fiber of family.

The year was 1988, and I had just begun to communicate again with the father of my two children, whom neither they nor I had seen or spoken to in the past 11 years. Our conversations were light and easy, and I remembered him for who he was when we were together, a kind and caring man, and not who I envisioned him to be during all those years I had not heard from him.

Through our telephone talks, we grew close again. So close, in fact, that I somewhat trusted him when he proposed that I bring the children to visit him in the town of Bryant, Texas, where he lived. Now, my sisters for some reason always considered me to be the most levelheaded one of us, the one who didn't get so easily led by my heart. But this time was different, because he was not only the father of my children, but my very first love.

He suggested that since we both had limited funds, I should pay our way down by bus or train. He would pay our airfare back home. This seemed reasonable to me. I wanted the kids to "meet" their father. However, because I had not seen him in so many years, I was still feeling a bit unsure. I consulted my older sister Marlene, and asked her what she thought I should do. She informed me I should wait until I had enough money to pay for round-trip transportation. She reminded me how Mama always told us, "Never put your welfare in the hands of someone else."

Of course, I didn't listen to her. I did what so many women do. I listened only to my heart, and that proved very nearly to be a deadly mistake.

Our visit started off great. He and the children were getting along very well. About a week into our stay, I inquired several times when he was going to purchase the plane tickets for our departure. His answer was always "tomorrow."

I became suspicious of his continuous stalling and called Marlene again for her advice. Never once saying, "I told you so," she told me to be adamant when telling him I was ready to go home. I took her advice this time and confronted him. At that moment the kind and gentle man who I thought him to be disappeared, and someone frightening stood in his place.

He became heated and angry, telling me we would leave when he was ready for us to leave. For two days he never let us out of his sight. We became prisoners in his home, until one night when he was called into work on an emergency. He knew I didn't have very much money and told me if I left, I wouldn't get very far. He would find me and kill me.

He was right about the money. I had a total of $90.00 to my name, but I knew I had to get my children out of there. I tried to get in touch with my family. After several attempts I was able to reach my sister Renee. In a panic, I explained my situation to her. She told me if I could make it to the airport in Houston, she would make contact with the rest of the family and together they would work something out. Not knowing when he would return, I had to do something quick. I called a cab service, gathered up everything we had, and proceeded to leave. That's when I discovered he had locked us in.

Afraid and confused, with my children by this time knowing something was wrong, I acted on impulse, the impulse to protect them at all costs. Frantically, I searched the apartment for an escape route. Finding none, I knew what I had to do. I smashed a chair through the front window, grabbed my children and what little we could carry, and got out of there.

He lived in an apartment complex, and as we were running toward the front gate, a taxicab appeared. Never so happy to see another human being in all my life, I flagged him down, learning he was indeed the cab I called.

Realizing someone would be reporting the broken window, I wanted to get out of there as fast as we could. The driver seemed a bit perplexed at our frazzled appearance, plus the fact we had no luggage. I pulled myself together, telling him calmly and precisely that I had a family emergency, and we needed to get to the airport right away. It was at this point I learned that the airport was almost two hours away.

A new wave of fear engulfed me. Did I have enough money to pay the fare? Would I be able to reach anyone in my family? Was it safe for us to ride with this stranger for such a long distance not knowing the route to where we were going? Numerous questions raced through my mind. However, there was one question I needed no answer to. I couldn't go back; I had to move forward.

Once in the car, not wanting my children to become more afraid by sensing my fear, I told them the same story I told the driver. Someone in the family was sick and we had to get home. They were tired and scared; it didn't take long for them to fall off to sleep. The driver informed me the fee would be about $85.00. I felt a little better; I would have just enough change to call home.

We arrived at the airport around 5:30 a.m. with the final fare being $87.00, leaving me with $3.00 and some change. My children were hungry, so I purchased two pastries and a carton of milk for them to share as we made our way toward a phone booth. I called my sister Yvonne. She was happy to hear we were safe and said Renee told everyone what was happening. She and Marlene were out attempting to collect funds from other family members to get us home.

Yvonne stayed on the phone with me for what seemed like hours, reassuring me everything would be all right. I was getting more worried by the minute that my children's father would track us down and do us harm. Finally, Yvonne informed me that my mother and Marlene had come in. When my mother got on the phone, I could hear the fear in her voice. She spoke with such concern and love when asking me if we were all right. I told her everyone was fine. I was scared and wanted to come home. We just held onto the phone and cried, it was all we could do.

At that moment, and as children will do when they see their mother cry, my children started crying, too. Marlene took the phone from my mother, assuring me all of the arrangements had been made. She told me all I had to do was go to the check-in counter and give them our names; the reservation clerks would be waiting for us. I pulled myself together and did just that.

Everything went just as my sister said it would. Once we were in our seats and the plane began to take off, I remembered to breathe again. It felt as if I had been holding my breath from the moment I got into the cab. My children were excited about being on a plane and were completely unaware of ever being in any danger. I was thankful for that, and also for the fact they would only have good memories of our stay with their father.

I did not want them to ever relive this horror, as I was sure I would for a long time to come. Eventually, I relaxed and looked forward to being in the safety of my family. It felt like forever, but the plane finally began its descent. Realizing I hadn't spoken to anyone since I hung up the phone with my sister, I wondered who would be picking us up from the airport.

What I saw when we came through the gates altered my life forever. My entire family was there: my mom, my sisters, my brothers, and almost all of their children. It was the most beautiful sight in the world. When they spotted us, everyone ran toward us, swallowing us up in a sea of hugs and kisses. I would later learn that Marlene, Renee, and Yvonne were the ones who pooled their own money to pay our airfare and were also the ones responsible for gathering the rest of the family together and getting them to the airport to welcome us home.

I would not hear from my children's father again for several years. By then my children were old enough to determine what kind of relationship they wanted to have with him, if any. What they learned from that day at the airport was that there are a lot of people who care about them. So whatever they decided to do in regards to their father would not be due to a lack of love. What I learned is that family is forever, my sisters are my sanctuary, and there is no place, no place like home.

Algebra You Can Use

I wasn't surprised to find out my oldest son, David Scott, was in prison. His whole life had led up to this moment—me visiting him in jail. I didn't want to be anywhere near prison because I had seen it far too close many years ago, when I was mistaken for someone else and picked up. I was homeless at the time and had left my driver's license over at Lucky Dogs, where I worked during the day and most nights, pushing a hot dog cart to earn enough money to eat and to pay for a cheap motel at night. I couldn't prove who I was, and the New Orleans Police didn't believe me.

I smiled at the guards and prayed they didn't know about my past. They went through my purse and made me take the box cutter off my key chain. I might hurt someone. Not me. I didn't want to spend any more time here than I had to. I was just going to see David Scott and go home. I couldn't shake the fear that as soon as I passed through the metal detector and into the barbed-wire-fenced yard, they weren't going to let me go. But I had to see my son.

David Scott had been on his own since he talked my mother into believing he was being abused by being made to clean the house while I sat around and did nothing. My ex-husband had given her custody, so I had no choice. She could dump him off at my house when he got to be too much just as quickly as she took him away. It was just one more way to hurt me.

Between my son and my mother, they both took pleasure in hurting me. Mom kept my son from me, and my son kept himself from me. It was easy because I loved them both and wanted them to love me back. I was an easy target.

When David was about a year old, he always wanted to go to strangers and be held. He held out his chubby, little arms to be taken and stubbornly turned his face away from me when I tried to take him back. I'd laugh and try to coax him away, but he pushed at me and cried. He didn't want me. But I wanted him from the first moment I discovered I was pregnant. At last, someone I could love who would love me just as much. But not David Scott. No, he only wanted me when I had food.

I waited in a crowded room full of families and lovers visiting the inmates. Children laughed and sat on their fathers' knees. Mothers cried over their changed sons with their buzz haircuts and their hollow cheeks. Fathers sat quietly, while their wives fussed over the boys and men. Guards sat at desks at the front and back of the building, well above the visitors so they could keep an eye on the prisoners in their bright-orange jumpsuits.

Just to go to the bathroom was an ordeal of being patted down and watched while the prisoner had to stay seated. They weren't even allowed to go to the vending machines for a sandwich or a can of Coke. They were escorted in and escorted out, their every movement closely watched.

I checked my watch, but David didn't show. Someone waiting talked to me, but I couldn't really understand what they were saying. My eyes were glued to the door. I was waiting to see my son and praying I could get out of there soon. I nodded and smiled, but I didn't understand a single word.

The guards came toward me. I gripped my wallet and prayed. Please, God, don't let them take me away. Not again. The guards passed me, and two more guards passed the other way. It must be a shift change.

"Mom?"

I turned around. David Scott was taller than the last time I saw him. His arms were covered with tattoos. When I stood up to hug him, I saw another tattoo peeking up out of his collar.

"I'm glad you came."

"Are you hungry?"

"Yeah, but I have to stay here until it's time to leave. You'll have to get it."

He told me what he wanted, and I got up and walked toward the vending machines with one eye on the guard at the front door. I wasn't taking any chances. When I brought the food and Coke back, David ate the food so fast I barely saw him chew.

"You're going to get sick," I said.

He shrugged his shoulders and smiled. Between bites he talked non-stop. "I'm getting my GED so I can go to college."

"College? You never wanted to go to college...or so you said."

"It's different now."

"Lord knows, you're smart enough, but you'll have to work."

"I'm ready for it," he said. His jaw was set. He was determined. I couldn't believe it. He had fought me every step of the way when I made him study at home. He was smart, but he didn't want to study or to work. He wanted the teachers to hand him the grades so he could run track or chase girls or fight. He didn't want an education.

As I listened to his plans, I found myself wondering what had changed him. After the drugs and the alcohol, it didn't seem he wanted any kind of normal life. Granted, I hadn't given him much of a life between his father and my mother, but I had always wanted my children to be happy and to go to college. He smiled as he talked about his schoolwork and how much he liked helping the other inmates with their studies. He was teaching some of them to read.

"Woodard!" one of the guards called. We both looked toward the door. Other names were called. Orange-clad prisoners said their goodbyes to teary-eyed mothers, wives, girlfriends, and children. Fathers looked on stony faced.

"I have to go, Mom."

"You only just got here."

David Scott shrugged. I stood up with him. He started to walk away, but he stopped and came back. He put his arms around me and hugged me tightly.

"Mom, I love you. Thank you for making me study algebra. Something must have sunk in, because I was accepted to college." He kissed my cheek and was gone before I could say anything.

For the first time in his life, he didn't want to go to someone else. I suppose no one wants to go to a prison guard, but that didn't matter. Somehow, some way, something I said or did had sunk in, and David Scott had been listening. I had been afraid the only reason he wanted to see me was to ask for money, but he wanted to thank me. For the first time in his life, my son wanted me. He may have been in prison, but it didn't matter. He wouldn't be there for long, and all my hopes and dreams for him would come true. He would go to college because I had taught him something. It was just algebra, but it was a start.

Birth Order

GERI SPENCER HUNTER

I stare at her sitting quietly on an uncomfortable sofa across the room and blink back the tears that threaten to expose me. She is attractive still. Her salt and pepper hair, with most of the gray clinging to the edges, is short and stylish. She has brushed it straight back from her forehead and pushed it forward with her hands until it surrounds her smooth, honey-colored face in wiry, complementing waves like she's done for all the years I can remember.

Her attire is as contradictory as she, a bold, rich, multicolored silk jacket over a simple, drab wool dress and flat shoes. She sits straight up, rigid on the formal, old-fashioned sofa, her legs properly crossed, and her hands clenched in her lap. She is not looking at me. She is focusing all her attention on the other people milling around the crowded room, though taking no part in any of their simultaneous conversations.

Neither am I. I am sitting across the room on an identical uncomfortable couch, ignoring the noisy chatter, concentrating on her. The talk does not interest me. It is just chitchat, frivolous words providing temporary distractions.

It has been two long years since I've seen her in another city on a different couch, but for the same reason. She was seventy-four then. She doesn't look her age. Her face is without wrinkles and her skin is taut. She is the oldest living of eleven children, and I am the youngest. Jake, the baby, they called me, and I loved it. I liked being the "baby of the family." I thought if I couldn't be the only one, being the last-born was preferable.

Having ten older siblings, six of them sisters, was way cool and powerful, not to mention the special privileges that automatically came with it. I wonder what she thinks of birth order, how she likes where she fits. She's probably given it no thought, and if I should right now stroll across the room, sit down beside her, and ask her that, she'd think it was a ridiculous question having nothing to do with anything. Or maybe, she'd laugh and say that's something to think about all right.

I continue to stare. She's wearing her stoic face, as usual. Seldom does she show her true self. I want to yell at her, shatter the mask she insists on hiding behind, but I'm not sure I want to see what lies beneath. I know she is grieving. She was close to the sister that just died. It was a strange kind of relationship, loud, boisterous, often volatile, sometimes ugly, but undeniably loving.

Regardless of the fussing, the arguing, the name-calling and finger pointing—the rage—they were an integral part of each other. She'll miss her. Who will she fuss with now, venting her anger and frustrations? There is only I and another sister. I am too far away, and the other refuses to accommodate her.

Finally, she looks in my direction, just a quick glance, a smile forming on her thin lips before moving her gaze. Is she afraid I'll recognize the painful truth in her eyes? I sigh and blink back my tears, again, as I suddenly realize I don't know her, not really. A wave of sadness washes over me. She was always there when I needed her, and I took her so for granted. We are separated by eleven years, but I know it's longer than that.

She grew up in the twenties and thirties. I grew up in the forties and fifties. She grew up when our mother was still having babies. I grew up after she had stopped. She had terrifying life experiences. Mine were laissez-faire. Her birth order was number three. Mine, number eleven. I'm finally willing to slip out of that position, sixty-plus years "being the baby" is long enough. I want to give it up, relinquish it to her. I want her to be pampered and spoiled and receive special privileges before it's too late, knowing it already is.

If we could talk, I'm thinking, just she and I really talk without the worry of politeness or hurting each other's feelings, being open and honest, what would she tell me? I want to drag her into the kitchen and slam the door. I want to pull a chair away from the old oak table, ease her into it gently, push it up close like I did my children when they were kids, to keep all the mess from spilling down their fronts and onto their laps.

I want to pour chilled white wine into a fancy crystal glass and place it on a crisp linen napkin in front of her. I want to pour me a glass, too, set the bottle between us, rush around the other side of the table, and sit in a chair across from her. I will stretch out my hands and squeeze her arm, tell her I love her and nothing, not one damn thing she says, can ever change that, and then, I will order her to talk, tell me her story in her own words, in her own way, and with her own emotions.

I already know her story. Mother told it to me long ago when I was gathering family history. I finally got old enough and bold enough to ask, and she confirmed my suspicions. I will never let her know I know. She has not told a soul, not one living soul. How has she kept it to herself for all these years and stayed sane? It's time to end it, relieve her of all that outdated pain. It's time to assure her that her secret will be safe with me.

I get up from the low seat, slip between the people that separate us, and walk to her. I grab her hands, pull her up from the sofa, and lead her toward the kitchen.

Mixed Marriages

RAMONA MORENO WINNER

I am the daughter of Pablo Lopez Moreno and Maria Magdalena Dominguez, the youngest of five girls, the rebel of the family. I was brought up in small mining towns all around Arizona, usually living in small trailers among other mining families. As a child, I roamed free, playing in creeks, exploring the desert, and running wild with my dog Poochie. Home was where I ate and slept and infrequently bathed. To stay in our trailer was to be subjected to the ravings of my three older sisters. Life was great until I entered puberty.

Five daughters to raise would have been a challenge for any man, and Pablo Moreno was no exception. For the first ten years of marriage, I think he drank as a means of coping. Once his pancreas was damaged, he was a lost man. Dad was a very traditional, over-protective Mexican male. My older sisters never went anywhere, never dated, and were seldom permitted to leave the house. This never bothered me until I was subjected to the same rules.

I witnessed my three older sisters, one after the other, marry just to leave our home. I also saw them struggle, as each one produced one child after another and dealt with immature and abusive husbands. Once they left, there was only one sister, who was two years older, and I, and I no longer escaped notice.

To my dad, my worth as a person was in my virginity. Being at home was like living in a convent. We were known as "the nice Moreno girls." I began the lessons that were to prepare me to be a wife and mother. I learned how to clean, wash, iron, and help in the kitchen. If my husband required a helping hand, I also received lessons on how to use the pick and shovel, to work with cement, to work with lumber and, like a good assistant, to run about for whatever tool was needed. When I finished high school, I was expected to find a husband. There were no plans for college; we were not to be trusted to work outside the home, and so marriage was my calling.

Of the five girls, I was the only one to complete high school and the only one to leave and totally change my life. With my mom's encouragement I entered the Marine Corps at age 17. The first thing I did—you guessed it—was lose my virginity! I was out to prove that I had value without it. The next year and a half was a whirlwind of parties and relationships until a young and handsome White boy caught my eye.

I didn't date while I was at home; it wasn't permitted. I had boyfriends on the sly, and they were always Mexican. My dad's other passion was his heritage. When I was small, I couldn't understand why White people would call me a dirty Mexican. All I remember was how impotent we all were to do anything about it. As a result, we too became prejudiced. We became snobs. If it wasn't brown, it wasn't pretty or good enough. Later in life I became a poor snob. You know, "Nobody knows the sorrows I've seen"—especially if you are White and have money.

My parents spoke Spanish at home, and once we began attending school, we were told to answer them in English. This was to practice our English and teach our parents more English. Needless to say, if you don't use it, you lose it! I understood Spanish, but I seldom spoke it, and when I did, it felt foreign.

My parents were born in Arizona. Their parents were born either in Mexico or in Arizona. My dad's father was half German. I believe his family left Germany during World War I and settled in Mexico. My dad's mother was said to be half Yaqui Indian and half Mexican. On my mother's side, my grandfather was Mexican and Black, and my grandmother was another Yaqui Indian. The reason I tell you this is so you can understand that marrying a German or a Mexican was acceptable to my dad. Anything else would wreak havoc. Bringing home a White boy was like dropping an A-bomb!

Rob and I had been dating for about six months before he invited me home to meet his parents. Rob's real dad died when he was nine, and his mother remarried a few years later. The step-dad was very successful in banking and they lived nicely. Visiting his family for the first time was like looking at a *Better Homes and Gardens* magazine—it was unreal! Both parents were wonderful and went out of their way to make me feel at home.

I felt like a fish out of water. I now tease them and we refer to my first visit as "the time you made me cry." I was so insecure; I thought every time they introduced me to something new they were pointing out how very different Rob and I were. At dinner, Rob's mother pointed out the tenderest part of a T-bone steak to me, and later, she was amazed I had never eaten blueberry pie.

That was it. The next thing you know, I was sobbing at the dinner table. I had to excuse myself to regain my composure. I was so embarrassed, and they were at a loss trying to figure out what they had said to offend me. What a hoot!

He was the man I chose to marry. He tried like a bandit to get away from me, but I knew I could lure him with my charm—better yet, my body. What of my family, you ask? They were not thrilled that he was White. He was not even a blue-eyed, blonde-haired German like my grandpa. Life is full of disappointments, and one of my most disappointing moments was the absence of my parents or any of my family members at my wedding.

Marriage was everything I had ever dreamed it would be. For two years I was on my honeymoon. How did Rob's being White affect me? I lost that closeness to my family. It was years later, once we had our first child, that they warmed up to him.

Rob and I left the Marine Corps and moved to Santa Barbara, where he attended college, and I worked and took college classes at night. My mother and sister would always tell me that once Rob finished school, he would dump me for a White girl. Nice, huh?

Santa Barbara has a large Latino community, so I was still able to celebrate some of our traditional holidays. I did miss, however, the dancing that was so much in my blood! Rob has never been a dancer. I'm in heaven each time I hear Latin music.

I spent a lot of time alone during our first few years of marriage. My tendency to "care for my man" drove Rob crazy. He kept pushing me to become independent. What really gave me wings was an assertiveness training class I took at the city college, and from that I began to soar!

What were some differences between our two races? One was my attitude about money. I didn't want to have any control over our finances, and my needs were minimal. Rob loved to spend. It took me years to learn that if I didn't control some of the spending he would spend it all himself. Most of my casual clothes were straight from K-Mart. I would often look with envy at women who wore good quality, well-coordinated outfits. I know I should have gone out and bought them for myself, and my husband often told me the same thing.

Well, I can't! I have tried many times. I pick up the items, carry them around the store, and then I can't get myself to pay for them! Sad, huh? The quality clothes that I do have, my husband gave to me. This man has wonderful taste in women's clothing, and I often get complimented when I wear something he has selected.

Another part of me that I attribute to my cultural background is my inability to decorate. What we considered a nice painting was a toro and a torero painted on a black velvet canvas, and I still do not buy furniture on my own.

As a youth, I wouldn't think twice about pilfering something I wanted. The unspoken rule at home was "just don't get caught." My mom had a socialistic approach to life and felt that abundance they won't share, we take. I had many friends; however, I never learned to spend a lot of time with them. My dad seldom let us leave the yard, much less visit friends. To this day, friends can't count on me for hours of entertainment. Rob, on the other hand, loves to spend time with his friends, and I had a hard time learning that he could obtain his solace from someone other than me.

Having children was my idea. After seven years of marriage, I wanted to see what gem we could produce. My son was a sick baby until age two, and I was a very protective mother. How could I be otherwise? I learned from the best—my own parents. Like my own mother, I cried whenever I made my kid cry. Fortunately for me, he was a good son. Seven more years passed and we had another boy. This child made me cry!

Growing up, I never got spanked. My dad ruled with a loud voice and a menacing look, and mom left all the discipline to my dad. I learned to discipline (my husband will guffaw) by reading books. And this caused problems in our marriage. Rob's parents used a belt on him when he misbehaved, and it took several years for him to ease up. You can imagine my horror and outrage when he smacked our oldest son on the butt. Boy, did we have some compromising to do.

My husband loves to go camping; the more rustic, the better. When my parents married, they built their house. I remember when I was small, having to use an outhouse or a bucket. Later, my dad started building a bathroom in the house, but since he was never one to finish anything off, it had an outdoor feel to it. The walls were stucco and the roof was an aluminum sheet covered with tarpaper. We lived in this house most of my childhood.

I remember when the monsoons would hit, the rain would beat like drums on our roof. Even though it was hot and muggy, we had to sleep covered with a blanket because centipedes would try to escape the rain and fall onto us at night. They would fall onto the blanket and get their clawed legs tangled in the covers. I know, you want to know what this has to do with camping, right? Well, as I see it, I camped most of my childhood, and if I have the choice of trading my bed for a tent and sleeping bag, my bed wins out.

Everything we owned when I was growing up was old and used, and I am always amazed at how people spend time and money acquiring antiques. You will never see me spending my hard-earned money on something old. My husband once bought friends two handmade rice bowls with chopsticks. When he was selecting them, I told him I didn't think it was a good purchase because the bowls were not identical. He just rolled his eyes as he explained that each item was unique and they would find that special. I thought to myself, he would have found eating dinner at my house a very unique experience; no two things matched!

I believe any two people have difficulty merging their lives. Perhaps this is the reason people confine their choices to groups of people with similar backgrounds. I believe at times my husband and I have been at a loss for words to adequately explain a feeling that would have been clear had we grown up in the same ethnic or economic group.

But to grow is to redefine yourself. I chose to risk the unknown, to go against the grain, to sacrifice the purity of my heritage, and I have found a life richer in experiences.

Chile Tales:
The Green Addiction

SANDRA RAMOS O'BRIANT

In Texas, when my parents were still married, we ate fried chicken, mashed potatoes laden with cream gravy, green beans flavored with bits of bacon, and buttery, light biscuits. Every item on the menu was in its own serving dish, and cloth napkins were always used.

"May I have another biscuit, ma'am?" I would say.

"You surely may, Sandra Mae," my daddy's mama would reply, and everyone would smile. Or we'd have fried pork chops and suck on the salty bones, but only when it was just my mama and me at the dinner table.

In Texas, there were black-eyed peas and ham, and all manner of greens and put-up preserves. There was watermelon and homemade ice cream from the hand-crank ice-cream maker. Daddy held a bourbon and water in one hand and turned the handle with the other, while Mama and my daddy's mama drank iced tea on the back porch and exchanged polite insults.

"Don't forget your manners out there, Sandra Mae," my daddy's mama said, after the divorce, and right before me and Mama set off for New Mexico. "Act like a lady."

In Santa Fe, we ate pinto beans muddy in their own gravy at my mama's parents' house. My aunts, cousins, grandparents, and, sometimes, neighbors ladled the beans into their bowls from the pot in the middle of the table. No other utensils were in evidence. Instead, tortillas wrapped in a dishcloth were passed around the table.

Each diner split their tortilla, usually into fourths, but the more adept could function well on thirds or even halves. Then, the tortilla was rolled into a half-moon scoop, and the eating commenced. It required dexterity and speed to fill the tortilla scoop and stuff it into your mouth before the bean juice had a chance to run out the back and down your forearm. I leaned over my bowl like the adults and soon shoveled like an expert.

"Hand me another tortilla," my Aunt Frances would say, not at all unfriendly, pointing her chin in the general direction of the tortillas.

The only green vegetable offered at my grandparents' table was chiles. Meat, usually pork, was a rarity and was reserved for the green chile pods.

If I wanted meat or vegetables, I was going to have to learn to eat chile.

Mama started me off slow, picking up the chunks of meat and sucking the chile juice out. She'd place the morsel on my tongue like a sacrament, and sit back and wait. I chewed tentatively, fearing the bite of the treacherous chile pod. Occasionally, a seed would sneak through, making my eyes tear and my nose run. I'd swallow glass after glass of my grandparents' icy well water, my face contorted in pain.

Then, I'd ask for more. By the end of that first winter, my yearning for the green was established. I was an addict.

"Hatch chile," the boy yelled from the back of the pickup. The truck drove slowly down our street, pausing when a homemaker ran out and negotiated with the chile vendor. The boy sat atop a truck bed piled high with shiny green pods, some plump and beginning to turn red, others long and thin or curled into a defiant C. I scooped up a handful of pods and breathed their spicy promise while my grandfather first sniffed and then bit into a pod to judge its quality, the latter variable not strictly related to taste or crunchiness but to the extremity of pain inflicted: mild, medium, or hot. He bought a bushel adjudged to be medium. Yeah, right.

In Texas, my father's new wife and his mama might be putting up figs and strawberries, tomatoes, or pickled okra, but in New Mexico, the women were about to put up chile for the winter. A certain macho bravado was necessary for this task.

The pods were laid out on cookie sheets and roasted under the broiler. Periodically, my aunt would reach in and turn the pods over. Soon, the house filled with the acrid scent of burned green. She dumped the black-mottled pods unceremoniously onto the newspaper-covered dining room table. The black skin of the roasted pods lifted easily, and my aunts, my mother, and I sat around the table and peeled chile.

Soon, our fingers burned, and we began to sweat and sniffle. Too late, my mother warned me not to touch my eyes. She refused to rush me to the emergency room. We flushed my eyes with cold water and returned to our task. At the end of the day we had laid 200 peeled chile pods to dry across the lines strung up in the screened porch off the kitchen. Adults and child alike gazed red-eyed, with nose and fingertips smarting, at our day's work.

I looked up at the glistening faces of the women in my family, each was content with her contribution. I had suffered, and wept, and done my share, too. I felt . . . full, and at peace for the first time since arriving in New Mexico. The lily-white hands of my Texas relatives might master a pecan pie or divinity, but they didn't have the cojones to deal with the sultry heat of chile. Feminine wiles and prissy manners had no place here. We were the real women.

REAL WOMAN GREEN-CHILE STEW
(only spicy-hot women need apply)

Ingredients:
6 to 8 fresh, long green chiles, roasted, peeled, seeds removed, and cut into coarse chunks
1 medium onion, chopped fine
3 to 5 cloves of garlic, minced
1 tsp oregano
1 tsp cumin
1 lb lean pork, cut into 1" cubes
Juice of 1/2 lime
Up to 1-1/2 cups chicken stock
Salt, black pepper, and hot green chilies to taste (New Mexico chilie preferred, but you can use Anaheims, Serranos, or Jalapenos, or a mixture of all)
1 tbsp olive oil

Heat Dutch oven or medium saucepan over high. Sauté onion, garlic, oregano and cumin until onion is clear. Add green chilies, sauté and stir. Add pork cubes and stir to seize all sides of the pork; add lime juice and mix.

Now add chicken stock, stopping when most of the pork cubes are covered with liquid. Stir well, reduce the heat to a simmer, cover, and set the timer for 30 minutes. Check occasionally to make sure the stuff isn't scorching on the bottom. When the timer goes off, check the consistency and either add more stock if it's gotten thicker/drier than you like it, or raise the heat and cook uncovered to thicken if it's too runny. Add salt and black pepper now. Serve with corn or flour tortillas. Delicious mixed with pinto beans.

Sistahs' Joys...
Life's Pain

Happiness is not a station you arrive at,
but a manner of traveling.
— Margaret Lee Runbeck

Press and Curl

JANET MICHELLE ELDER

Even after all these years, I still remember the sweet smell of Royal Crown hairdressing and the orange, waxy Bergamot pressing cream my mother used to press our hair. Growing up in the Deep South during the '60s meant getting your hair pressed and curled for school and church. There were no such things as relaxers, jheri curls, dreads, or hair weaves.

Lisa, Ronn, and I were two years apart in age, so my sisters and I went through the press-and-curl phase together. We all had thick, shoulder-length hair, so press and curl lasted all day when Mama did it at home. First, she would lay out the towels on the kitchen counter, and each in turn we lay on the counter with our heads hanging over the edge of sink to be shampooed.

This would be one time you were very sure your mother loved you dearly, because without a spray attachment at the sink, drowning seemed like a distinct possibility. Since we didn't have blow dryers, either, we were detangled, oiled, and put up in Bantu knots (little did we know that we were a fashion statement back then) to dry.

Mama always had a gentle hand when pressing our hair, and rarely did we get burned, maybe a little singed when we moved at the wrong time. Although the way my little sister, Lisa (the tender-headed one), carried on, you would think she required treatment at the nearest burn center when her hair was done! I think every family has one tender-headed one who screams at the sight of a comb and brush. Lisa was always good for a least an hour or two on press-and-curl day.

When we got a little older, we would go to Mrs. P's beauty shop, you know the kind, attached to the back of her family home. Lisa liked going to the beauty shop even less than letting Mama do her hair. However, if the truth be told, Mrs. P's assistant, Jane, was much better at doing hair than she was.

Mrs. P liked to talk on the phone while wielding that smoking-hot comb, so your chances of leaving the shop with a second-degree burn somewhere around your head and ears was pretty good. Mama usually made sure we got in Jane's chair, but one day only Mrs. P's chair was open when it was Jennifer's turn. When Mrs. P called her to come and sit down, she loudly announced to my mother and the entire shop, "I don't want her to do my hair 'cause she always burning somebody."

Jane shook all over trying not to laugh, and we children knew better than to laugh. Mama, of course, was mortified. Later she explained to Jennifer that you can't say everything you think out loud.

The afro era brought an end to press-and-curl day, but every now and then I put a little Royal Crown on my son's hair. The scent always seems to carry a little whiff of smoke.

My First Trials of Puberty

MARGARET HURLEY

At ten years of age I could climb every tree and win any foot race that was run between the boys and girls in our neighborhood. I was a thin, tomboyish girl growing up in the Gibbs Street projects of Alameda.

One day things changed. I looked in the bedroom mirror to straighten my knee-high socks, and noticed I was getting quite tall. I paid closer attention to how my soft, frizzy hair was combed on my face. I also noticed my face was pretty; I had a nice mouth with small lips, for a dark-skinned girl. I had a small nose that wasn't flattened, and eyebrows that needed only brushing with my toothbrush each morning to be arched. I was growing up oh so fast! My body was growing much faster than I knew what to do with.

One morning while getting dressed for school, I looked in the mirror to straighten my sweater. I was still growing quite tall and thin. I looked at myself sideways in the mirror and didn't like the reflection staring back at me. I didn't like the way I couldn't smooth my sweater down to cover my protruding chest.

Several months went by, and I was continuing to grow taller and thinner by the day. My tee shirts could not hide the way my chest was bulging outward. I couldn't express my feelings or the shame I felt. I wasn't able to cover up and hide this monstrous thing that was happening to my body.

Playing sports was not as much fun as it once was, because my monstrous chest would heave and jiggle. My friends would laugh at the way I looked, running around the school grounds, my chest bouncing all over the place. My older sisters teased me, saying it was time I wore a bra.

None of my friends were having this problem, even though they seemed to be envious of my developing body. Anyhow, I just didn't get it! Mama finally noticed me struttin' and playing around the apartment building and called me inside the house.

"Here, gal, take this five dollars and go to town and get yourself a couple of bras. Go to Woolworth's and get yourself some training bras, and don't mess around and lose this here money, cause there ain't no more where that came from," she said as she handed me the money.

I took the money and stuffed the five-dollar bill deep inside my pants pocket and went around to pick up my two girlfriends, Vicki and Debbie. Now, in my neighborhood back then, shopping at Woolworth's and the 99-cent store was like going down to Macy's department store and the K-Mart shopping center today.

We walked at least two miles to the get to the store. The lingerie department was discreetly located in the back section of the store, for privacy, of course.

They had such a variety of sizes and styles; plain cotton, lacy, sheer, and padded. They even had several different colors—white, nude, black, and red. I had no idea what size bra to pick. What was the difference between an A cup and a B cup, I thought to myself. I asked if either of my friends knew, and all they did was to shrug their shoulders and look as lost as I was. Well, I knew I was a beginner, and Mama had said to buy a training bra.

Well then, the smaller cup size had to be for me. I figured the 32A cup would be plenty big enough. And I could buy two of these for under five dollars and have some change left over to buy a couple of Betty and Veronica comic books. I was so proud of myself and the choices I'd made. I had really stretched my money!

We went home and I showed my mama my purchases and she seemed pleased. My girlfriends and I ran into the bedroom so I could try on my bras, which wasn't allowed in the department store. I put one of the bras on, clasping the two hooks that secured it to my chest, but I couldn't get my breast to go all the way inside of the A cup. I took it off and tried on the other bra, which was fancy and padded.

Even though it looked bigger, I had the same problem.

"Oh no, what am I going to do?" I cried. Woolworth's had a no-return-of-lingerie policy, and I'd just messed up Mama's five dollars. I was so ashamed, to have to go and tell mama I'd messed up the whole five dollars. Money don't grow on trees, you know. Well, I did tell Mama late that night, and she just looked at me, and didn't say anything. Finally, she just told me to go on to bed. I barely lifted my eyes to hers, and just walked out of her room and went to bed.

The very next day, while I was in school, my mother went to Woolworth's department store and bought me two brand-new beautiful bras, size 32C, and they fit just perfect. Thank you, Mama.

Behold, She Stands

JOAN MCCARTY

Behold, she stands on Prairie Avenue
With outstretched hands, she welcomes me and you
Where pupils learn to keep the golden rule
What you should learn is taught in this dear school!

—The Bennett School Song, 1957

I t is the cold Chicago winter of 1957. I am eight years old. My hand is in my father's hand as he walks me from the school office up to the third-floor classroom. As we come in the door with my registration slip, the teacher in the front of the class looks surprised and at the same time sad.

"Children, say hello to Mr. Foster," Mrs. DeYoung commands.

"Hello, Mr. Foster."

"Now say hello to Joan."

They repeat after Mrs. DeYoung, and a sea of faces like Timmy from Lassie and like Shirley Temple seem to peer through my flushed little colored face. I have not seen many white children up close, only the ones I have seen on television. This seems like a different, but exciting new world. I have come from the all-black Carver elementary school, where teachers, staff, students, and the community have embraced me. This is my first day of school at Bennett, and I will be the only Black child in this class for one year. At this moment, I do not understand how very, very different this world will be for me. At this moment, I am protected by the wonderful innocence and hope of youth.

Behold she stands, on Prairie Avenue

My father leaves to go to work, his task of registering his children having been accomplished. I know to wait for my big brother and sister at noon so that we can walk across the bridge back to our house, where Mama will be waiting with our lunch. I hang my coat in the cloakroom. I am assigned a seat and given some textbooks. I print my name carefully on the slip of paper in the front of each book, as instructed.

The class is working on spelling, but I do not understand how we are supposed to write our heading at Bennett. We did it differently at Carver, and I do not want to get it wrong. I was on the honor roll at Carver every year, and I want to start off right here at Bennett. I ask the girl in a pink-and-gray felt poodle skirt behind me for help. Helen seems friendly as she answers my question. Maybe she can be my friend, I think. Suddenly a booming voice from the front of the classroom breaks through the air.

"I don't know what kind of place you came from, Joan, but we don't talk in class here."

Mrs. DeYoung's face is red and she is looking at me with the meanest look I have ever seen. I am too embarrassed and ashamed to even respond. I put my head down and will myself not to show the tears that have begun to fall down my cheeks. I peek at the kids around me who seem to be snickering and talking about "the new girl."

With outstretched hands, she welcomes me and you

Before I know it, it is recess time. We hurry to put on our coats and to line up. We walk through the hallways in an orderly, quiet fashion, but once on the playground, a burst of third-grade energy takes over; children run in the snow to the swings, the daddy-long-legs, the seesaw, and the merry-go-round. I stand by the door surveying everything, looking for my sister or brother, but they take recess later than the third graders. I silently pray that someone will ask me to join in with their jump rope game; I can jump rope really good. But no one does. In order to avoid looking completely stupid, I skip over to the merry-go-round, wait my turn in the line, and then begin to take a seat. Eva Landers, a big kid, (I find out later that she is in the fifth grade) looks at me and announces loudly, "No niggers allowed on the merry-go-round."

Where pupils learn to keep the golden rule

I wish that I could tell you that I came up with a smart response like, "Oh, I didn't see your mama in line," or how I was suspended for punching Eva in the face, smashing her cat-eye glasses as we wrestled in snow turned bright red from her badly bleeding broken nose. But I did none of those things. I paused, unsure for a slight moment that she was even talking to me. I actually remember looking behind me for the unfortunate recipient of such a bad, mean word.

When I turn back to face Eva, there was no mistake—she was sneering at me. I remember the blood rushing to my face, and the kids waiting to see how I would respond. I was flustered, lost in a sea of white kids. I stepped out of line and said, "Oh. I'm sorry." That being done, the kid behind me jumped onto the merry-go-round, and in a moment, all I could see was a blur of colorful scarves, hats, and coats while shrieks of youthful glee filled the air. I stood there alone. I had a new identity—the new girl—and a new name—nigger.

At lunch time I cried and told Mama all about how mean Eva had been to me and how I didn't have any friends, and I asked if we could go back to Altgeld Gardens, a housing development (most people call it "the projects") in Chicago, where I had friends.

I didn't care about our new house or anything; I begged to go back to Carver. I also wanted Mama to cuddle, coddle, and console me, but anyone who knew my no-nonsense mother could tell you that was not to be. After duly listening, she looked down at me.

"Joan, you don't go to school to make friends. You go to school to get an education. You got sisters and a brother to play with after school. If those white kids don't want to be nice, that's they problem. Now if anybody puts their hands on you, I'll take care of that. Your job is to go to school, do what the teacher say do, get good grades, and get on the honor roll. You learn your lessons. Can't nobody take that away from you. You just make sure you learn your lessons."

My mother had spoken, and that was that.

Recess became hell. I did not have friends with which to play, and those fifteen minutes became unbearable. I found a solution by volunteering to help in the classroom during recess. I cleaned blackboards, clapped erasers, washed milk bottles, and placed them back in their crates. I counted books, sharpened pencils, ran off mimeographed assignments, and took solace in smelling the purple pages.

I was a regular little indentured servant/homeroom slave. Sometimes, when Mrs. DeYoung was not looking, I would linger at the tall windows of Room 308, which looked onto the playground where everyone seemed to be having the times of their lives. I remembered the wonderful times I had at Carver during recess, racing, laughing, pigtails flying behind me as the cold Chicago wind beat across my face. During the spring, I could hear voices on the playground because the windows were open. I could imagine myself in the volleyball game or jumping rope with the other girls in saddle-oxfords. Of course, I had to get back to my duties, but I derived a measure of pleasure from my vicarious, secret life. And so it went, that first semester at Bennett. Although I was no longer innocent and unaware of racism, I was not without hope.

What you should learn is taught in this dear school

One day, as school was about to end for the summer, I stayed after school for a half-hour to clean out my desk. I had proven to Mrs.

DeYoung that I was nice by that time, so she allowed me to stay as she drank coffee. When I finished, I went outside to begin my walk over the bridge to the black neighborhood where I belonged, but something caught my attention.

There it was, the object of my desire and despair—the merry-go-round. I approach it with trepidation, almost as if Eva would instantly dart from around the field house and deny me once again, but the playground was deserted. I walked boldly to the merry-go-round. I put my book satchel on the ground, not taking my eyes off the glorious plaything.

I pushed it once and it went around. I pushed it a second time and it went faster. I pushed it a third time and jumped on it, braids flying in the air. I remember I laughed, holding on tightly, kicking my feet with joy as I leaned back and felt the soon-to-be summer breeze over my caramel face. I was finally riding it, alone, but I was riding, damn it! And I was not to be denied.

I'm learning my lessons, Mama. I'm learning them real good.

My Son, the Australians, Mrs. Spain, and Me

CAROLE MCDONNELL

I don't know why I think they were Australians. They might have been Americans, or British, or white-skinned Jamaicans, but I have always remembered them as Australians; therefore, Australians let them be.

They lived in the large house beside my grandfather's, a rectangular house, and the pale color looms as untouchable and indistinct in my memory as its vague eggshell color. Its architecture is also a vague memory. It is possible that I have forgotten it, because a ten-year-old child—it would be safe to say—would not be an expert on the Tudor or Spanish stucco architecture prevalent in that wealthy section of Jamaica. But also because the house seemed unapproachable, and the everyday invisibility of the house's inhabitants never really made the house come alive for me.

I remember that their house was large and rectangular, and that the bare yard that surrounded it was separated from ours by a chain-link fence that began in the front yard and continued all the way to the back, where both properties ended at the borders of a deep gully.

Whether these were Australians or white Jamaicans is unimportant. For a ten-year-old girl whose sister was playing elsewhere, the important thing was that a young boy about my own age—the youngest of three brothers—was playing in his yard, too, seemingly as alone and as bereft as I.

Jamaica is a country of many class and racial issues. Among children, these issues are often shown by whether one is allowed to play in the streets or not. It was normal for my sister and I to be locked away in our grandfather's yard. The neighborhood of Kencot, in the parish of St. Andrew, had a variety of people, very rich, very poor, very holy and upstanding (like my grandfather and myself), or very low-life. The fact that the young boy was locked away only proved his class. So we were prisoners for our own good.

I remember the family as blond. But who is to say if this is true? Perhaps I remember them as blond for the same reason I remember them as Australians, to push the family to some far ethnic extreme. It is quite possible that they were redheads or brunettes, and swarthy and dark. But I will remember them as blond and pale.

I remember the young boy bouncing a ball on the patio near the side door of his house. Alone, he stared back through the fence at me. I don't know how long he had been looking at me or who saw whom first or who initiated our silent communication, but we were aware of each other and that we both had balls in our hands.

I don't quite remember the game we invented. But he would bounce his ball under his mango tree or throw it in the air. And I, under the Ackee trees on my side of the fence, would throw my ball into the air. Whatever the unspoken rules were, at the time we seemed to understand each other well enough. His face is a blur now. All I remember is its whiteness, a whiteness that has now subsumed itself into blondness. I imagine his eyes might have been a kind of pale blue or green. I remember his curiosity, however, and the timid smile that spread across his face as the rules of the game solidified and we matched skills ball-toss for ball-toss.

On the other side of my grandfather's house lived a poor family whose lack of class was generally and specifically commented upon by my preacher grandfather and by everyone else in the neighborhood. They were a thoroughly dirty and poverty-stricken lot, and my grandfather made it quite clear that my sister and I should have nothing to do with them. An order we readily obeyed, for the most part.

My grandfather was a well-respected minister and his yard was a continual feast for our hands, noses, mouths, and eyes. The yard was full of fruit and flower gardens, jade leaves, soft petals, mango trees drooping with heavy fruit, hyacinths, and humming birds sipping from nectar-dripping flowers. The yard, with its bronze grate work and stucco walls, its European-style gardens, its well-kept hen-houses, verandas, stoops, and balconies, was full of roses, hot peppers, Ackee, tamarind, and lime plants. All these showed our class and showed us to be proper British subjects, if nothing else.

As we played, my ball accidentally—or perhaps it was on purpose—made it over the fence and the little boy ran after it. He had the ball in his hand and was about to throw it to me when the door of his house opened.

It was his mother. It is quite probable that she had been gazing at our interchange from the kitchen window. It is also quite probable that she might have allowed us our parallel play if my bouncing ball had not intruded upon her space and upon her son.

I heard the boy's name being called. And even now I laugh when I consider how sharply my memory remembers this: his name was Andrew. Yes, Andrew. His mother took the ball from Andrew's hand and threw it over the fence at me. Anger was written all over her face. Then she hurried him into the house, far from my contaminating presence, with such aplomb and maternal fear and disgust on her face that for a moment I feared she had mistaken me for the dirty riff-raff on the other side of our house.

That night my grandfather called me to the living room. I don't quite remember the exact wording of his warning. But the sum of his comment was two-fold: the Australians next door were very offended because I had played with their son, and did I not realize that boys like that were dangerous and would hurt little black girls.

I had not realized such a thing. I hadn't even imagined it. And, frankly, that was the kind of thing my grandfather should be saying to the riff-raff next door and not to me.

On a purely intuitive level, I sensed that my extremely class-aware grandfather was both guarding the family's purity (my virginity) and hiding his hurt that the Australian mother had dared insult him by accusing his low-life ten-year-old granddaughter of attempting to seduce her son. When I consider now that this extreme upset on the part of both adults was caused by the innocent actions of two ten-year-olds, I find myself wondering about the priggish racism of times past. Then, my only question was, "But we aren't like those bad people next door. Don't they know that?" But, although I could not articulate it, it had begun to dawn on me that whites did not differentiate between good blacks and bad ones.

Nevertheless, I was grounded for the next day and told not to talk to the Australians again. For the next few days and all throughout that summer, as I played under the Ackee and mango trees, all I did was watch that little side door, waiting for the smiling face of Andrew to appear. I don't remember that it ever did. Perhaps they were vacationers and not native Jamaicans; perhaps that is why I never saw Andrew again. Perhaps they kept the doors closed and never ventured outside again. Perhaps they moved out stealthily by night—or by day—and I have conveniently forgotten. As I've said, my memory of the day is none too clear.

But despite my vague memory of the events of that day, whether it was sunny or full of looming clouds, whether they were indeed Australians or not, whether they were vacationers or native inhabitants of Jamaica, the events of those long-ago fifteen minutes remain with me always. Among my grandfather's trees was a small plant called the Shamed Old Lady that we shamed and bothered all the time. The leaves of the plant were very much like those of the mimosa plant, with this one difference: when touched by human fingers, animal paw, or even the slightest rain drop, the leaves of the Shamed Old Lady would shrink away from the offender's touch; hence the name.

The memories from that day rise within me as a shaming accusation, an accusation that I could not defend myself against. They float before me, rejection as deep as the gully at the far end of my grandfather's yard. They oppress me like an eternal loss, a loss brought about by power and spite. I never knew Andrew. I don't remember ever speaking with him. Sometimes I think I'm still looking for him. It's the removal of Andrew that I remember. Other friends have been gained and kept, but it's what I don't have that stays with me.

You may imagine, then, my perturbance when my son encountered a racist teacher in his high school, Mrs. Spain.

My son eats, breathes, dreams, and vomits Mrs. Spain. He imagines and re-imagines each of her insults. And in his imagination, his staircase wit is now at the ready, not delayed until she has slammed the door. The words at our dinner table, breakfast table, and bedtime prayer are all of his might-have-been mental triumphs. But these are only imaginary weapons, mental power.

Unlike Mrs. Spain, my son is not cruel. But like me, he is sensitive. I had grown up with a sense of injustice and loss. I did not want my son's life being weighed down by a sense of injustice. But neither did I want him to be argumentative with a chip on his shoulder.

There was imbalance in the situation. Mrs. Spain was his teacher, with power to do harm and to affect his future. My son has always been a conqueror. When he was five, he painted a poster of Strongbone Man, his alter ego. Strongbone Man never rescued little girls from drowning. He never returned the sun back to the sky.

Strongbone Man merely stood there, exulting in his strength. The thick charcoal lines of Strongbone Man's muscles swooped tight around his torso, taut, crablike. Strongbone Man's blue cape wafted in the paper breeze and "m" birds hovered around his head like a crown. But how does one conquer someone who, for all intents and purposes, already rules an empire?

I tell my son that although Mrs. Spain is cruel, he must do nothing. Mrs. Spain is to be watched. Mrs. Spain, I tell him, will become a byword. Years from now, I prophesy, he will hear news from afar: Mrs. Spain will have died in infamy. Mrs. Spain will have died from a horrible self-inflicted death. He says I sound as if I am wishing it. I tell him I am. What goes around comes around; this is the patience and the endurance of the saints.

These are spiritual weapons, spiritual power.

When my son was two or three, he developed a fear of Chucky, the homicidal doll of the *Child's Play* movies. Trailers and coming attractions of *Bride of Chucky* would cause my son to flee the living room and the TV set. Then, after the trailer ended, he would return from the dining room, free for the moment from the specter of the vicious doll. I grew to hate Chucky because of the power he had over my son.

One day, the owner of Monument Video put a poster of Chucky on the entrance of her store. This was troubling because we had to walk by the store whenever we went downtown, and my son would not venture past Chucky. From that day on, we walked on the other side of the road. And, always, he averted his eyes.

One day, as we were walking downtown, I remembered that we had to walk past the poster. As we neared the store, I stopped at an intersection.

"We'll cross the street here," I said. "And you won't have to look at Chucky."

My son said, "Mom, don't cross the street. I'm going to walk on this side, today. I'm going to walk right in front of Chucky."

"Are you sure?"

He nodded.

We approached the video store. But his head still faced outward towards the traffic. He continued walking, though, feet moving ahead, head turned.

I said, "I'll tell you when we're coming closer to Chucky. I'll cover your eyes now. Then, after we've passed the door, I'll take my hand away. After that, you'll be free to look straight ahead because Chucky will be behind us."

When the door to the video store was only two or three steps away, I put my hand on his head, ready to slide it over his eyes as soon as we reached the poster.

I stopped to make sure he was all right. "Ready, son?"

He nodded.

I slipped my hand over his eyes. "One more step and we'll be in front of Chucky. We're just about to reach Chucky. Okay, one more step, one more step. Okay, here we are. Don't look."

When I said this, he did a surprising thing: he removed my hands from his eyes and turned to look directly at the poster; he stared Chucky down. His hands were clenched, his stance was sure as he held Chucky's stare. We toppled Chucky, who stood there pinned against the door. He was two or three years old then. And now, at age 14, he meets Mrs. Spain.

I warn him over and over: the secret of his power will be to do no harm. Mrs. Spain is powerful. She has authority on her side. She has collective adult immaturity on her side. No son, whatever the plans of your imagination, you must not harm Mrs. Spain; for in harming Mrs. Spain, you will be harming yourself. You will lose your allies, those people who walk beside you. And allies are always a necessity.

Every day, he enters the high school and walks past Mrs. Spain. Mrs. Spain wears her poster grimace, crueler in its cunning than Chucky. But Chucky had his witty, kinder moments. Chucky had a method to his madness. And Chucky does not hide his cruelty for his reputation's sake. In short, even in his cruelty, Chucky fought fairly. Chucky felt no need to strip his enemies' mental armor. Chucky was honorable. Mrs. Spain is not.

But I remember the walk past the poster. And I am heartened that my son's life will not echo loss as mine has. How can I describe to you my love for Chucky? I love Chucky, I love Chucky, and I love Chucky. To this day, and forever more, I will love Chucky, because Strongbone Man mastered him. One day too, I will love Mrs. Spain, because Strongbone Man will conquer her.

Who Is This Woman?

FELISICIA WILLIAMS

Early one morning I woke up, placed my feet upon the carpet, and thought how clear everything looked. This was quite unusual, since I am legally blind without corrective lenses. I started my regular routine: turned the television on to the Today Show, poured a glass of juice, and proceeded to the dressing area.

This is where I usually put in my contact lenses or put on my glasses. I decided to wear my glasses, so I looked on the counter, went back into the bedroom, and checked the nightstand. I even went back into the kitchen and checked the counters. No luck. Hmm, that's strange. I frantically began to search, with no luck. I finally gave up and went back into the bedroom to wake my husband. He can usually find things when I can't.

"Lamar, have you seen my glasses? I want to give my eyes a break from the contacts today. I can't find them."

"Baby, you fell asleep in them last night. They are on your eyes!" We both fell out laughing. Who is this woman? I never looked once in the mirror, and I have worn eyeglasses since the fifth grade. My frame is lightweight and I am so used to having them on, but this was scary. Is my memory this bad? Where did my 20s, and my 30s go?

I am 44 years old and can't remember where I put most things. Sisters, my body is going through some serious changes. I resisted the changes initially, but I learned (the hard way) that this makes it worse. The more I tried to cover up my short-term memory loss, the more things I forgot. Lesson: Covering things up can cause stress; stress can cause short-term memory loss. As I age there are other challenges and other lessons I have learned.

Lotion was once a wanted item. It didn't matter if I had any or not. Not a necessity. My skin was soft and supple, never dry. Lesson: Aging can cause dry skin; lotion is now a necessity, and I need a brand that is best for my skin type. Dry skin is no fun. Itching in all areas and at some of the oddest times can be downright embarrassing. I began to feel like a seven-year-old who has rolled around in sand. Lotion is a must for me.

The most significant change and the one that brings tears to my eyes at times is—I can barely share this now without a tear. I cannot eat everything I want anymore! I fought and fought, lied to myself and to my husband. I made up all kinds of excuses, for example: "Lamar, that food we ate last night stayed in the fridge too long, or I have premenstrual symptoms or I have postmenstrual symptoms; it's my nerves." Anything!

Lamar would gently say, "Felisicia, your digestive system is changing, and you're going to have to change your eating habits."

I hated him! (smile) He was only telling me the truth. Lesson: The digestive system ages along with us and I can't eat hot dogs or ice cream or drink juice after 9 pm and fall asleep. A "little" problem called indigestion creeps into my body, and I have a night of tossing and turning. In the morning I have a lot of bloating and feel awful. I probably need to give in to the "little purple pill." This brings me to one more lesson I would like to share.

My favorite seasoning is salt. My favorite meat is pork. I loved it long before it became the "other white meat." In 1996, my primary physician informed me that my blood pressure was high. This was after I altered my diet, decreased my salt intake and was no longer eating pork. I could not believe it was still high.

How much more could I take? I was born and raised in Rocky Mount, N.C. Home of the best pork barbecue money could buy. She was crazy. I wanted to get a second opinion. These and many other thoughts were going through my mind. I only heard bits and pieces of what the doctor was saying. Finally, with a deep breath I asked, "Will I have to take medication?"

"Yes, you will."

This was it, sisters. I knew it would only be downhill from there on.

Initially I was not compliant. I took the pill when I wanted to, but after a wake-up call in September 2002, I now take my medication. High blood pressure can lead to strokes, heart attacks, and many other major health conditions. I didn't like any of those. Lesson: Even though high blood pressure was prevalent in my family, I could have possibly avoided it by eating a healthier diet in my younger years. I now enjoy eating all the wonderful food I want and I also enjoy all the wonderful seasonings (salt free)!

Peace and blessings!

Menopause:
The Madness and Mystery

SANDY KAY

There I was, 39 years old—happy, healthy, and confident in myself and with my purpose in life. My life was like being in a womb in the last two months of gestation. I had worked hard on my personal development and was on my way to full-on enlightenment. I felt good in my body and had just begun to enjoy the fruits of my labor when I turned forty and midlife contractions began.

The first contraction came in the middle of the night. I woke up and I was soaking wet, as was my bed. I didn't know if I had already reached my second childhood and was back in those diaper days, or had met with early senility and the world of incontinence. I got up, changed my sheets, and called my mom. She reassured me this was normal in menopause and said the first "night sweat" was the worst. She was right. This exciting adventure of night sweats went on for a few months and then disappeared for the most part.

The second contraction started right around the time the first one let up. Hot flashes. I felt like I was stepping into an invisible microwave off and on throughout my day, being cooked from the inside out. A wave of heat would roll through my body like thunder, making me want to strip on the spot. A few minutes later it would pass and I would freeze. This experience lasted a few months and only returned a few times in the last five years. Those were physical contractions, which I could handle because I still had my mind and emotional stability. Contraction three took care of that.

The third adventure affected my short-term memory. I had always cherished my ability to recall names, faces, dates, and phone numbers, and now I was wandering the parking lot looking for my car because I forgot where I parked it. I would walk into a room and forget why I was there. I would lose my train of thought right in the middle of my sentence. Just for fun, try going on a job interview in this crazy state. Things got a little harder, and my sense of humor was slowly leaving. My self-confidence was turning into self-acceptance.

Now, I knew how to lose weight, and when I put my mind to it, off it came. However, because of contraction three, I no longer had a mind, and my short-term memory had no recollection of eating all the chocolates in the box. To intensify this adventure, the cravings were so strong I woke up when the box or carton was empty. This was and continues to be the fourth contraction.

I am now gaining weight, and the biggest joke is contraction five. I have to eat like a fasting yogi to lose one measly pound. I read a wonderful book, Outsmarting the Mid-Life Fat Cell by Debra Waterhouse, M.P.H., R.D., an expert in menopause issues. She states that it's necessary and healthy for menopausal women to gain a few pounds of fat. The operative word here is "a few." But when I can't button my jeans and my blouse pulls across the chest, I am not laughing and this is not a funny joke.

Contraction six is the inconsistency and unpredictability of that ever-so-familiar monthly occurrence. Before mid-life labor, I knew every 28 days, almost to the minute, to be prepared. Now I haven't got a clue, and being prepared becomes a guessing game where nature usually wins.

As if all this isn't enough, the most challenging contraction is number seven, emotional insecurity, and the one that creates madness. I can handle the inconvenience of physical challenges and the temporary loss of short-term memory, but the emotional roller coaster in contraction seven amplifies any challenge. If I am feeling the physical effects of contractions one and two and my emotions are up and down, I truly feel like I am dying. If my memory is fading in and out and I am riding that emotional roller coaster, I really feel like I am developing Alzheimer's, and I will never be normal again.

When all three hit at once, just give me a cave far, far away for about a week. I remember starting a new job and having one of these "cave days." I started crying over nothing, took a question my new boss asked me completely out of context, and couldn't remember a single thing I was learning. I was never like this before. I wonder if I'm alone in this menagerie of the mind.

So, the comfortable days in the womb of the thirties are long gone. I am now 45 years old and most of the contractions have diminished considerably. Maybe I have just gone through Mother Nature's mandatory class of Personal Growth 102.

What I have learned and continue to discover is I am giving birth to unconditional self-acceptance, a sense of humor I never knew I had, unbelievable strength, courage beyond my imagination, unrelenting perseverance, and surrender born from a desperate need for peace. But the most profound and beautiful lesson has been that of self-love, continually burning and glowing from the mysterious depths of who I am.

In those Zen moments of being detached from my personal experience, I feel myself chuckling at the paradox that embraces this time of life. I am falling apart to come together and shine my own personal light brighter than I ever have before.

THEME III.

Love, Humility, and Other Spices That Flavor Relationships

*A Woman's life can really be a succession of lives,
each revolving around some emotionally compelling
situation or challenge, and each marked off
by some intense experience.*
— Wallis Simpson

LOVE'S LEGACY

Time has passed
since that first kiss, so fierce.
Passion-bruised evidence
lingered on my neck for a week.
I felt, I had dissolved into you.

Your kisses aren't as fierce now,
softened by the pummeling of problems
rock-sliding through the years.

The force and frequency of kisses
are less important
that the love-legacy
bestowed.

A heart-branded love,
fire-tested love
only connected souls could bare.

Some miss the mania
young lovers own;
but, this morning
my body welcomed the warmth
ignited by your touch
and the security that is mine
tucked away inside your arms.

— *Paula White Jackson*

The White Dress

CYNTHIA REGINA HOBSON

I was sitting at the kitchen table today, reading *The Rescue* by Nicholas Sparks. I got to the part in the book where Denise meets Taylor in the store unexpectedly and they are subtly attracted to one another. My mind drifted back to when I first became attracted to my husband Lawrence. I was seventeen years old. It was January 14, 1958.

I was with a girlfriend at Lawrence's eighteenth birthday party. There was lots of folks there, and the party was live. The latest 45s were on the box, everyone was dancing, and there were lots of laughter, good food, and drinks. My girlfriend Miller Earl and I had bought new, white sheath dresses. My dress shimmered when the light hit it because it had tiny threads of silver throughout. I was built nice back then, and the dress fit just right.

We knew we looked good, because everyone stopped to look at us when we entered and as we walked around the apartment where the party was taking place. I was always a little on the shy side, but the admiring looks made me glad I had worn my new white dress. Little did I know that my white dress would change my life forever.

I was standing with a group of people when someone said, looking over my shoulder, "Hey, there he is, the birthday boy—Happy birthday, man!"

I turned around, and there he was walking toward us. He was looking me up and down, starting from my face, down and back up again.

I said, "Hi. Happy birthday, Lawrence!"

He held out his hand and said, "Cynthia, would you like to dance?"

It was a slow dance. "Baby, It's You" was playing, by some singing group whose name I do not remember anymore. I do remember the dance, though. Lawrence held me close as we danced as one, then pushed me slightly away, looked into my eyes and down at my white dress, then held me close again.

I must say he had my attention. Lawrence was looking good as always. He had on an olive-green, Ivy League-style suit with stingy lapels, a light-tan shirt with a skinny, striped tie, and pants pulled slightly over his waist-line with suspenders. His shoes were spit-shined black Stacey Adams. Not only was he handsome, he had a beautiful, muscular, 5-foot-8 physique.

When girls looked at him, they would go, "Mum—Mum—MUM! I wish he was mine!"

Lawrence and I grew up together. We had the same friends, who all hung around together. We were a tight-knit group. I had never thought of him as someone who would be attracted to me, or me to him. I always thought he was cute, but we were just friends. For one thing, he had a reputation for being a playboy. I knew to stay clear.

Somehow, this night it was different. I don't know why, but it was. So, when he asked me to dance, I said yes. When I stepped into his arms, it was familiar, like something I had always known. I liked dancing with him. It felt good, and we seemed to just fit together. When the music stopped, to my surprise he kissed me softly on the lips, took me by the hand, and said, "Come on."

We went into the kitchen to get some refreshments. When I turned around from the table, he put his arms around me and gave me a deep, long kiss. My knees buckled. I got embarrassed and hoped he hadn't noticed. He took me by the hand. We were a couple the rest of the evening. Folks checked us out, wondering what was going on.

Then, he asked if he could walk me home. All my intuitive alarms went off. My heart skipped a little beat and I said, "Yes!"

A couple of years later, we said "yes" at the altar at Holy Angels Church.

After we had been married for a while, I asked Lawrence why he picked me out of all the girls he could have had. He answered, "Baby, it was the white dress. "

"The white dress? You mean the one I wore to your eighteenth birthday party?"

"Yes!" He went on to say, "Actually, Cynthia, I had been attracted to you for some time, but couldn't figure out how to approach you. Plus, I already had a girlfriend at the time, and you knew her, too. I knew you had a lot of integrity and would not think of moving in on someone else's game.

"In fact, that was a problem you asked me to solve before you would even consider being my only girl. But baby, when you walked into my party with that white dress on, all of my scruples went out the window. You always have been pretty, but that night, you were scrumptious. The guys were looking at you. I knew I had to make a move. Besides, I knew I had better make my move right away, or lose out. I'm glad I didn't wait."

I smiled at him and said, "Yeah, you'd better be glad you did not wait, 'cause look what you would of missed out on."

Then he asked me, "Why did you decide to say yes to me? There were plenty of guys who wanted to be in my shoes."

"It was the kiss."

"What kiss?" he asked.

"The one in the kitchen at your birthday party."

"Oh, that kiss," he said. "It was something else, wasn't it?"

"Yes it was. I felt it all over. I said to myself, 'self, what is happening here?'"

We both laughed, and I thought to myself when it's good, it's just good, and there ain't nothing else like it. Sitting here, reading this book really brought back memories, things I had not thought about in a long time. It's amazing how something you read or see can do that. All I know is that 47 years later, my knees still buckle when I think about that kiss in the kitchen. Mum—Mum—MUM—I'm glad he's mine!

PHOENIX

I'm going to pick you out of
my hair
unconditional freedom.
I've got the pick,
rake, comb,
wide and narrow
and a money-back guarantee
erase you from
my twisted marrow,
my brittle roots
that aching abandon
my fro
perm
weave
twisted incantations,
momentary
surreal, unrealities,
shattered time
and time again
with poisoned
lice lies.
"heal thyself,"
reclaim my mind
from the bumpy,
beaten, deceitful
path you have
so cruelly
so relentlessly
traveled with
my hands clasped
frozen in
your image
numb and broken
in betrayal
self-hatred.
Water unravels
twisted sister's

braids and such
Tiny bits of your
ego vanish in
the first rinse,
Residue of
non-stop betrayal
flushed down
the drain along
with confusion
Endured for
so long,
Hope reigns brilliant
against worn,
war-torn tears.
I'll greet my day
sunshine bright
From top to toe
beginning with my
fresh, new hairdo
Totally and completely
absent of you.

— *Lynette Velasco*

The Can't Pick a Nigga Club

CAROL NOWELL

F lo and I ordered our usual Saturday morning breakfast of grits, eggs, bacon, toast, and coffee. We settled back in our seats, saying good morning to people we knew and did not know. When the waitress brought our coffee, it was the signal to stop the pleasantries and get down to the business of what had happened in our lives the past week.

Flo had been married for six years and had the same joking complaints of her husband's male ignorance and stupid behavior. She credited him with being the best man she ever had, and in the end she was happy and content in her marriage. My update did not have a happy ending. Once again, I was ending a marriage where I had given my all. Still, it had failed because my man was just trifling and no good. So, I was lonely and starting my life all over again.

That really bothered me. I was starting over again at age 43. Hell, I should have been settled in a nice house in the country with an attractive and financially secure husband who I knew and understood inside and out. Instead, I had just moved into a mobile home, had no savings, and had started a new job. My only blessing was that at least my son and daughter were grown and out on their own. They would not have to be packed up and moved again.

I stirred the cheese around in my grits and stared at it as I complained to Flo, "I should have known better than to even speak to Vick."

After the second date, I knew he was an ex-con and did not like working a boring 9 to 5 job for the White Man. And worse, he was broke on our first date. But I smiled and compromised my way through the relationship, until we married after knowing each other for only four months. Then I struggled with him for a year. He could always get a job. He just could not keep it for more than two months.

Large amounts of money appeared from the "side gigs" he was doing. My sweet and considerate husband then decided to just stay home and take care of the house. He would have my dinner ready when I came home every day. The ultimate pain hit me when I discovered he was having sex with women in our house while I was at work. Only then was I able to drum up a little self-respect and dignity and put him out.

"Girl, don't feel bad, you are one in a million sisters. All just trying to fix and understand a no-good man. At least you finally saw the light. Just learn from your mistake."

Flo was supportive and always gave solid advice. Yet, I still felt trampled and dumb.

I sucked in my feelings, changed the subject, and after breakfast we headed for the mall. Later that night, after downing a bottle of wine, I lay in bed trying to figure out just what I had learned. Two marriages had gone down the drain, and numerous serious relationships had proven empty. Once again I was alone. It seemed I never met any good men.

And why was that? I was educated; I had a master's degree. I was attractive, a beautiful "high yella gal" who looked ten years younger than my age. I had a good state job with benefits. And I was willing to do whatever it took to make my man happy. Why did I always end up with a sorry man?

Flo's words came back to me as I pressed my mind and soul for an answer. Then it hit me. I did not know how to pick a good man. I was one in a million sisters, all members of "The Can't Pick a Nigga Club."

The next day, I told Flo about my realization. We laughed and rolled at the name of my club. But when we stopped, seriousness took over Flo's face as she said, "Girl, you don't have to settle for anything. Decide what you really want and need and don't stop or waste your time on anyone if they can't deliver."

Flo's words were stern. She was no longer giving advice. She was demanding I take care of myself. Her words seeped into my mind, soul, and heart. Another night of wine drinking and hard crying brought me out of my pity party. I decided I had been a member of "The Can't Pick a Nigga Club" for too long. I was getting out.

Four months passed. It was the longest I had been without a man in my life since I starting dating at the age of 17. Proudly, I realized I was fine. I liked my new job and had settled into a comfortable routine at work. My new place was furnished and felt like a real home. I met my new neighbors and gained a few more friends. After buying a new professional wardrobe, I put some money in savings. I joined a health club and was feeling more energetic and even lost some weight. Every Sunday I was in church, and I started going to Bible Study classes. For the first time in my life, I was focusing on me.

Oh yeah, there were a few knuckleheads that had tried to enter my space, but I had closed my door to them quickly. I followed my instincts and prayed to God for a good man. But this time I asked him to give me the wisdom to know him when he came in my life. This time I wanted to be able to recognize the signs and have the strength to act in my best interest. The signs were there before. I simply chose to ignore them. Now they blazed before me, and I felt embarrassed just thinking of them.

My first husband, Gray, was overly complimentary of me from the start. He was constantly telling me and anyone else who was around how beautiful I was. He loved to tenderly touch my face and whisper how lucky he was to have such a beautiful woman. After six months of marriage, he was beating my beautiful face every weekend. So, after staying home from work for a week because his handprint was branded over one side of my beautiful face, I gathered my babies and left.

Don helped me move. He was the kind, classy-dressing guy in two of my evening classes. Well, he did not come to class much, but when he did, he was very concerned about me, and what I was going through. He suggested I escape my troubles and get a clear head. Don introduced me to good weed, fine wine, and strong liquor. It shocked me when he got fired from his job as a parole officer because he was buying drugs from a client. And I cried for days when he left me because a mother with two kids was too much of a burden for him.

So, I moved back home to North Carolina to start over and find a good Southern man. Lucky me. I met Kevin, 14 years younger than me, sinfully handsome, and hung from heaven. He made me scream every night, and he loved a "mature woman of beauty." I was so busy screaming every night; I did not realize Kevin had a gambling addiction until I came home to find we were being put out of our home because he had not paid the house payment for the past five months.

He suggested I calm down and go stay with my mother for a few days. He would take care of our problems. He was going to Atlantic City where he would win big at the blackjack table. I just needed to give Kevin a few dollars to get in the game. Of course, I did that to show I believed in my man. When Kevin called a few nights later asking me to send him money by Western Union to buy gas to come home, I decided to kick him to the curb.

Meanwhile at work, Jean was smiling and coming by my office with coffee and donuts on a regular basis. A quick kiss in the elevator one day led to a night of lust. Which led to more nights of lust in his car and local hotel rooms. When I questioned why we never went out together or spent time at his place, he explained he had a housemate who was nosy and nasty. As soon as he got rid of him, I would be able to come over all the time. Until then, he had to save money because he would be pressed for cash until he found a new housemate. That was understandable.

When he was out of work for three days with the flu, I found his address from a friend in Personnel and decided to surprise him with some homemade soup and juice. I got surprised when his housemate turned out to be his wife, who opened the door and threatened to drown me in my soup. There were more, but that was enough of the past. The memories were too painful.

I had been disgracefully blind and stupidly needy. Tears filled my eyes when I thought of the example I had set for my son and daughter. One Sunday afternoon, the guilt burned so bad I called them and apologized for my poor behavior. I promised them and myself I would be a stronger, wiser person and mother.

Seven months passed. Then he walked by my desk at work. My heart jumped and my brain geared up. It was him! Now, he did not look like my dreamboats of the past. He was older, shorter, shy, and not a city boy dressed in fine clothes. But I knew it was him when our eyes met.

William was the one God had sent me. Trouble was, he did not know it. He could not believe I was truly interested in him. He was meek, ten years older than me, and just a "plain ole country boy." Most important, I was able to recognize the goodness in him. William was kind, respectful, hard working, intelligent, and generous.

We had known each other for five months and still William had not asked me out.

He would come by and speak to me, offer to carry my briefcase, and just make small talk. Finally, I asked him out on our first date. He picked me up with flowers in hand, and from then on we have been a couple. After two years of peaceful loving, he gave me a stunning engagement ring. Next year, after he finishes having our new home built, we plan to get married.

My son and daughter think he is the best thing that has ever happened to me. For once, my grandmother approves of the man I have in my life. Now I have chosen a good man, and I am living the good life I deserve. My membership has been cancelled. I am no longer a member of "The Can't Pick a Nigga Club."

I had to realize I deserved the best before I could get the best. There is one other important note. I now give the best as well. I find myself happily doing things for William I would have wrung my neck and snapped my fingers at before. Like cooking what he wants for dinner, fixing his plate and bringing it to him (with a smile), and getting up from the table to refill his glass. Flo was shocked when she saw me jump up and get him a roll when he said, "Baby, that bread is delicious. I could eat just one more."

She pulled me aside later and asked what I was on and joked I was setting a bad example. I laughed and reminded her, "My man buys all the groceries, pays the bills, takes me out to eat whenever I ask, gives me extra money to spend every week, buys any clothing item I mention I want, and reimburses me every time I get my hair and nails done. In addition, he has never raised his voice or hand to me. However, he makes his feelings known in a firm, yet subtle way. William has not come over to my house since our first date almost three years ago (when I told him I loved chicken) without a box of my favorite chicken from KFC. So, if bringing him a plate of food or filling his glass with iced tea makes him happy, he will be happy forever."

I finally figured out how to pick a good man. I stopped looking for fashionable clothes, a fine car, a cute face, a hot body, a lot of sweet talk, or a smooth dancer—all that outside stuff. I saw the light shining in his eyes. It was the light of inner kindness and honesty. In William's arms, I feel safe, secure, and protected from harm. The best feeling of all and the most comforting is I know he will not harm me.

I Blew Right Past You

You know, I blew right past you
Like the coolest of evening breezes
My eyes danced all over you
Did a sexy peek-a-boo
Trying not to stare or make you aware
Of the talent your mere presence brings

So, I just blew right past you
Leaving you with a casual wave
And the scent of China Musk in my wake
You looked up and saw the space I used to occupy
Because I developed wings to fly past you
And those like you who would choose misery
Over a lifetime of delight

Oh, yes, I blew past you like a mighty hurricane
Not plain, and kind of insane
With my passion for living and giving all I've got
To the great big pot of life
A meal I partake of voraciously
But, not you 'cause you TOO COOL
And, school's been out on you for a while, child
The winds of time have caught up with you
Stuck in our own personal time warp
You've missed the most important part
Of the meal—the real deal
Big wind whirling, swirling on gossamer wings
With a bit of a sting
A wind with just enough bite
To whet your appetite—for adventure
But, you're too immature to try
That's why…

I blew right past you
Like soft summer sighs and harsh wintry goodbyes
Like autumn leaves rolling down fog-filled streets
Like a sensuous breeze from a time long ago

But whose scent takes you back to when…
I blew right past you
Like a willow-the-wisp, too quick to catch
Too hot to hold, with a bite that can leave you cold
Unless you're bold enough to
Catch the breeze that blows
Right—past—you!!

— Katherine A. Parker

Learning to Breathe As
We Wait to Exhale

CONSTANCE DIGGS MATTHEWS

When sister friend Terry McMillan created our public looking glass into (Black women's) issues and challenges with relationships through her critically acclaimed novel and movie of the same title *Waiting to Exhale*, we were able to laugh, cry, reflect, and shout amen with three snaps and a circle at how common and deep our issues were in this area. There was a dose of reality for all of us to grab hold to.

I've personally watched the movie over a dozen times, with the last six times followed by *How Stella Got Her Groove Back*, to remind myself that the possibility of a B-side to my relationship soundtrack does and can exist. I love Terry and her gift to use the written word to make us look at pain in a charming and less alarming way. She makes us smile and laugh at ourselves in stereo. It's good medicine but not a cure.

When the popcorn, Häagen Dazs, chips, dip, and Diet Coke were gone, the sun came up and I was forced to leave the soothing world created by Terry, who had become my self-proclaimed personal analyst and motivational speaker. As I came back to reality, I sometimes cried because, like many of my sisters, I searched hard and long to find my groove and was blue in the face from waiting to exhale. All along forgetting the most important weapon in the struggle to maintain a healthy life. I simply forgot to breathe.

To breathe, according to most medical dictionaries, is the process of circulating air in and out of one's lungs to provide oxygen to vital, life-sustaining organs—specifically the brain and the heart. Hmm. So in other words, if we do not breathe properly, we can surely die.

Well, beyond the need to circulate oxygen to my heart and brain, I needed to breathe (process in and out) those things that are vital to sustaining my spirit. At one point, I found myself drowning so deep in tears, fears, and the anguish of past and present relationships that my spirit began to fade.

Without going back as far as my father's poor example of a husband and father in my youth, I'll fast-forward to about nine years ago, when a dear friend and mentor noticed a change in me as I struggled in a relationship that would end in tragedy. My friend and mentor, who also happened to be my boss, pulled me aside after our weekly meeting. He looked me in my eyes and said slowly and clearly, "Never let anything or anyone steal your joy."

I was shocked and embarrassed that my life was written so eloquently on my face and in my body language. After all, I had a wonderful career as director of publicity at a major African-American children's book publishing house. I was a lieutenant in the Army National Guard. I was in peak physical condition at a shapely, model-size eight. My pre-war garden apartment was beautifully furnished with parquet wood floors and Black art everywhere. Books and music smiled on me from wall to wall. I was a walking testimony of one of Terry's put-together sisters and the inspiration that many of my girlfriends admired and all of my relatives lectured their girls to look at as a picture of what they should be.

As work pulled my spirit in and lifted it up, my relationship with my then-boyfriend pulled it out and apart. Even so, I really thought I had it together. I hadn't even noticed, as my boss did, that my joy had gone into cardiac arrest. After all, I was doing my job–very well.

Eight months later I found the beautiful Black man, who I loved very dearly, murdered in his apartment, leaving me with unanswered questions about his life, the circumstances of his death, and the truth about the life we shared.

Had I stopped to breathe, not only would I have maintained my joy but also the clarity of mind to see the road of destruction that would claim his life and forever change mine. I would eventually rise from the ashes this experience left me in. Scared and scarred, I moved on to a new career, a new address, and several new men without the privilege of knowing who and what I know now. That in order to live or survive, we must practice the type of spiritual breathing that can and will bring the relationships God intends for us to engage in.

Fast-forward again to 1999, where I found myself diagnosed with another relationship polyp. It was a terrible time in my life. I was experiencing a meltdown of gigantic proportions. I had lost another man, two jobs in a row, bill collectors had me talking to imaginary representatives, and I was convinced that I was destined to die a childless old maid. I went to church "religiously," fasted, prayed, sang in the choir, worked with the youth, but was still lost in my own relationship wasteland.

To top it all off, the man "I lost" this time was actually the man who dumped me, and it was a bad breakup. At least for me it was because he basically told me I was not "good enough" for him. I wasn't pretty enough, trim enough, and lived too far away. Ours was a bicoastal relationship. He lived in California and I was in Harlem, New York. He was the second man I ever brought home to my family. For the first time in my life I had self-esteem issues. It was a devastating spiritual blow that would take over a year for me to heal from.

I entered into a self-imposed isolation and quarantined myself from everything social. All I did was worship, work, and worry. This time I had lost my joy and control of my spirit. In my efforts to heal, I surrounded myself with the Word of God, prayer, and a vision to start my own businesses. Juanita Bynum and TD Jakes replaced Terry McMillan as my personal analysts and motivational speakers.

My cousin, best friend, and prayer partner Marlo (who lived in California) grew quite concerned for me. After all, she was the one who had introduced me to the relationship that now poisoned me. Next to prayer and God's Word, she truly was my rock. I learned quickly, in that year's time, the value and importance of building healthy relationships. My relationships with God and Marlo taught me the importance of learning how to breathe spiritually.

Toward the end of my social sabbatical, I realized I had stayed single for over a year (by choice), and was forced to focus on the most important relationship of all—me, myself, and I. Shortly after the breakup, I took a job at a teen magazine as marketing director and cried at least once a week by phone and daily via the 'net to Marlo. Sharing my disdain for 9 to 5's and men full of jive, I needed a miracle and prayed for it.

Well, in true form, Marlo wanted to help me bounce back and told me about this gentleman (a "brother" she called him) who needed some (wink, wink) "tips on putting together a media kit for a music project he was working on." I quickly reminded her of the foils of her first and only attempt to match-make me with her friend, who broke my heart, and of my vow to never date another man long distance, especially one from California.

Marlo quickly denied my accusations, but I smelled a "matchmaking" brewing. Nevertheless, I entertained my cousin's request to be my "keepin' real, down for my people" self and lend my experience to her friend. "Coni, just call him," she said as she finally admitted her motive was more than finding her friend some professional advice.

"You have to hear his voice. He puts Barry White to shame. He writes poetry. He loves the Lord. He so cultured and did I mention he's easy on the eyes? Just help him out and maybe, who knows, you can just have dinner the next time you come to town. I'm not asking you to marry him! Just have some fun. You work hard and you deserve it."

"Fun?" I asked. "I'm living in a state of emergency. I have no time for fun. I only have time for God and me. I don't want or need a man. If he's mine I'm going to need a 'burning bush' experience to convince me. I'm not calling that man. Call just to hear his voice? That is so high school. What would I say?"

As much as I bucked, her plea worked. I gave in and called his job. He was a commercial business representative at a Kinko's in San Diego where he was well known as the man with a voice like butter. He answered in serenade, "Thank you for calling Kinko's, home of the 99¢ Kodak Picture Maker. This is Leon speaking. How can I help you?"

I stuttered, "Uh, uh, where are you located?"

As he recited the address, my heart literally jumped. I responded with a thank you. Hung up the phone, called my cousin, and shared in agreement with her that "the brother had it goin' on," and girly and giggly as he made me feel, I was not going out with him. "Give him my number at work," I instructed. "I'll talk to him about the project and that's it!"

The rest, well, let's just say we spent about five minutes talking about his project and the next two months in one of the most beautiful courtships a girl could ask for. Leon Alexander Matthews became my friend. I imagined how he looked. Offered to send photos so as to get the whole visual thing out the way. He insisted that it was not necessary, proclaiming that he knew I was beautiful.

As great as it all was, I constantly referenced mental notes of scriptures God had diagnosed for me, Juanita's warrant against getting soul tied, and TD Jakes' declaration of Woman Thou Art Loosed, which made me step with extreme caution and pay attention to my own reactions to him and more importantly his treatment of me. I had finally learned how to breathe spiritually. I knew how to believe and receive. How to let go and hold on to what was important and relevant for my soul survival. I didn't have to wait to exhale anymore because I no longer held my breath. I was in control of the process and my spirit was aglow.

Leon and I exchanged poetry, wrote letters, sent cards, and held marathon conversations before we came face to face. On August 12, 2000, we finally met. I was in California pursuing a long-time dream of owning my own company. I'd wanted to start my own business since I was 12. Between jobs and encouraged by my new friend (Leon), I went for it. I had lost my last job about two weeks into our getting e-acquainted and his immediate response to my tears and anger was: "It's just your time to step out and do your own thing. And you can do it." This, after only 14 days, 5 hours, and 3 minutes of getting-to-know-you time. Wow!

Well, through our conversations, I'd learned that Leon also had an entrepreneurial spirit, and we shared a common vision and outlook on life. What a premonition that would turn out to be!

Fast-forwarding to the present: I've lived in San Diego, California, since August 2000 when Leon and I officially started dating. I moved in with my cousin Marlo and her family, an offer she'd made many times to me in the past. I took on a few temporary jobs while I finalized the business deal that brought me to California. Leon continued to be a very good source of spiritual oxygen, providing me with financial and emotional support as I grounded myself, but was not the air that I breathed. That was a privilege I finally learned to reserve for God and myself.

On October 13, 2002, Leon proposed during a ceremony celebrating his pastor and first lady's 60 Years of Marriage and 40 Years of Ministry. He plays the saxophone and had been rehearsing for two weeks prior to the celebration with an acoustic guitar player, pianist, and two beautiful, young ballet dancers for what I thought was his gift to his pastor and first lady in honor of their lives together.

While it was just that, it was also a serenade for me. I sat in a second-row, aisle seat, praying that he would hit every note, and everything would be what he wanted it to be. Not knowing my life was about to change. Midway through the song (Kenny G's "Innocence"), two dancers came to get me from my seat in the standing-room-only church house.

They dropped rose petals for me to walk on as they escorted me to a center stage seat, where in front of God, my family, our friends, and our respective churches, Leon (on bended knee) said, "Constance, you've been my princess for two-plus years, now I'm asking you to be my queen." After about five seconds of staring into his eyes in shock, I said yes and we were married on August 2, 2003, at an Afro-Cuban themed wedding in San Diego's beautiful Balboa Park.

Our company, Epiphany Management Inc., is a marketing and publishing services firm that is now over three years old and growing daily with our love and respect for each other and the life we look forward to sharing.

I've learned and am learning that the process (and it is a process) of living requires that we first learn to breathe on our own. That the relationships and experiences that we are blessed with are meant to help us grow and build a tolerance and understanding of who we are and who we are meant to be. Most importantly, relationships, familial, professional, or personal, are not meant to be life-sustaining respiratory systems. Instead, they are sources that help us build our own stamina and ability to be our own respirator.

Relationships in their purest form are platforms from which we learn to take in and absorb strength and power and let go of the toxins and waste that plague our ability to exhale.

Rebirth of a Woman

I'm most irate when I pretend to be at ease. My heart aches more when I try to please.

The audience keeps laughing, that's well and fine, but it's drama not comedy, and I'm falling behind.

They say ignorance is bliss, and a wise woman's cheeks are never dry.

Well, I've seen the good and evil of love, and now I wish I had closed my eyes.

A woman demands attention, and all the love she can bear.

No man or woman to be equal, so she alone can reap his care.

But once the ransom had been paid, unlike selfish love, more demands were made.

I stagger from the love of my man demanding my full attention; yes, his desires were grand,

But the nails were from my foundation. You can't build a relationship on mistrust,

and broken promises. After a lifetime of living in misery, you soon run out of options.

I look within my isolated heart, through my crumbled walls of despair, and thank God

I got out of that relationship, 'cause after awhile he no longer cared.

I tried to bake him a cake with humility, and a smile to quench his thirst,

a vow to love him forever, with pure honesty and everlasting trust.

My jaws were clinched so tightly, that my gums began to bleed.

My screams echoed through the rubble, as I dropped down on my knees.

I quickly turn to my man, but his eyes were blinded by his own fixes and needs.

I put my right hand on my chest, and I swear, I could feel my own heart bleed.

It was the first thing I would forgive, and the last thing I would ever forget.

I was the essence of his life, yet he was afraid to let me live.

Emotionally he stripped me of everything I had; after awhile my love finally died.

I was afraid to leave and afraid to stay; this wasn't a real marriage, there had to be a better way.

There was only one thing left to do: I packed up my two kids, and told him we were through.

It's been twenty years since I walked out on him; I never looked back, and I don't even hate him now.

I just close my eyes and thank God, that I opened my eyes in time.

— *Debbie La'Sassier*

Flight of the Black Butterfly
(an excerpt)

REGINA A. BRADFORD TARDY

"**C**alling all members! If your life has been knocked off balance by the unfaithful, disrespectful, or inconsiderate actions of the opposite sex, you are welcome to join!" For years I stood at the forefront as the self-proclaimed president of one of the most damaging clubs known to womankind. There were a variety of tactics utilized in stirring up conversations that would help to prove my point of view. "If you're emotionally wounded or enslaved by self-pity and blame men for your state of mind, financial ruin, or sexual deprivation, then sign on the dotted line." (The names have definitely been changed to protect the privacy of the not-so-innocent) "Is there a membership fee?" asked Sad Sally. Her husband left her for a woman ten years younger then she. Imagine that, he left three days before his 50th birthday. "How often do you meet?" asked Runaway Rhonda. Her Mr. Right Wrong was filled with secrets, and had four children by three different women. This information was a complete surprise to her until her paycheck was garnished for his previous indiscretions. "Do you provide childcare?" asked Damsel in Distress. Damsel's old man was diagnosed with cancer. After she quit her job to care for him, he got better and filed for divorce, claiming she had gotten too fat for his taste.

Then, of course, there was my story, overflowing with indiscretions, and secrets. My life went from marginal prosperity straight into isolation, girlish temper tantrums, and, of course, the famous "I can't" statement. There was one ex-husband that helped to set the stage, and one live-in mate to later help continue the saga of buried pain. Lights, camera, action...then bam! Fade to black!

Act I: I said, "let's get married, have babies, and enjoy one another's company until we're old and grey" and he said "O.k." From there we strolled down the aisle in front of 500 people. We looked good! The pastor had to ask me twice if I was going to "obey" Eventually we got through the vows with a few added chuckles, said I do, and we had a passionate honeymoon. Our marital bliss produced a beautiful son. I enjoyed consistent companionship and the dream of someday owning a home with a white picket fence and a dog named Skippy.

Unfortunately, these and other dreams weren't meant to manifest themselves during that particular season. Divorce papers soon would solidify the end. The other baby's mama gave birth to a bouncy baby girl eleven months and three days after our first son was born. Little did I realize that healing must come before self-love will appear.

Act II: Before the ink on the divorce papers was dry a sexy, fine, young man just happened to walk into the club at the right time. Vulnerability alert was in effect! He never knew a thing was going on. Yet the red flags let me know something was going on with him. He was as smooth as butter and gravitated straight toward my red dress, freshly manicured toes and nails, not to mention the brand new multi-toned auburn and jet-black 14" hair weave.

Dress up was one of my favorite games to play. After a few drinks and lots of love songs he and I were convinced that this was worth pursuing. With lust on our sides, away we went. Within a few weeks of dating, the highly sexual suitor's toothbrush was next to mine. Imagine that! He was entrusted with the keys to my new apartment. Little did he know that he had only received the physical keys to the front door of the apartment, but my heart was off limits! Pass the ice-cold beer, and medicinal cigarettes so we can loosen up during this saga. After five years and nearly dying in a car accident, the sexy suitor found love elsewhere.

Suddenly, the first line of one of Freddie Jackson's most famous songs became mine. "You've got your heart securely locked away, and you won't let nobody in!" Love was all around me, yet digesting any other stanza from the love song of the year would be too much like right. The residual effects of a hardened heart, compounded by self-sabotage, had sent a beautiful sistah into hiding.

"Girl, what's wrong with you?" echoed healthy, productive members of the single and loving it club. You'd better get over him and go on with your life!"

What life? Mine was wrapped up in his and he was wrapped up in someone else's.

"What are you talking about? "I'm fine! Leave me alone, damn it!"

Work and occasional church attendance became excellent escape routes.

"Good morning! Praise the Lord, how is everybody doing on this fine, fine day?" I'd ask in a bold boisterous tone.

In the "World" I could wear a very different hat than the one that waited for me at the front door of my 675-square-foot apartment. At work I was insulated by 40 convenient hours of weekly workplace dramas. On a daily basis I spent what psychologists term as co-dependent behavior (whatever?).

Maturity was knocking at 30's door! Finally, I shut my mouth, closed my legs and kept the keys to my apartment. An oath of celibacy allowed time to review how sex had become an invaluable tool of manipulation. I returned not to the back pew of the church to hide, but straight forward to faith and more forgiveness. This time I was praying for my well-being.

After intense soul searching, therapy, support groups, and a rededication to my Baptist roots, I shifted from being pitifully isolated to peacefully sipping tea. The love I was looking for was in me and shined back through the eyes of my son. I had lied to myself for years. I loved everything about men. For the first time it dawned on me that I was raising someone's husband. What was he seeing, what was he hearing, and most of all, what was he missing out on?

That summer I'd be challenged to complain less, and live more. Like Paul and Silas, the prison doors were opening and the opportunity for freedom awaited my arrival. I was alone, yet filled with more companionship than I'd ever experienced. Most days were spent learning how to play (my son taught me that one), listening, and walking in rhythm. My mask was slowly being removed as the "real me" began emerging. It hurt to see how much time had been wasted; yet I had to get on with it. I was a daughter being told, "go and be healed."

After two years of occasional dating and a marriage proposal that was almost accepted, I continued to receive valuable insight from sistahs sharing their testimonies. They were free, and I wanted in!

Ok, bring him on! My spirit is rejuvenated, my freedom is here. The moment I stopped looking for a man to provide something that I already had within myself, he walked into my life to accentuate my existence. On one of the most calm and confident days of my life, his sweet face appeared. While my eight-year-old son was visiting his "forgiven" father in Arizona, I had an entire summer to regroup and reprioritize.

Another dear sistah friend that had spent plenty of time motivating me to move forward suggested a girl's day out in San Francisco. Off we went, cruising over the Bay Bridge in a sexy little sports car with the top down. That day the winds of freedom blew through our hair. We had only one plan, and that was to have some good clean fun. When we arrived in the "City" the streets were covered with people dancing to Caribbean music. We got out of the car ready to blend in the midst of feathered dancers, drummers, and nice-looking men of all shades and sizes dancing to the rhythms.

There's something beautiful about a brotha's face. Suddenly, out of nowhere (only to realize years later he was from somewhere), a gentle member of the male species was caught taking our pictures. I pretended not to even see him but kept him in view out of the corner of my eye. I smelled his fragrance before I even noticed his smile. The scent of his body oil permeated through the gentle wind that trailed behind him. Who was he? Where did he come from? He must be here for my sistah. This rhythmic dancer approached us to lend a warm introduction.

"Hello ladies my name is "King." (Reginald)

I nearly passed out. In a soft, unconcerned tone I replied, "My name is Queen." (ReGina) Before I could rehearse a scenario that would protect the innocent, my mind called out,

"Lord, what are you doing? What am I supposed to do now?" Secretly I thought, run for your life!

"No, dance girl; continue dancing and don't stop!"

Of course there were questions that wanted to instantly find a lie hiding in his pleasant smile. He was nice? Oh, that's unheard of! Honest? He couldn't be! I was terrified. Should I run? I was standing there looking crazy. I couldn't even look him in the face. I was feeling...Oh Lord, take these feelings away. I was scared. Yet there was something there, bigger than the man, calling my attention.

My inner woman was about to start analyzing, when spirit stepped in and said, "Relax enjoy this moment, you deserve this connection." I tried to start the cover-up... (You know the one, when we act disinterested, and perhaps a little stuck up to get them to go away.) His confidence was cutting through each one of my hidden lies of unworthiness. My knees were buckling as I tried to keep up with the music.

For the first time in a long, long time I could hear the rest of Freddy's song. "I can teach you how to love again." My soulmate was bringing one of the many gifts straight to my heart. The first was assurance that he was mature, confident, and mildly assertive in his approach. He called every day to tell me to have a good day. Then, there was a true respect for me as a woman. Every door opened, as it should be. He had the patience to develop a solid friendship. This man made no disrespectful moves with even the hint of sexual manipulation. Lastly was a commitment to form a relationship with my son, on baby boy's time, not his own.

He took my son on outings that didn't include me. (Now ladies, you know I really wanted to go). He led the way for discovery by inviting the virtues of passionate romance. Rose petals, candles, and a silk kimono followed by a lovely Japanese dinner and a nicely chilled bottle of apple cider were amongst the birthday gifts marking my 31st year on this earth. No other man had brought forth the very gifts that my soul yearned to unite with.

Romance was indeed leaping off the pages of a dusty old novel from my teenage years. The only difference was that I had blossomed into a woman that was no longer blinded by a hardened heart. At 40 and 50 now, our life together has had its share of struggles and setbacks but together we've continued coming back, over and over again! One of the most enlightening attributes of a soulmate is acknowledging that there will be someone in your life who has insight into the past without using weaknesses to gain strength.

My husband has his own strengths and understands that my strong will is nothing to be afraid of. We both understand the impact of being abandoned. We've both been there and done that, for he was once a Mr. Right Wrong, and I once a Damsel in distress. The only difference is that was then, and we are here now. When he sees a blank stare in my eyes that reveals a dark memory popping up to sway my attention his response is usually the same–"Hi, I'm King." And I say "Hi, I'm Queen."

Sweethearts: A Luv Story

JOYCE GITTOES

Prologue

I have always hated it when someone said, "It's better to have loved and lost than never to have loved at all." There's so much pain in loving and losing. Is the pain worth the brief pleasure? The pain lasts forever. The pleasure seems to just fly by. My pain has lasted for thirteen years, the past thirteen years of my life. It was caused by the death of my first, and truly, only love. I have had many loved ones leave me through death, but none of them have haunted me like this one.

Well, maybe haunt is too strong a word. He comes to me in my dreams. I think he wants me to tell "our story". Whenever I would mention meeting someone new, he would ask, "Do they know our story?" He thought it was amazing that we were together after almost 40 years, even though we never married.

The Story

We met when we were both fifteen, in 1951. It was love at first sight as far as I was concerned. He was tall, dark, and handsome, and he was also very well mannered and intelligent. What more could you ask for? We were very mature for our young age, and got very serious very fast. We were inseparable. If we weren't talking on the phone, he visited me Wednesday nights and all weekend, even though he lived in the Bronx and I lived in Manhattan.

Unfortunately, the "course of true love" didn't run smooth. My mother found out that we were "having sex," and she forced me to stop seeing him. He joined the Air Force that summer and I was sent upstate to my aunt. That's when I self-medicated for the first time. This was an awful time in my life. By this time we had both been drinking socially for a couple of years. I realize now that we probably drank more than other people our age, but we didn't think we had a problem, because it was social drinking.

My aunt kept a pretty hefty liquor cabinet, and every night after she and my uncle went to sleep, I'd drink until I got that nice warm feeling, call him and discuss our plans for the future, then go to bed and cry myself to sleep. This went on for the whole summer, but when the new school term started, I went back to my normal, excessive, social drinking. The Air Force proved to be an excellent training ground for Leroy's drinking, too. I was to soon find out.

When he finished Basic Training, he came home to visit. It was just before Christmas. We met briefly, and planned to meet again on New Year's Eve, but he couldn't wait. He showed up at my door on Christmas morning. I was angry because he changed the plans, and I didn't go to the door. A month later I found out he got married shortly afterwards.

I graduated from high school in 1953 and started college. He eventually got out of the service and out of that marriage, and I was expected to marry him then, but I had met someone else while he was away, and instead of marrying Leroy, I married the other man. I know now that I only hurt myself when I made that decision to marry someone else. But, I wanted to hurt Leroy like he hurt me years earlier. I convinced myself that I really loved the man I married, but I knew it was a big lie.

Eleven years and five children later I met Leroy again at a funeral. I had gained quite a bit of weight over the years, so I came up with this elaborate plan. I would wear a dark blue dress with a large straw hat to match and sunglasses. If he didn't recognize me, I wouldn't speak to him.

It was daytime when I left Queens. By the time I got to the Bronx by train, it was dark. I took a cab from the train station to the funeral home. When we pulled up across the street from the funeral home there was a car in front of us. As I was getting out of the cab, I noticed a man getting out of the car. It was him.

By the time I paid the cabdriver and slowly walked across the street to the funeral home, he was already seated inside. Chairs had been placed outside the chapel for the overflow crowd and he politely motioned to the chair next to him. He didn't recognize me.

After a few awful moments I whispered, "Excuse me, don't I know you?" He glanced at me and said, "Should I know you?" My heart was in my throat, and I couldn't speak, so I just took off my sunglasses. He jumped up and screamed, "Joyce!!"

The floodgates opened up; he talked about what he'd been doing for the past eleven years—why he had married so many times —,"looking for you in all those women." I had to take him outside; he was so loud.

We continued our conversation across the street in a bar, and later we went to visit his mother. On the way home, he asked me if I was happy. I said, "Yes." He said I was lying, because if I were happy I wouldn't have gained all that weight. I didn't want to admit it, but he was right. Aside from my children, I hadn't been "happy" for a long time.

He wanted to drop me off in front of my house, but I had him drop me off around the corner. When I walked up to my door, my mother, father, and husband were out front waiting for me. I made up a story about problems on the subway, and not being able to find a phone that worked, and everybody bought it, except my mother. As I passed her to go upstairs she said, "You've been with that Black bastard, haven't you?" I ignored her, and just kept walking.

We started seeing each other again. He was about to end his third marriage. I had started having problems in my marriage too. I didn't start out creating opportunities to see him. I'd wait until my husband was out of town and then I'd have him over.

I remember the first time he came over. I had never entertained a man as an adult. He brought a bottle of champagne. I had to wash out two champagne glasses that I probably hadn't used since I got them as a wedding present.

I brought out the wedding album. I don't know what I was thinking about. His eyes welled up as he turned the pages. He said he should have done what Dustin Hoffman did in *The Graduate*. I put it away. I don't know what we talked about—everything, and nothing. He didn't want to leave, but I put him out about 4 or 5 o'clock in the morning. We kissed a little, but did not have sex, although we both wanted to. I only saw him one more time at my house.

That time it was different. After a while, I began to create elaborate scenarios to be able to see Leroy. I met him at various spots all over the city and we went to motels in the Bronx, Queens, and New Jersey. Eventually, he got his divorce and his own place, and I started going there.

The first afternoon I went over, I told my husband I was going to lunch and the opera with friends. Naturally, I had to let my friends in on the secret. Leroy had to run some errands and I went along. I remember thinking, "We could split up and get this done faster." I was on a schedule. Years later, I realized he just wanted to be with me.

That day he cooked for me and we had a picnic on the floor. We had roast chicken, French bread, and white wine. I thought it was so romantic. We didn't go out in public much, because I didn't want to get found out. Once when my mother was babysitting for me, he called my house. My mother and I sounded a lot alike. Years before, sometimes when Leroy called, he would mistakenly have a conversation with her thinking it was me. My mother answered the phone and she knew who it was. When I got home she said, "That Black bastard called!" but nothing more.

A couple of years after I began seeing Leroy, my mother died of cancer at 57 and Leroy left for California. Again, he didn't tell me, but I found out he had gotten married to #4. I started to self-medicate again. This time it escalated for 22 years.

After my mother died and Leroy left, I went to work as a paraprofessional at a junior high school. I took advantage of their special program for paraprofessionals, and went back to school. I eventually got a degree in English-Theater in 1978 and started to teach.

I didn't see Leroy much from 1970 to 1975. He came through from Boston in 1975 and then moved back to California. I stayed with him one night in 1979 on my way to visit friends in California, but we weren't intimate. I didn't talk to him from 1980 to 1984 because of a misunderstanding.

My marriage ended in 1982. His fourth marriage dissolved, and in 1984 he was in a long-term live-in relationship when I started seeing him again. My father died in November 1983, and in June 1984, I got Leroy's new address (he was back in NY) and sent him a birthday card. I included my telephone number. He called me in August, after they had gotten back from vacation, and we met about a month later.

He was very thin, but still very handsome. As usual, we talked and talked for hours—actually he talked—about what he had been doing since we last talked—1979. Dinner was ready when I got there, but neither of us was hungry. So, we drank copious amounts of some expensive wine that he brought from California, and talked. I have many special memories of this time together. One morning when we were sitting in the living room, he ran his hand across my head, smiled and said, "My little girl with gray hair." Then thoughtfully, "Your little boy with gray hair." We were both almost 50 years old, but we were acting like teenagers again. We sang show tunes to each other; he sang "S'wonderful" to me and I sang "Make Believe" to him.

In retrospect I realize that by 1979 I had become a chronic alcoholic. I was drinking on a daily basis. And so was he. Shortly after I started seeing him again, he free-based in front of me. On New Year's Eve, I asked for a hit, and that was the beginning of my drug use.

In 1985, crack cocaine made its appearance and we started doing that. He had been steadily going downhill, but once he met Crack, he plummeted. By this time he had sold all his stocks, pawned or sold most of his jewelry, borrowed money from most of his friends, and his health was deteriorating rapidly.

We didn't just drink and do drugs, which was probably why we didn't think there was anything wrong with our lives. We went to plays, movies, concerts—watched TV and read the Sunday newspapers in bed. There were also frequent periods when I would be angry with him for having women in his bed. His argument would be, "That's just sex. I don't love them."

In 1987, my youngest daughter was murdered. My drinking escalated to first thing in the morning and the last thing at night. I had the care of my grandson, who was 4 at the time, and that's the only thing that kept me from turning into a full-out crackhead. I started to go into treatment facilities shortly after. One of them told me that Leroy was my drug and that I wouldn't stop as long as he was in my life.

Leroy had been talking about going to Maine to get some real lobster. In February 1990, he said we should go. I tried to convince him to wait until the weather got better, but he insisted. He rented a car and came over to my house the night before. We left early on a Saturday morning. To this day, I don't know how he drove that distance without his drugs. He had a terrible skin condition by this time that made him itch and scratch constantly, but he drove to Maine without crack and without scratching. He seemed so happy and so proud of himself. It was only the second time we had been away for a weekend together.

We hadn't made reservations at a motel; he said there wouldn't be a problem at that time of year. There wasn't; he found a nice little motel in Ogunquit, and we got a room. We went to a great restaurant in town, but we didn't have lobster. He had a particular place in mind. He said we'd go "tomorrow."

When we woke up Sunday morning, it was snowing—pretty hard. So, he decided we'd better head for home early. He never got his lobster. His health took a turn for the worse in April. In June, he went to live with his mother in Mt. Vernon, and in August he was gone.

While Leroy was at his mother's, he discouraged me from visiting him. I talked to him frequently, but he'd tell me not to bother coming up there because he'd be better soon and he'd come see me. The first week in August, his mother convinced me to call and tell him that I planned to be in the neighborhood, and just come by. I did.

I had no idea what it took for him to drag himself downstairs to see me; he was a proud man. He looked like he was 80 years old. He couldn't sit up very long, so I said I'd leave and come back another time, but he didn't want me to leave. He went back upstairs, straightened up his room, and put a chair out in the hallway for me to sit in, because it was so hot in the room. I visited for several more hours that day, and came back the next day, going straight upstairs.

He went into the hospital the following day. I guess he didn't want to die in his mother's house. I called him every day. One day, a few weeks later when he answered the phone he said, "Who's this?" That was the last time I heard his voice.

Leroy never thought his mother really loved him. When she called to tell me he had died, she told me that when they were moving him to another room, they held hands and cried. No words were spoken, but I think he got the answer he needed.

After Leroy died I tried to stop drinking again. But, I couldn't handle the pain, and I only drank more. Because I wasn't his wife, I couldn't grieve like I felt I should. Only my closest friends supported me. I couldn't take time off from work or share how it felt to lose my heart. On my job, I had to go into neighborhoods we used to go in together. I rode around on the bus looking out the window and crying every day for weeks.

In 1992, I went into a detox facility, hopefully for the last time. When I left, I got involved in a 12-step program, and have been a member ever since. I moved to Phoenix, Arizona, in 1994 and started acting in 1995, and have been doing it ever since. I haven't had a drink or a drug in all this time, and I have a very strong connection with my Higher Power, whom I call God.

I no longer feel the need to self-medicate, because I know now that all I have to do is ask Him to help me. I have heard it said that "Alcoholism is a low bottom search for God." It took what it took, but I'm glad I found Him.

Epilogue

When I was looking for a title for this story, I thought of a few different ones: "The Course of True Love," "The Story," and then, one night (or morning), Leroy came to me in a dream. He was singing, "Sweethearts," a song from an old '30s movie with Jeanette McDonald and Nelson Eddy; how appropriate. Some of the words are: "Sweethearts make love their very own, Sweethearts can live on love alone, For them the eyes where love light lies Open the gates to Paradise."

You know, the definitions of "Love" and Addiction" are almost the same—a strong feeling, affection for, and even need for someone—or something. So, it really doesn't matter what you call it. The story's the same. I still don't think it's amazing, but I do think it was what it was supposed to be—all of it; the good and the bad. And, I think it was a love story.

ANNIVERSARY

I
my skin is light enough
but my hair too defiant
too deliberately nappy
my mind my ways
too black too Africa
for his straight hair fetish
and snow-white cravings

II
October 25 marks the day
he christens my new tape
with baritone message
much akin to rape
of hopes future plans
icy angry words
cowardly delivered to a machine
words that are bold mean
meant to smash a dream
convenient easy
no human voice to reply
no need to continue to lie
just talk to a machine
no answers in between
my freeze-burned heart
dries up all my tears
over cold callous end
to a relationship of 14 years

— Virginia K. Lee

THE APOLOGY

"our relationship is dead"
his stinging words said
because I became too old
to remain in his fold
and much, much too fat
"don't want a woman like that
smoking 60 cigarettes a day"
his complaining ass would say
maddening mid-life crisis
sent him searching for Isis
found Misery instead
who swelled his head
she was 13 years younger
sent his finances under
and led him around
like a harnessed hound
then he decided to break free
humble-pied back to me
renewed standard of pulchritude
but I had a changed attitude
in a different direction
affirming my disaffection
I smile triumphantly
at his 12 years of apology

— Virginia K. Lee

Mothers Use Love, Forgiveness, Compassion, Wisdom…

When you are truly joined in spirit,
another woman's good is your good too.
You work for the good of each other.
— Ruth Senter

Letter to My Daughter
So I Can Sleep

ROBERTA ORONA-CORDOVA

My plan was to give you up for adoption, until I saw you the first time. There you were, skinny, long, and covered with blond peach fuzz.

"Is that my baby? She doesn't look like me," I thought as the doctor lifted you in the air. But I held my breath, turned my head to one side, and waited for the doctor to pull you out feet first. Dr. Carl told me the umbilical cord might "strangle the baby" because you would not turn around to come through the birth canal headfirst. You were in danger, and although I did not know it then, the seed was planted—the desire to keep you was like a spark, which gives light to life—your life with me.

"It's a girl," Dr. Carl announced.

The "baby" became "she," and you came into the world "brand new," your dad said. My heart spoke and quietly sang, "I want to keep my baby."

I was as innocent as my new baby girl. I wondered what your grandpa would say. And how was I going to tell the social worker that I had changed my mind, that I did not want to give my baby up for adoption? Would I be able to tell my confessor-priest, "I'm going to keep my baby"?

Your grandpa said it for me the day he came to see us in the hospital. First he went to look at you in the infirmary. Then he came into my room and greeted me with: "You can't give away your baby; it's your blood!" It lifted my heart when I saw his big Mexican tears, and he sang the sweet melody of love I heard from him all my life, "I'll help you, Jita."

That was the end of that. It was settled. I only needed his stamp of approval. The nurse would not let me hold you at first. It was a rule for all the unwed pregnant girls at the Daly City hospital where you were born. The social worker said they did not want the girls who were giving up their babies to get too close to their "own flesh and blood."

It was a rule set by St. Ann's Home for Unwed Mothers—the place where Catholic girls hide so their families do not have to face a scandal in their communities. I never could figure this out; usually everyone found out anyway, because when one other person knows something, just one other person besides you, the whole world will know.

It wasn't my idea to hide out at St. Ann's. Father Moore made all the arrangements. In Catholic school we were told unwed mothers were not able to bring up children properly. "A child must be in a home with a mother and a father to be raised right," Sister Frances taught us this in catechism, over and over. Sister Joseph told us, "Don't ever let a boy French kiss you, because it's a sin." Babies born out of wedlock were "illegitimate." What the heck did that mean? Of course you were legitimate. You were my baby.

I remember that day I had to tell your grandpa about you. He sat across from me at the kitchen table when I finally had the courage to tell him, "I'm going to have a baby, Dad."

He surprised me when he answered, "I noticed you were getting fat and beautiful." According to your grandpa, the prerequisite for beauty was you had to be fat. He always used the two words together, "fat and beautiful."

I was quick to explain my big plan. "I'm going to give the baby up for adoption," I said in my mature manner—a baby myself making grown-up decisions—always settling problems by thinking them through alone, never discussing them with family or friends, only with my spiritual advisor. What a horrible phrase—"I'm giving my baby up for adoption."

He was supportive and understanding. "Whatever you say, Jita. Don't worry about anything," he said, his heart heavy with love. I wanted to reassure him that I knew what I was doing.

"It's all arranged. Father Moore says I should go to a home where girls who are not married stay while they are pregnant."

Everything I said, your grandpa went along with. "Okay, Jita, that's a good idea."

Then I told him I'd move there one month before the baby was due, because it was expensive. I also let your grandpa know that something called "welfare" would pay the bill, and we didn't have to worry about it.

Your grandpa was quiet and non-judgmental. He had seen so much of life at his young age of 71, and was now living on social security and railroad retirement. I had to tell him, because I quit working at Pacific Telephone in Oakland. He had to know why I was going to be staying home every day. When I first arrived in California, my best friend, Bea, helped me get hired at the telephone company. Imagine me working at the telephone company! This was the last place in the world I wanted to work, because my dream was to go to college. When I resigned, my boss lectured me, and told me I would never be rehired. Well, I had bigger ideas and was more than happy to say adios.

"It's your blood. It's your blood," echoed in my ears the five days I was in the hospital after your birth. Those nights were sleepless ones. I knew I wanted to keep you; your grandpa helped me make the decision, but I had to think it through over and over because everything anyone ever told me up to then was the opposite of what my heart wanted, which was to take you home with me.

Those sleepless nights were wasted hours after all, and I should have just gotten my rest, since my heart would never change. I decided I was going to keep you. I wanted to hold you in my arms—but the rules did not change so easily simply because I had changed.

A rule is a rule. All the girls from St. Ann's Home, the girls who were in the same situation as me, were able to see their babies through the infirmary window, but they could not hold them. It was unfair. I was no longer like the rest of the girls. You were going home with your mommy. But rules are rules. Good Catholic girls understood this. I walked to the infirmary several times a day and stared and stared at you through the window. A baby, a real baby. My baby. Blond, blond, blond! I expected you to come out with a head of furry black hair. I have to confess I was disappointed you didn't look like me. Little did I know you were your own person from the get-go—separate and distinct.

I remember lying in bed one night when I was six months pregnant, and I felt you move. I thought, "How beautiful a baby feels." I put my hand on my stomach and felt your heart beating. "What a wonder it must be to await this baby with a husband, with the two making plans to care for a new life. If this movement was beautiful, what beauty it must be to have all the ingredients in place." I loved you then—at that moment I bonded with you, and fell asleep feeling warm and good, and for the first time, not so alone and lonely.

There you were in my dream—you came out head first with a mop of thick, black, straight hair; round, dark-brown eyes; and olive skin. Imagine! The next morning there was a smile on my face. How was I to know that nature has its own way—that Spanish genes would win over indigenous roots; that you would be fair, while I was dark; that you would be a free spirit, while I was a Catholic girl?

Once a Catholic girl, always a Catholic girl. My decision to raise you non-Catholic set you free. A decision made because the Church dictated pregnant girls "should give up their babies"—the infamous "should" word.

Father Moore sent me on my first adventure alone to San Francisco to visit St. Ann's. I'll never forget that day because I lost my favorite ring. St. Ann's looked like my high school, St. Vincent's Academy. The halls were buffed like spit-shined French-toe shoes, Pachuco style, like your dad's.

There were statues of the Virgin Mary, and Santos on every wall. An antiseptic aroma permeated the air. I saw pregnant girls as young as 12. The atmosphere was sacred, Catholic, and familiar, yet "aloneness" enveloped me. A million thoughts crossed my mind. Was I doing something wrong, like a mortal sin? I was scared and ashamed. No one in my family knew where I was. Did I make the right decision to give my baby away? Never mind. It wasn't my decision, for it was made for me long ago in Catholic school. Where was my mom when I needed her? Why did she die and leave me when I was in third grade? Why did she leave me way back when I was seven to become a woman on my own?

Three weeks later I moved into St. Ann's. You were due in a month. In the director's office, the sister explained the procedure. I was assigned the fictitious name "Louise O'Brien" and advised not to reveal my real name to anyone. All the girls went by phony names, and this is how I met "Bernadette." She was 14 years old and very pretty, as pretty as her name. I passed the first few days praying in the chapel and meditating in the garden.

One night, a few days after my arrival, I walked the smooth, slick hallway to the nurse's room. "My bed is wet," I told her.

She was startled. "It's your water bag, Louise. The baby's early."

The nurse made a phone call, and soon an ambulance carried me away to Mary's Help Hospital in Daly City. The doctor looked at my chart before he examined me and said, "All one has to do is look at you to know you're not Irish."

I was puzzled, but more simply naïve, and wondered why it was necessary for him to make that comment. It wasn't until I went to college at Cal Berkeley and became politicized about ethnicity and identity that I understood that I was not white.

The nurse "prepped" me and then left the room. She checked on me from time to time. The doctor came in and examined me. "We are waiting for the baby to turn. If it does not happen soon, we will have to perform a C-section." He turned and left without another word.

Several minutes passed, and I rang for the nurse. "Something is tickling me," I said, scared. She looked between my legs. "Oh, the baby's foot dropped out," she said and left the room in a big hurry.

The doctor came in and when he saw your little foot, he ordered the nurse to wheel me into the delivery room. When she looked between my legs again, I saw your toes reflect off her glasses, your tiny foot greeting life with a kick. The nurse helped me sit up and while she gave me a spinal, I dared to look down and there you were—a pink wrinkled appendage waving at me—stuck, with no place to go.

"Babies always come out head first," I heard the doctor say. "We will have to pull the baby out with forceps. I don't want you to worry, but there is some danger the umbilical cord may wrap around the baby's neck while we pull on the baby's feet."

The doctor's brow glistened with sweat beads as he gently began to nudge you out, first one foot then another. "Push down on her stomach," he told the two nurses, one standing on each side of me. They pressed and pressed to help you move through the birth canal, and I heard only silence.

I braved a glance and looked toward the doctor. There in his glasses, I saw two little feet; then I turned away and prayed you would arrive alive and healthy. An eternity passed. Finally, I heard the doctor announce, "It's a girl," and saw his face soften. A baby! You were long, white, and blond. I watched as he slapped your bottom until I heard you cry out. I wanted my baby. You worked so hard to make it into the world, doing it your way; you were special.

The nurse took you immediately away to the infirmary. I was rolled into the recovery room for awhile, then to my regular room. It was then grandpa came in and sang his Mexican tune, "You can't give away your baby. It's your own blood."

"Thank you, Dad. Thank you for saying it for me."

While we were in the hospital, you were baptized. One day the nurse came and said they would baptize my baby. They didn't invite me to witness your baptism. I didn't know enough to ask questions—to ask to be present at my baby's baptismal. But that's how it was—you were baptized in Mary's Help Hospital—and so you are a Catholic.

The nurse said I was to give you a name for the birth certificate. Your dad came to see me, and I asked him if he had any ideas.

"Maya," he said.

No. I had to make this decision myself. I asked the nurse if I could have some time to think of a name. I spent a couple of hours writing lists of girl's names. I remembered the pretty girl with the name "Bernadette," and I knew you were going to be prettier than she, so that's how you became Bernadette. "Maria" was my best friend in eighth grade at El Rito, where I met your dad. She was the first female I felt genuine love from, unconditional love, without jealousy or competition. Her affection was pure, honest, and clean. I wanted to honor her by giving my daughter her name. She was Anita Maria Archuleta, from Ojo Caliente. So you have roots in Ojo, too.

The girls from St. Elizabeth's were to leave the hospital on the fifth day. This was a big day, because I was able to hold you for the first time. The social worker was there, also. She smiled quietly as I examined your feet, your hands, your belly button, and all your little features.

"Bernadette's going to have pretty legs," I said to the lady. Then I asked, "When can I take my baby home?"

The social worker gently said, "I will have to change the paperwork and make new arrangements. The baby will have to stay in a foster home for a while. In the meantime I can help you apply for AFDC."

I had never heard of AFDC, but if it meant I could keep you, I'd accept it right away. The social worker promised to call me at home to give me the appointment to fill out the forms that would give my baby back to me. I was happy that day, but sad, too, because you were not leaving the hospital with me. The earlier plan was to place you in foster care while waiting for you to be adopted. Now that I reversed the adoption, I couldn't just take you home. The social worker had to undo all the prior adoption arrangements.

I was making new decisions, sound ones, good ones—all by myself—and thus it was my first step toward letting go of the Church. Everyone else at that moment was in control of you and me, everyone but me. My heart sank, and there was nothing I could do. I was told I could visit with you for 20 minutes. Rules!

"Don't worry you'll be home with me soon. I have to buy you clothes, bottles, diapers, and a baby bed," I whispered in your ear. Then the nurse came and took you away.

Your grandpa and I looked for a new apartment where they accepted children. He was excited, too. He even wanted to adopt you. After three weeks we found a two-bedroom apartment near Lake Merritt. I bought baby bottles, diapers, and auntie Flora sent cousin Frank's baby clothes. After two weeks, I called the social worker and made an appointment to pick you up a week later at the county welfare office in downtown Oakland. On my way there, I stopped at Sears Roebuck & Company and bought a car bed that became your bassinet for several months.

I arrived at the welfare office nervous and excited. I wanted to park right in front of the building so you wouldn't have to be in the sun too long. There was a space right by the main entrance, with lots of time on the meter. I've had a parking angel ever since that day!

It seemed like an eternity waiting in the small office. The social worker said the foster mother would arrive soon. In the meantime, I glanced through two baby books, which answered many basic questions about how to take care of you. Suddenly the door opened, and there you were in the arms of a very nice lady. You had grown so much in three weeks. I never learned the woman's name, but she said the best words I ever heard, "Bernadette is a very good baby," and then she put you in my arms. She also handed me a bottle and a diaper bag.

"Thank you," I answered, with a small smile. I examined your one-piece outfit and noticed it had two tiny milk stains. As I looked at you sound asleep, I wondered if you knew you were going home with your mommy that day. Just as I got to our '56 Pontiac the meter turned red. I placed you in the car bed and lay a diaper over you. I sat in the driver's seat and gripped the steering wheel. I looked back at you, and then stared through the windshield at the big world that lay before us.

I Am Your Mother...
I Know You

JANICE SMITH

When my son was an adolescent, I began a poem about him that I never completed. While his formative years progressed into young-adult status, I felt disappointed I never completed the dedication that had been burning in my heart. I felt further disappointed as a working mother; I had cheated him in not completely bonding with him as an infant because of a mandate to return to work only six weeks after his birth. Most of his life as a youngster was spent being co-nurtured by babysitters, at day care facilities, and by preschool attendants; later, he elevated to latchkey status.

In his latter high school years, I prayed to be blessed to be able to stay home as a "real" mom until he graduated. Unfortunately, that never happened. One warm summer evening, when he was sixteen, we were sitting in the kitchen having a conversation. He told me I only knew about him and did not know him. In light of that startling news, I wrote the following letter to him in remembrance of the wonderful, many-times–tested relationship we have shared.

From this letter, I realized that not only had I earned stripes as a "real" mom—even though I also had to work outside of the home—but also, I was equally blessed to complete the dedication that was buried deep inside my heart.

Dear Son,

I am your mother and have known you all of your life. I know you better than anyone else on this earth knows you. I have gone through your triumphs and your trials. I have witnessed your personality development and behavioral changes, and have lived with you all of your life.

I know your likes and your dislikes, and the foods you like and don't. Know what you do well, mediocre, and do not do well. I know of every developmental stage you have experienced. Every time you changed a shoe size—I was there. I know when you were 1 foot, then 2 feet, and 3 feet . . . and now you're approaching 6 feet.

I know every grade you have made, classes you have succeeded in and those you've failed. I remember things you have forgotten. Do you remember you were expelled from school for pulling the fire alarm? You simply could not resist the sign that said: "Do Not Pull." Or the time you were in a school play and were too frightened to say your lines?

How about the excitement we shared when your team won the little league baseball trophy? I bet you don't remember I was a chaperone on the trip to the zoo with one of your classes, nor the trip you took with your father to Barbados. Or, when you were very young, I helped you write a letter to the mayor about why there was no amusement park in the city.

I am your mother . . . I know you.

I know the day a tiny, little puppy chased you home, and you were terrified. When you couldn't get inside the house, it terrified you even more. When I finally opened the door (which probably seemed like an eternity), you shoved me against the wall as you ran inside. I excused your moment of brutality, in view of the shock and fear you were experiencing. But even after you were safe and secure inside the house, you cried an additional five minutes—with an accusing look upon your face—like I deliberately locked you out.

I know the Ninja Turtles and Super Boy characters you tried to imitate. You thought wearing a black belt made you a karate expert. Do you remember I enrolled you in a karate course at a recreational center? You only completed one semester because you didn't want to endure the physical discipline it required.

How about the time you packed your suitcase (with toys only) at four years old? You were running away from home because I wouldn't allow you to watch a program on television, and because your room stayed messy, which you blamed on me. You said, "I go live wit' my otha' mommy." (Grandma.)

I am your mother . . . I know you.

I know the time you amazed the doctor's office staff by delighting in your visit one day, whereas most of the visits you resented. Every time you scraped a knee, I knew about it. I had to nurse you back to health every time you were sick. Every tooth you lost, I knew about, and most of them I pulled personally.

I know the times you were afraid of the "tooth fairy," but not afraid to walk in the dark because I never played "boogieman" with you.

I know when you declared that Santa was a fraud! It was such a disappointment to you. Afterwards, you went on a mission to convince a cousin of your verdict. She was five years younger and simply could not support your claim.

I know the time you discovered that you were the intelligent one. I did not have much sense. 2 + 2 no longer equaled 4. You were so clever!

I know the day you let go of my hand. You decided you were too big for that now. We kissed when no one was watching.

I am your mother . . . I know you.

I know the time when your appearance became your number-one priority and your hair brush replaced your school books. I informed you that "vanity" was taking all of your money and urged you to let vanity go! You did take time out to regroup; but after much thought and ten fewer telephone rings, you informed me that vanity was here to stay!

The day you told me, "Mama, you can't choose my friends." Because I cautioned you about the ones who were undesirable to me. I agreed with you, and reminded you that neither did I choose the friends who were desirable to me. But, as your mother, I will advise you.

I know the day when you were a little boy and said you would never want to drive a car. Now, as a young man, getting your driver's license is your life's dream.

I know the day we drove past your girlfriend's house. Later, I overheard you tell her, "Me and my cousin just passed by . . ." I smiled and mentioned later, "So, we're cousins now?" Then I knew hanging out with your mother was not very popular.

I know the boys who bullied you and those you bullied. The girls you loved and didn't love.

I know the day you told me that you had changed your birth name, and your friends would be calling our home referring to your new name. It never occurred to you, "The truth will set you free."

I know the times when you were very young and told me God could do anything. Now, you question His existence because He won't do everything you ask. Also, the time came when you decided to challenge all authority. When all the why's were put to the test.

I know when you were learning a very painful lesson about life. It lasted at least six months. You labeled me your enemy and accused me of not caring. You wondered how I could color this picture with love. Even though my record should have spoken for itself. You didn't know it then, but I was saving your life!

I know the very first check you received from your summer job. You were so happy. But, sharing your money with me was not an option. I do thank you, though, for the lovely rose you presented to me for a Mother's Day gift. How did you know I like roses?

I may not know what you're thinking, nor the ideas you've planted in your mind, nor all of your hopes and dreams. But, I'll always know you, son. My love for you requires I get to know you . . . I Am Your Mother.

I presented this letter to my son, and he read it very attentively. He looked at me with a smile and said, "Okay, but you don't know what me and my girlfriend do!"

I smiled and said, "I do know. I was your age once."

Daughter,
I Traveled That Road

DORIS HOUSE RICE

My late son inspired "Daughter, I Traveled That Road." During those dismal days after he was murdered, I thought about his advice to me when my oldest daughter and I were at odds over some of her choices.

"Mama," he said, "Chris can't relate to your perfection. She might listen if you shared your experiences." He was right. In memory of my son, Officer Reginald R. R. House, I dedicate the poem to daughters and to mothers who find it difficult to confess, Daughter, I traveled that road.

Daughter, I traveled that road
Looking back, I wonder why. It hasn't been that long ago. My footprints are barely dry. The thought of you traveling that same road makes me cry.

It was a place in time without reason, during my life's spring season. That road was so inviting, lured me with excitement and adventure. The grass was so green, and it didn't cost anything. At least, that's what I thought.

Daughter, I traveled that road
The trip was a shortcut I believed I could quickly make, took that path for curiosity's sake. Before I started on that road my mother warned, "Take the other road, child. It may be straight and long, but it will take you safely on."

I gave my mother a look of scorn, didn't wonder why she was so tired and worn. Really, I didn't think there was anything on the road, that could do me harm. Daughter, I was so very wrong.

Back in the day, youth made me think I was very smart. Didn't believe evil was lurking in the dark. As a teenager, I thought I had earned my life's degree. I was blind and naïve, you see.

Daughter, I traveled that road
Met betrayal, denial, and deception. Those evils will attack anyone; you'll be no exception. Please pay attention and hear, don't want to control

and cause a lot of fear. I know it's the same old song. But that road is dangerous with winding curves. On it the innocent don't belong.

Many will persuade you to take that road, and they will walk it with you for a while, but when the road takes detours down strange aisles, there won't be a crowd. Then, you'll have to walk along those lonely miles.

Daughter, I traveled that road
Walked in its trails, took its exits, too. Went to taverns, joints, and discos, yes, I hung out in a few. Speeded in the nightlife and bright lights. The thrill of going up and down the road's hills made my head swell. Didn't use cruise control. Hanging out was a quick fix. Once I got caught up, sure was hard to quit.

Daughter, I traveled that road
Know what you're going through. I went through it, too. Burning the candle on both ends and longevity don't blend. On the road are those who'll look like the epitome of men. You'll trust and mistake them to be friends. Most will be nothing but male body parts in fancy pants. But the piper must be paid if to his music one chooses to dance.

Daughter, I traveled that road
Listen, honey, listen and learn. That road is a mass of crooks and turns. My journey took me to places where the road didn't run. The signs warned of disappointment, sorrow, and pain. The sun did shine sometimes, but mostly, there was nothing but rain.

Daughter, I traveled that road
It's rough, with lots of bumps that seem like fun. The missing bridges are some I have burned. Honey, don't take that same road, not the one I roamed. Don't fall in the same pitfalls and drink my brimstone. Take the straight road; it has obstacles, but those can be easily hurdled. The road I traveled has no genuine laughter.

Love compels me to tell you, the road is wrong. I promised the day you were born, you would not travel that Jericho road alone. You are beautiful, intelligent, and strong. Daughter, I traveled that road, but I believe you will rise above my pitfalls and move on.

A Salute to Mama

Mama started it when I was a little girl. On a normal summer day I wasn't allowed to play and get dirty like other girls. Me, Mrs. White's darling little girl, had to sit on the porch dressed in a "made by Mama" party dress. On my feet I wore the whitest of white socks, boiled on the kitchen stove by Mama in hot lye and water. Underneath the dress I'd wear an itchy petticoat.

Of course, the panties and undershirt were also white. Mama only permitted white underwear, none of those kinky panties with little pink or yellow flowers for Mama's girls. When I asked Mama why she didn't let me wear jeans and get dirty like the other girls, Mama responded, "Because you're not like everybody else."

Mama didn't work, other than preparing three meals a day of homemade rolls, pot roast, greens, sweet potato pies, fried chicken, cabbage, and such. She'd somehow get around to washing (by hand) the clothes for our family of four and ironing (in the days before permanent press, Mama ironed everything). This included the bed linen, towels, curtains, even our underwear.

She kept the halls of the six-unit building where we rented an apartment clean (for no pay). She was a co-Girl Scout leader of my Brownie troop, was present at all of my school functions and PTA meetings, and sang in our church choir. Whew! Is that enough?

When she did get a real job at the pillow factory where her own mother worked, she arranged a babysitter for my younger sister and me.

"A babysitter!" I complained. "None of my friends have babysitters at twelve years old."

She said, "You're not like everybody else."

In eighth grade my peers were wearing makeup, nail polish, and cinnamon-colored nylon stockings held up by garter belts. I already knew what Mama would say about this, so I sneaked and wore stockings to school one day, praying Mama was only kidding when she said she had eyes everywhere and would find out if ever I disobeyed her.

Of course that prayer was not answered. She found out. I had to be reminded, by Mama once again, how different I was from everybody else. By the time I made it to high school, Mama no longer needed to remind me I was different. I was part of the Permissive Transfer Plan, the city of Chicago's answer to school integration.

I traveled via public transportation from the West Side of Chicago to the North Side Lake View community. If all went well, this was an hour and a half passage each way. In my junior year we moved to the far South Side, which upped the travel time to two hours each way. I was one of the first fifteen colored kids to walk the halls of Lake View High.

Oh boy, was it different! Time itself did not allow much room to continue friendships from my West Side neighborhood. Once we moved, extreme shyness and a lack of social skills prevented me from making new friends in the new neighborhood. I spent a lot of time on trains and buses, feeling quite different. Even as I enthusiastically participated in Lake View's extracurricular activities (I was the only dark spot on the pom-pom squad, the only dark face on the student council, most often the only dark face at the lunchroom table), it was very clear to me that I was different.

To the white kids at Lake View I was often an interesting phenomenon, a colored girl who could be invited to dinner in their homes to be questioned by their parents about my life in the ghetto.

During my sophomore year I knew it was time to start sporting a natural, these days known as an Afro. I was no longer colored but now Black. As I recall, there was frequently some white classmate, lacking the sense that they might be offending me, sticking their fingers into my hair without asking my permission. There was commonly a surprised exclamation, "I had no idea it was so soft!"

The summer between junior and senior year, my best friend at Lake View met a young man who was involved in an underground, revolutionary movement. This brother blessed us both with African names. I became Oroki, a Yoruba name that means "a protector." Soon afterward, my younger sister incorporated African culture as a way of life for herself and adopted an African name, Rakina. We became known as the Lumumba Sisters.

We insisted that everyone, including our parents, give up the use of our old slave names (Ella and Adrienne) and refused to answer to anything else. Mama went along with us without much fuss. After all, she was the one who encouraged us to be ourselves, not like everybody else.

African culture opened the door to a whole new world where I felt at home instantly. I gave birth to a daughter and gave her an African name, Asabi, that Mama helped to choose. My sister and I became wholeheartedly connected to an African organization. There I met and married a man who adopted my daughter. As part of our African wedding ceremony he was given an African name. From that union were born two more daughters, Mandisa and Uchefuna.

Integral to this new way of life was our involvement in the development of an African-centered educational system. I was one of the key teachers in a school we founded with other families. We saw the need for a place where our children could feel safe and supported and would not be ostracized because of their names, diets (we were vegetarians), and the unpopular political views that we chose to indoctrinate them with.

Unlike some of our peers, my husband and I made the decision not to alienate our daughters from mainstream culture. This meant they were encouraged to interact with cousins, neighborhood children, and children of our friends who were not part of our way of life. Bear in mind these girls were named Asabi, Mandisa, and Uchefuna.

They didn't eat pork or any red meat. Both my husband and I come from families where soul food is the norm. We now did not celebrate any of the traditional American holidays, including Christmas. We had to struggle with most of our family to get them to believe that our children were not being socially and educationally deprived and that we were not part of a cult. I believe the fact our children excelled academically was what brought us some sense of acceptance, even respect.

Our children learned early in life that they would be looked upon as different.

Sad to say, demons from my past that had haunted me since childhood caught up with me. I succumbed to drug addiction, which heavily influenced the destruction of my marriage. Fortunately, I was blessed and found a recovery program that allowed me to choose a life without the use of drugs.

Even today, these ghosts continue to instigate war against my sanity. I have discovered I must vigilantly abide on a spiritual path in order to stay true to my call of uniqueness in a world that persistently demands me to conform. I am discovering that not being like everybody else becomes increasingly comfortable as I age.

I am proud to say each of my daughters has found her distinct way of living life differently. Two of them are mothers of daughters whom they have named in the African tradition, Asafoni, Nia, Faith-Kimani, Amaya, and Akilah.

I have remarried. Far too often, I find myself involved in a heated discussion with my husband about how my choosing to approach life on my terms ill-affects our marriage. He has reminded me often that I told him early in the relationship I was attracted to him for his stability. He has told me he wants an ordinary wife. Well, I'm no ordinary woman. I'm the grown-up version of the girl whose mother instilled in her early not to be like everybody else.

I struggle daily with what this could possibly mean to our marriage. I admit fear regarding feelings and thoughts of losing my unique spirit if I turn into what I imagine my husband sees as an ordinary wife. Even as I love my husband, I acknowledge I am uncertain I have the willingness to compromise in a way it might take for this marriage to work.

These days my heart goes out to my oldest daughter, who is currently incarcerated for a felony she admits committing. I admire her dignity and inner strength as she serves her jail time with few complaints. I have observed her, as she has been able to hold her head up proudly in spite of some folk who judge her harshly because of the mistakes she has made.

I know from personal experience how difficult it can be to not give up and not give in, refusing to be devoured by demons that feed off self-pity and depression. Some may see her as a failure. I pray that the Creator of my soul will keep me humble so I may always see myself in her.

My middle daughter, who is the mother of two young children herself, made the decision to allow her three nieces to live with her, rather than see them separated from each other, which would add additional trauma to their young spirits while their mother is away serving her time.

My youngest daughter has made personal sacrifices by assisting financially and taking the children on outings when her schedule as a flight attendant allows. I am very proud of each of my girls.

January 1999, Mama made her transition into the world of the ancestors. The essence of her spirit remains alive as I teach my granddaughters about whom she was on earth. She loved butterflies. I have taught them that whenever we see butterflies, to know Grandma is reminding us she's still here and still loves us. I believe it is her spirit who wakes me up in the middle of the night, bursting with the taste of foolish, wildly improbable, yet oh-so-real dreams to be lived.

I see myself writing books, dancing barefoot in rainforests throughout the world, hosting talk shows, protecting and nurturing the spirits of broken-hearted women and children, meeting heads of state and writers of books that have inspired me to be the writer I am. Mama was an avid reader and passed this gift on to me.

I ask that you take a moment to salute some woman in your life who has encouraged you to live your dreams. The next time you see a butterfly, I ask you to remember my mother and women like her who dare to teach us we don't have to be like everybody else! I ask you to honor some woman who has given you permission to be yourself. Thanks, Mama.

Toothsome

SANDRA RAMOS O'BRIANT

In her thirties, Nellie wore miniskirts and go-go boots, false eyelashes and hairpieces, and seemed oh so with it, up to date, and modern. Her small, square teeth gleamed in a perfect line behind a red-lipsticked mouth. She laughed and giggled weak-in-the-knees through days where nickel-and-dime tips forestalled economic disaster.

Her life was hard work and more work, and raising kids, and sexual trysts on the sly, nothing long-standing, nothing lasting. Even the children became upwardly mobile wraiths that disappeared, and then reappeared with babies. But Nellie was strong, looked younger than her age, and there were her teeth. Perfect. She had no cavities.

In her fifties, she finally needed dental work. Nellie traveled to Juarez, Mexico, to get the work done cheap. The dentist suggested gold fillings for three of her front teeth. "Special price for you," he said, and patted her knee. Later, her smile sparkled.

"Why?" her children asked. They'd only seen gold teeth on winos and the occasional rap-music star.

"Oh, well," Nellie said, and shrugged her shoulders. "He said gold would last forever."

Her children cringed every time their mother flashed her golden smile. They gave her $500 to get the gold taken out. Nellie bought a new water heater.

"I changed my mind," she said.

In her seventies, her teeth began to trouble her. They would have to be removed.

"Give her the best dentures available," her children told the dentist, secretly relieved that the gold-lined teeth would go. Nellie would look like every other senior citizen equipped with porcelain choppers.

"Don't let the dentist keep that gold," Nellie warned her children when they took her for the surgery.

"I paid a pretty penny for it!"

"Everyone wants their teeth blazing white these days," her children told her. "You'll look modern."

"I don't want people to know I'm wearing false teeth," Nellie said.

The dentist fitted her dentures perfectly to her mouth and handed her a mirror. Nellie smiled at her reflection, turning her head to the right and the left. She ran her tongue over her small, square teeth gleaming in a perfect line and nodded at the dentist, satisfied.

Her children waited in the lounge and stood to greet her as she exited the office. She gave the dentist a hug before turning to them.

"Surprise!" she said, smiling wide at her sophisticated children, gold now lining every single artificial tooth in her mouth.

Wallflower Mom

UMA GIRISH

You don't get to choose your mother. You inherit her. Good, bad, attractive, blue-eyed, dark-skinned, gentle, stern, wild-tempered...you get the picture. And when I was fourteen, all other moms—neighborhood moms, moms of friends, TV soap moms, and movie moms—seemed perfect, almost made-to-order. All except mine.

Other moms held fancy jobs. They were secretaries with nails painted crimson, teachers with crisp, convent-school accents, and bankers whose fingers expertly counted wads of crackling rupee notes. They were moms who stepped out in cool, cotton saris to face a new working day, or shimmered in their colorful salwar kameezes as they clicked off on their two-inch heels to well-paid jobs. Mine just stayed home and worked in the kitchen. All day long and well into the night.

Other moms made regular trips to beauty salons for manicures and makeovers. They glowed and sparkled with fresh life. Mine was oblivious to her greasy, limp strands that showed early grey. Her hair grew thinner and thinner until it curled and trailed away. Her skin was turning sallow from bending over steaming pots for too long.

Other moms spoke their minds, made decisions, and were involved with their kids—what courses to take, how to make scary masks, how to plan a surprise birthday party. Mine stared up at my father with big, dark eyes that spilled confusion and waited for him to make up her mind for her.

Other moms marched purposefully as they went about their business, whether it was shopping for a get-together, getting curtains tailored, or cashing a check at the local bank. Mine wouldn't cross the road without fearfully clutching my fingers. There was so much wrong with her, I forgot to see what was right.

My eyes casually skimmed over the neatly ironed pile of uniforms that stood ready for me on my cupboard shelf every school morning. My fingers grabbed the hot mug of cocoa that was offered to me, the curling steam a welcome at the end of a long day. But my mind was miles away as the cocoa warmth left a trail down my throat.

I bolted my dinner in a frenzy of hunger, barely tasting the tangy lentil broth my fingers mixed into the mound of soft white rice, forgetting to even ask if mom had eaten. The skirt I tore off in a tearing hurry, the handkerchief I lazily tossed aside, the leather bag I carelessly flung on the living room sofa to put away later and always forgot—they all somehow found their rightful places.

The house was a neat, well-ordered haven to return to. The bathroom tiles sparkled as long, golden panels of afternoon sun slid across them. The coffee tables shone, proof that someone had used a rag and polish with plenty of loving care. The clothes smelt of lemony detergent and warm sunshine. And yet I roamed through the house, day after day, blind to the generous toil it took to maintain it. It was ten years before the truth hit me with the force of a sledgehammer.

It hit me as I turned the key and entered my one-bedroom apartment. It hit me as I waded through tossed-aside newspaper supplements, dog-eared and limp from re-reading. It hit me as I stumbled over mugs that were caked with coffee stains and strewn about the place. It hit me as I walked into the kitchen and gagged at the congealed grease on dinner plates and soup bowls haphazardly chucked in the sink.

On my bed was a hillock of clothes—stale, crushed, and scattered all over. Dust motes jigged up and down in wicked glee as the light beams caught them. Dust sat thick on my bedside table and bookshelf, the odd finger striation where I'd grabbed a pencil or a notepad as I rushed out. All I could do was drop my face into my palms and cry. And then I got down on my knees for the first time in years and thanked the Lord above for the stay-at-home mom I'd taken for granted all along.

She had, for two whole decades, ordered my life into neat little slots, almost invisibly. Standing at the sidelines, she had conducted my life with such care that it was a harmonious symphony. Blending into the backdrop, she had given every ounce of her energy honestly and daily to what she did best—raising her kids and making a happy, comfortable home for the family to return to.

She didn't expect applause or accolades. No one ever thought to give it to her. There were never any words of gratitude at the end of a long, hard day for a job well done. And yet she was there every day, reliable as the morning sun, a rock for the family to lean on. She never called in sick. She simply popped an aspirin and got on with the mountain of beans she had to string. She never threatened to quit, not even when the kitchen grew too hot. She shrugged aside her needs, her desires, her entire self, putting her husband and kids ahead of all else.

My mom put in twenty years of service as a stay-at-home mom. She receives no pension or retirement benefits today. But she sighs contentedly at the thought that her kids have grown into responsible adults; that they carry with them the road map of values she handed them. And she prays that the map will safely see them through the journey of life.

As the daughter of a stay-at-home mom I can't think of anything more precious one could give to one's child. As a tribute to my mom's legacy, I, too, am a stay-at-home mom. I have kept the tradition alive for ten years and ...Oh! I have to get the door. My nine-year-old is home; she needs me to help her unravel at the end of a school day.

Miss Bea's Style

BEATRICE M. HOGG

My mother was old and she dressed funny. She was interested in comfort, not fashion. She liked nothing better than flat shoes and a starched cotton housedress. To me, she was a relic from another age. She wore a scarf wrapped around her head like Mammy in Gone with the Wind, tied with a knot in the front. Her dresses came from the local five- and ten-cent store, or from the door-to-door salesman who sold cotton shifts and other staples of old-lady life.

Stylewise, she had more in common with the babushka-wearing immigrant grandmothers of my white friends than with the mothers of my black friends, who wore form-fitting dresses and slacks and had perfectly curled, shiny hair. Momma never wore slacks. She looked more like Mrs. Troskin and Mrs. Manduzio than like Miss Mamie, Miss JoAnn, and Miss Norma.

I loved her with all of my heart, but sometimes I did not want to be seen with her. Hills Station, the Pennsylvania town where I grew up, had a population of 500 coal miners and their families. There was nowhere that I could hide, nowhere to hide. Everyone knew I was "Miss Bea's little girl." Why did my mother have to be so different?

Beatrice Harper Hogg was born in Lenoir, North Carolina, somewhere between 1892 and 1899. When she and my father adopted me as a baby in 1957, Daddy was 57 and she was in her late 50s or early 60s. By the time I was a preteen, she was around 70 years old, and they had been together for 50 years. In those years, Momma had worked many jobs, such as running a hotel, taking in laundry, and doing volunteer work with churches, women's clubs, and political groups.

As I was growing up, Momma devoted herself to taking care of Daddy and me and our house. She was always doing something: cooking, canning, or sewing. She made the best meals from scratch. She showered attention on me and made our home a place of light and love. She had a multitude of friends, who were always calling, writing, or visiting. From my first grade teacher to the priest of the local Catholic Church, everyone in town was her friend. Why was I so embarrassed then?

Momma's skin was the color of the honey that she liked to put on her homemade pancakes. In the summer, brown freckles dotted her nose and cheeks. Only a few wrinkles belied her age. Her morning ritual involved smoothing her face with Pond's cold cream. I could hear her singing through the closed bathroom door as she prepared for the day. When she came out, her face shone with the luminescence that the cream provided. She never wore make-up or cologne, but I loved her smell. The mixture of Dove soap, Cashmere Bouquet talcum powder, and lotion sweetly scented the air around her.

Her short, unruly hair was wavy in the front, straight in the back and nappy on the sides. The mixture of textures was a reflection of her mixed heritage, as her father was half-white, and she may have had some Indian blood, too. Her hair was rarely styled but always combed neatly. All of her life she mourned the fact that her hair never grew longer than a few inches. But she was proud of the fact that she had few gray hairs.

She was only gray at the temples, with no more than a smattering of gray interspersed throughout the rest of her head. Momma loved it when I combed her hair. Many nights I sat behind her on the back of the sofa with a comb, a brush, and a jar of Royal Crown Hair Dressing. As we watched television, I greased and massaged her scalp and combed her hair. Her coarse hair was soft to the touch. It was so short that I could only make little plaits, and those usually sprang apart as soon as I moved on to the next one. I could commiserate with the effort that it took her to do my hair.

She had to tie ribbons or strings to the ends of my plaits to keep them together. On the few occasions that she got her hair straightened, with soft curls in the front, it never stayed curled for longer than a few hours. She always talked about getting a wig, but she never did.

Momma didn't wear any underwear. When she went out, she wore a whole slip, but nothing else. They were a lot fancier than her housedresses: the white or black slips were always edged in lace, adding elegance to an ordinary garment. She said that bras and panties were too binding.

But in her bedroom there was a drawer of intricately constructed girdles and pointy bras. I used to play with them, imagining myself to be a grown-up woman. I used to watch her get dressed. I sat on the bed as she covered her flaccid breasts and her round stomach with its long hysterectomy scar. She was never ashamed of her body; it was what it was.

She wore red fox-hued stockings that she kept up with pieces of elastic. Her sensible shoes had low heels or were flat and were not very stylish. When asked what size shoe she wore, she would always say, "I wear fit'ems."

At school functions, my mother was always the oldest mother in the room and the frumpiest woman in the room. She was usually older than the oldest spinster teacher. But everyone was nice to her. I wondered what others really thought about her and her appearance. What did the white people think?

When I got my first Communion, my mother and father were the only black people at the Mass. They looked proud but uncomfortable, sitting alone in a pew at the back of the church. Did she have to wear that headscarf and that dowdy coat to my church?

Diabetes took my mother in 1970, when I was 13. After her death, I discovered what people really thought about her. Everyone remembered her kindness, her friendliness, and her concern for others. After her funeral, friends and neighbors talked about her love of flowers and plants, her sense of humor and her warmth. But no one ever described her by the way she dressed.

Every so often, I look at the photo album I inherited from Momma of old, yellowed photographs from the '40s and '50s. My favorite picture is of a man and a woman sitting on the hood of a big, fancy car. The woman has on a light-colored, short-sleeved shirt with dark buttons and matching pants. Stylish shoes adorn her feet and a big, floppy hat surrounds her face like a halo.

The man has a similar outfit, with a newsboy-style hat perched on his head and tipped to one side. They are smiling into the camera, parked on a dirt country road. The picture is of Momma and Daddy, looking good on a summer afternoon long ago.

There is another photo in the album, a portrait of a young, smiling woman perched on a bench. She is wearing a fur-trimmed velvet coat. She has on a wide hat adorned with feathers on the top and a pearl necklace. Her round glasses match the roundness of her cheeks. I remember asking Momma if it was her picture, and she always insisted that it was her sister. But her dark-skinned half-sister looked nothing like her. I also have a one-inch-square photo of Momma, with a rolled brim hat and a swing coat. She sure loved her hats.

When my mother died, I gave away her two mink coats and her muskrat coat. I threw out the threadbare but still stylish hats, pocketbooks, and gloves. Her fabulous brooches have all lost their rhinestones by now, but I keep them in my jewelry box. My middle name is the name of her favorite jewelry company, Marvella.

These days, I have my own skincare rituals. From Momma, I learned the importance of taking care of my skin. The products I use may be fancier than those Momma liked, but the effect is the same. My skin is smooth and brown as the syrup that I put on my homemade pancakes. When I look in the mirror, I am pleased with the mostly firm skin that smiles back at me. I only wear makeup on special occasions, and then only sparingly.

Like Momma, I have few gray hairs. I don't pluck them out, but acknowledge them for the stripes of honor that they are. Like Momma, I rarely straighten my hair. She would laugh if she could see the funny little coils springing from my scalp. Momma didn't live long enough to see me in an Afro. Eventually she would have embraced the style for her own unpredictable hair. Sometimes when I'm doing housework, I'll put a scarf around my head.

As I fold it in half and tie it with a knot in the front, I remember the countless times I watched Momma tie her scarves the same way. When I look at my reflection in the mirror, it doesn't look old fashioned at all.

After many years of gazing at bumps, humps, curves and valleys, I am finally comfortable with the landscape of my body, too. My bras and panties are practical and fit well on my full breasts and round tummy. I have given up on wearing sexy but itchy lacy undergarments. If I have a lover or go to the hospital, they will have to deal with my clean but unadorned undies. In the evening when I am at home all alone, off comes the bra. I welcome the loss of pressure on my shoulders. Now I can relate to the unencumbered freedom Momma felt.

I even have a few cotton dresses I wear around the house. But my animal prints and Polynesian patterns are a little racier than the checks and flowers Momma used to wear. She would have liked them, though. In the back of my closet are some fancy high heels, but my everyday shoes are low-heeled and comfortable.

I wear the same size Momma used to wear. She would have approved of the soft, pliable leather loafers I prefer. Maybe she would even have wanted to borrow them. Sometimes I dream we are adult women together, going shopping and sharing secrets. The fun we would have together—caressing soft fabrics, sampling the latest fragrances, trying on the latest hats and telling each other stories. Whenever I pass a jar of Pond's in a drugstore, I am tempted to open it up and sniff that familiar scent of my girlhood, a scent that takes me back to Momma.

Love Is Kin to Sadness

CYNTHIA REGINA HOBSON

I t's ironic. The people you love deeply, and who are the source of many of your happiest moments, will cause you sadness. Not out of their own doing, but just because you love them. There she stands, one of my main sources of happiness and objects of love, waving good-bye to me with a smile. I wave back smiling, thinking, how many times have I watched my mother do this? I feel she is the only person who has been part of my life, all of my life, and I am sixty-five years old.

Oh, I have so many wonderful memories about her and the special, close times we have spent together. I have to laugh because she is the one person whose approval is still so important to me.

My mother is very wise, but I do not think she knows this. She is brilliant as a morning star competing with the sun. She has many sides to her personality. She can be soft and gentle as a feathery breeze against your face (especially with children), or hard and sharp as the edge of a rock when she is taking a stand. She will argue a point she believes in until she wears her opponent's hide out. She will extend her arms as a place of comfort and compassion to those who are in need. She is very soft spoken most of the time, but if riled, she can shriek like a banshee. And she is still independent as hell.

My mother looks fragile and a little faded now. When we talk, though, her inner spirit is still strong as ever and full of abiding love and humor. She once stood straight, a highly intelligent, bronze beauty, but her stature has become slightly bent. Her focus is perceptive, broad, purposeful, and active, if to a lesser degree caused by time. Somehow, she seems smaller now. Her gait is slower and her hair almost all gray. Well, after all, she is eighty-eight years old.

Eighty-eight years old—how did that happen? I worry about my mother because she is getting old. It makes me fearful and sad. I am sad because I love her so, and afraid because I know someday I will lose her.

Those thoughts slip in and out of my mind on an unconscious level, but I do not like to dwell on them. The truth be known, my thoughts of her also make me think about getting older myself. What it will be like and my own mortality. That is, if God, in His wisdom, blesses me to live to my mother's age. I sometimes think about the aging and mortality of others I hold dear. Those thoughts make me afraid and sad, too.

Oh well, I know it is important to take each day at a time; and to take the time to experience, appreciate, and enjoy the people you love. Life is short, the inevitable is in God's hands, and love is truly kin to sadness. However, true love is a bridge from God, to good memories that lift us up during times of sadness, and I believe carries over into the hereafter.

MATERNAL CONVALESCENCE

Reverse deja vu!
I doing for her
what she once did for me.
A strange sense of grace,
an exchanging of roles
without rancor.
An awesome dissolving of taboos;
for I have rarely seen her
sans clothes.
The casualness of the hippie generation
was not hers.
Modesty protected at all cost,
now lost.
As I assisted in all basic ways,
a strange new bond was formed;
not of words but touch.
As I read an adult Bible story,
put her to bed, kissed her cheek,
and left the nightlight on.
How strange, how dear
the memory of that time,
now that she has gone Home
and the room is empty.

— *Diantha L. Zschoche*

Birthing Maelou

ELAINE RUTH LEE

In the silence of meditation I heard a faint click. Opening my eyes, I saw a large, pink lily gracefully unfurl as it stood majestically amidst a lovely bouquet of tulips, roses, and daffodils. They were nestled in a tall, cut-glass vase, which sat atop a lace tablecloth surrounded by lit votive candles and framed pictures of our beloved mothers.

Janice's eyes, opening in amazement, met mine. She later told me that in her eight years of leading bereavement groups, she'd never seen or heard a lily open like that before. "This must be a sign," I thought, my standard response to mysterious happenings, especially since my mother's death.

After the meditation, Janice gave her opening prayer and the meeting began. During the sharing that night, one attendee told of a woman who made commemorative teddy bears for surviving family members from the favorite clothes of their departed loved ones. While listening to her talk, an exquisite feeling of joy welled up in me. I instantly knew I wanted to have one made to honor my mother.

As Janice closed the meeting with a moving, heartfelt prayer, one of the votive candles exploded, propelling glass and melted wax across the table and around the room. Startled, we sprang to our feet and began cleaning up the hot wax and retrieving the shattered pieces of glass.

"Do things like this always happen when you pray?" I asked Janice, only half-joking.

"No," she said, "This was a first."

We wondered aloud what these occurrences could mean. I thought that my mother was "sending word" again via the media of things, nature, dreams, and animals—our newfound language. There had been many such occurrences in the last eight months since my mother's passing, such as:

• I took my car in for the annual smog test and found out that it would require an expensive repair. The mechanic said that in view of my car's age, it was his recommendation that I donate it to charity and buy another car. Within a matter of weeks, through a serendipitous series of events, I encountered a friend's mother who was about to donate her car to charity, a barely used deluxe-model Volvo. I was able to acquire the car for a nominal cost. My friend's mother's name was Mary Lou, the same as my mother's.

• During a cold Halloween weekend, I asked a friend to bring some firewood around from the back of the house. Since it was raining and he didn't have a coat, I offered him my mother's rain jacket because I thought it might fit him, which it did. After loading up the firewood, he happened to put his hand in the pockets, and lo and behold pulled out a handful of Halloween candy—the taffy kind of candy wrapped in orange and black paper twists. We both stood there stunned. She had apparently left it there from a previous Halloween.

• On Valentine's Day, I went to my health club for my thrice-weekly swim in their outdoor pool. Afterwards, as always, I lay on a chaise lounge to recuperate. That day I happened to look up and see a seagull flying overhead with something unusual in its beak. The bird was quite far away, so I couldn't quite figure out what it was carrying. But the bird circled back around and came closer, and much to my surprise, it was carrying in its beak a large, shiny, flat object that looked like a wrapped chocolate heart. Perhaps the bird had looted someone's valentine basket or found it discarded somewhere.

"Coincidences" such as these made me feel as if my mother was presenting me with gifts and letting me know she was there, watching over me and taking care of me. They comforted me and reminded me that death is the end of a life, but not necessarily the end of a relationship. Each time, I felt the power of such marvels nudge me to unravel a bit more of the grief that had bound my soul for the past eight months, since my mother's passing.

She and I were very close. In addition to being parent and child, we had also become sisters and best friends. It was just the two of us. My father had died 18 years ago, I had no siblings, and we had very few extended family members, being transplants to California from Michigan. Consequently, her death represented the end of our family...a double whammy and perhaps why I have been blessed with an ongoing plethora of miracles since she made her departure from the physical realm.

Several weeks after the infamous bereavement group meetings, I attended my friend Susan's annual New Year's party, and I noticed several wonderfully large African-style rag dolls resting regally around her house. More than just dolls, they were enchantingly colorful works of art, full of life and personality.

Suddenly, I flashed on the commemorative teddy bear story and began visualizing a beautiful doll made out of my mother's favorite African dress. As the thought gradually mushroomed in my head, I asked my friend where she got the dolls; she said her sister, Lashaun, made them.

It took me a couple of days to muster the courage to call Lashaun. Bracing myself for possible rejection, I painstakingly dialed the number. After nervously exchanging pleasantries, I posed the question about her making a doll from one of my mother's dresses.

Lashaun responded with a resounding YES. She said she would consider it an honor and a privilege. In her voice I heard such a tenderness and earnestness that it brought me to tears as I savored what seemed to be her sincere desire to share with me in this new-fangled way of grieving. After hanging up, I found myself engulfed in an inexplicable constellation of emotions, as feelings of joy, excitement, sadness, gratitude, peace, and exhilaration swirled through my tears and me.

Lashaun, an extremely talented and multifaceted artist whose media included fabric, metal, wood, and clay, told me to bring her a dress, some of my mother's jewelry, and any small, special mementos I might have. Deciding on the dress was the easy part; it would be my mother's favorite lavender African dress with elaborate gold embroidery. In my most cherished picture of her, she sashayed down a Hawaiian beach in her flowing African garb, her footprints trailing in the sand, her face aglow with a sunbeam smile, her arms reaching out in a hearty, spirited wave...a joyous hello that her passing had turned into a poignant goodbye.

The hard part was getting the dress. I had given it, along with most of my mother's clothes, to my friend Jewell, who loved my mother's style and was about the same size. Jewell and her boyfriend had graciously helped me organize and move my mother's belongings from her apartment after her death. As a way to thank her, it seemed like giving her the clothes was the least I could do. I didn't know how I could frame my mouth to ask her to give me back what had since become her favorite dress.

But ask I must. In a nervous phone conversation, I danced around the subject and finally, awkwardly blurted my request. I offered to swap the dress in question for an even more elaborately embroidered two-piece outfit I had gotten for my mother while traveling in Kenya. Somewhat reluctantly, Jewell agreed. Mission accomplished, I called Lashaun to schedule our meeting.

I arrived at Lashaun's totally jazzed with the dress in hand, as well as a few other scraps of fabric, fur, and jewelry harvested from my mother's hope chest. When I showed her the Hawaii picture, she asked if she could keep it on her altar while she worked on the project. It was a magical time as we held up the huge dress, turned it around, and flipped it upside down, trying to find just the right configuration and patterns for the layout. As we discussed trim, direction, eyes, mouth, belly button, our creative juices soared, and the vision of the doll was born. We slipped into an alternate reality that felt like Holy Communion—artist-to-artist, sorceress-to-sorceress, conjure woman-to-conjure woman, healer-to-healer.

Several weeks later, Lashaun called to tell me the doll was ready. When she brought it into my house, I was dumbfounded by the brilliance of her creation. The doll was huge, over three feet long. The mixture of printed fabric and plain was exquisitely positioned for maximum symmetry, and the edges were ensconced with gold piping. The doll's head was adorned with simulated curls made from the garment's intricately embroidered neck trim of overlapping concentric circles.

One embroidered heart taken from part of the dress was sewn onto her chest, while a second heart was sewn inverted in front of her womb. Lashaun handcrafted the doll's multidimensional round eyes and belly-button in her metal-smith class. She adorned the doll with one of my mother's favorite necklaces, and I later made earrings to go with it.

I named her Maelou, the nickname my mother's mother used to call her. Maelou now sits majestically on my living room couch, holding the scepter my mother won at an epiphany celebration—poised to bless and be a blessing.

She is a wonder to behold; all eyes fasten on her when they enter my front door. To those who visit my home, Maelou serves as a symbol of welcome, love, ancestry, and the power of art to embody and evoke the deepest mysteries of life, love, and death. Maelou is also a reminder of the possibility of recapturing and reintegrating into our present lives the language of our ancestors, and receiving the magnificent blessings they still hold out to us if we are willing to heed their wisdom and yield to their guidance.

Seasonings for Our Self-Esteem

And the day came when the risk to remain tight in the bud was more painful than the risk it took to blossom.
— Anais Nin

The Christmas Wrinkle

JOY COPELAND

There it was, bold as you please. A crease under my right eye. A trophy for having reached the ripe, old age of fifty. Was this my future? Ugh. But why now? Why would a wrinkle show up today of all days, Christmas Day?

Again I looked in the mirror, adjusting my blurry eyes while gently pulling at my skin. Somehow I could see it even with the morning crust still in my eye. "Oh my." But then I saw it wasn't as large as it initially appeared. It was only an indentation, a half an inch long. "This is nothing," I told myself, trying to be blasé in light of this aging milestone. There'd been other signs, signs I'd managed to ignore, like the tiny spider lines that would appear and disappear seemingly at will.

I focused my eyes on the wrinkle again. This time I used the magnifying mirror, that unmerciful microscope that often showed me more than I wanted to see. "Yep, this is serious." For one thing, this wrinkle was set off to the side, crowding out the other hairline squiggles around it. I could see this one without glasses or contacts. Maybe I'd just slept wrong. Or could it be loose skin around my eyes, the blessing and the curse of a ten-pound weight loss? My skin would bounce back. At least, that was my hope.

But, wait a second. How did I end up with a wrinkle anyway? Wrinkles were the purview of pale-skinned women; those who worshipped the sun or frequented those tanning salons. I did none of those things. My olive complexion, which darkened in summer and took on a yellow tinge in winter, wasn't supposed to wrinkle. I'd done all the right things: not smoke—at least for the last fifteen years; drank plenty of water—eight glasses when I could; and slathered my face in moisturizer—one of the inexpensive brands from the supermarket. "Don't forget your good genes," I reminded myself. Black women didn't wrinkle until well into old age. It was my birthright not to wrinkle. What the hell was this?

I scanned my mental gallery for the portraits of my female ancestors. There were figures in shades of honey beige, caramel, walnut, and milk chocolate. All were beautiful women in their time. My grandmother, my aunts, and my mother, there wasn't a wrinkle in the lot. My mother's oval face was prominent. It'd been two years since she passed. Her picture lingered in my mind, then washed away, as if taken by an ocean tide. I pressed my mental faculties to find her image. But my concentration couldn't make her reappear. As long as I had a picture of her, like the one in the gold frame that sat on my dresser, I could always bring her face back. For now, my mind was blank.

The fact was, women in my family never lived long enough to see their skin deteriorate. Their flesh would sag, of course, especially when the underlying fat melted. But weight loss never came in time to save them. Nor did the lessening of stress. Never in time to spare their vital organs from the ravages of life's disappointments, or the hardships faced by women making it on their own. Diabetes, hypertension, stroke, or cancer always arrived first. It was only after they'd achieved mental and physical overload, like factories on self-destruct, that their smooth skin would give way. If only they could've stayed alive to enjoy a nuisance like wrinkles.

I washed my face and looked at the spot again. The indentation that was there wasn't my wrinkle. Not yet. Not to keep. In the minutes I'd lingered thinking about my family's medical history, it had failed to disappear. Perhaps I'd squinted once too often. Pulled the skin too many times putting in my lenses. I applied a thin coat of moisturizer to my face. Then I stuck my pinky into the cold-cream jar, scooped out the thick, white goop, and patted it right on the spot. At first, the cream felt cool. Then it melted, leaving a shiny film that looked like a treatment for a black eye. I downed two cups of water, a futile attempt to moisturize from the inside out. It might work, but not right away.

"Oh well, Merry Christmas," I said, staring into the mirror. I waited for some kind of response. But the face looking back didn't answer.

"Mom! Are you coming?" came the call from downstairs. It was my daughter, Renee. "What are you doing up there? We're all waiting for you!"

"Yeah, I'm coming…just give me a minute." It was already 9:30. I'd been the last one to bed, staying to clean up from the previous night's festivities—our traditional Christmas Eve party. Now I was holding up the show in the family room. And what a show it would be. I knew everyone was already gathered by the tree, positioned to pounce on the pile of presents. That pile was a spiral of packages. It consumed all the available space under the nine-foot spruce and threatened to avalanche the entire room. As usual, we'd gone to excess. Our Christmases had become an embarrassing demonstration of consumerism. Every year, my husband, daughter, son-in-law, and friends made faint-hearted promises to spend less and give to charity instead. We'd make the donations and shop anyway. The truth was we were all multiple-credit-card-carrying contributors to the U.S. economy. And Christmas, it seemed, was the season of our largest donation.

I thought about what was waiting downstairs. I knew in a couple of hours, the gifts representing three weeks of shopping and two more weeks of careful wrapping would be lost in a sea of ripped paper and ribbon. In the frenzy, no one would notice the gold tissue matched the gold-wrapped box or the embroidery on the sweater inside. No one would mention the red and green tissue coordinated so nicely with the plaid pajamas that it covered. Only I would know all the stripes on the silver and blue boxes were lined up perfectly at each package seam.

I slipped on my red fleece robe, last year's gift from my husband, and shoved my feet into the matching slippers, a gift from my daughter. The father-daughter team collaborated on gift giving. I wondered what their teaming would yield this time. Over the years, I had learned to rely on my daughter's good taste, and funneled any special wishes through her. But there was no more time to think. I was keeping them waiting. I took a deep breath, forced my mouth into a smile, and slipped down the stairs.

As I entered the room, I could see the eager faces ready to begin our Christmas ritual. My husband, John, sat in the oversized chair sipping coffee. He looked with pride over the elaborate holiday decorations, as Nat King Cole's Christmas CD played softly in the background. My grandson, Dean, with cheeks that looked like they'd been smudged by a candy apple, ran to me on tiptoe. He'd already discovered his new blue and yellow tricycle, the one that had been hiding out, unassembled, in my car's trunk for several weeks.

"Merry Kismus, Gama," he said as he shoved a small, red package with a white bow into my hands.

"Thank you, sweetie." I reached down to hug him, but he escaped before I could get my arms around him. He rubbed his little hands together and jumped with excitement, ready to take on the mountain of presents. There'd be no hugs for Gama until he'd conquered it.

My daughter and son-in-law were half-prone on the floor, recovering from too much Christmas Eve cheer. Their dogs, Dolly and Dude, wandered at the edge of the pile, sniffing for doggie-scented items — the packages they could tear into with impunity. Our good friends Angie and Mike, morning people, sat with wide eyes on the couch, poised with cameras to record the event.

"Gee, Mom. We thought we'd have to start opening without you," Renee said.

"No, we wouldn't do that," my friend Angie said. Mike was busy taking candid shots.

"Well, I'm here now. Have at it." My son-in-law, with newfound energy, leaped up to distribute gifts. With the efficiency of military mail, he read the nametags and jostled each box in a shameless attempt to guess its contents.

"Sit," my husband said, tugging at my robe and patting the ottoman near his chair. So, I sat. I sat and I stared. The stack of gifts bearing my name was growing. Each box looked bigger than the one before. I was frozen. I could only watch the frantic ripping, and listen to the oohs, aahs, and thank yous, as Christmas morning played out as it had many times in the past. But something was missing.

"You'd better open your presents, Mom. You'll be here all day. Open the little one first, the one that Dean gave you."

"Okay, okay," I said, overwhelmed by the stack of boxes. Overwhelmed by all the decorating, the shopping, and the wrapping, not to mention the cooking and cleaning for the Christmas Eve party. And the kicker was, it wasn't over. More effort was still required to make Christmas—Christmas. There was still that night's dinner and the whole week of parties and entertaining until the New Year. I was already exhausted. And I was feeling a little sad, even with friends and family surrounding me. I couldn't help wondering, was all this really appreciated? Did any of it really matter?

"Honey, what are you waiting for? Open one of your gifts," John said. He held up his new moss-green shirt and smiled at me with approval.

The true Christmas spirit will hit, I told myself as I tore the paper from the small package. Everyone except for Dean stopped unwrapping to watch me fiddle with the box's tight lid. I pulled hard and was finally able to lift the top. Inside was a small locket, gold and heart-shaped. I opened it. It was a picture of my mother. Her face smiled back at me. She seemed alive. Christmas was her favorite holiday. And it'd been more special because of her. She expended the effort to make things perfect for everyone else, even though Christmas Day was her birthday, even when her poor health made that extra effort a struggle. We'd always put her birthday presents under the tree along with the other gifts. Christmas was a double celebration.

Angie left the couch and made her way through the mass of paper to where I sat, choking back tears. "Oh, how beautiful. How thoughtful," she said, complimenting my daughter. Then she gave me a hug.

My mother was the one who'd kept the Christmas spirit best. She was the one who had the smoothest skin.

Shifting Gears

ROSAMARIA SAGASTUME

For twenty-three years I had been driven around in either an orange '70s Volkswagen van, a yellow Hornet, or a cranberry Buick station wagon. I went from grocery store to mall to home to grocery store. Everywhere I went I had company—the kids in the back laughing uncontrollably; the stern man I married, once upon a time, in the driver's seat; the groceries in the back, and me sitting in the passenger seat. Always the same scene, the same actors, and props in the same set, in the same play.

Sometimes I dared to dream of the future. When the kids were at school, the husband at work, and the groceries in the kitchen, I would think about what life would be like if I made a decision. Not just any decision, the decision. Divorce seemed the only way out. I needed to be. Up until this point I had never been anything but a passenger, sitting through life while someone else took all the turns, beeped the horn, locked the doors, and pumped the gasoline. So when the kids finally were in college, I made my dream a reality.

It took twenty-three years for me to take the plunge. Twenty-three years, which had brought me two wonderful, intelligent, and independent children. They were everything I wanted to be, when I was their age, and still today. They say something and do it. Just like that. Well, I finally just said something and did it. I saved money from my part-time job and paid for the divorce. My husband had nothing to say; he knew it was coming.

He had known it many years ago when he'd come home and found his rice burnt. That was a sign of daydreaming taking hold of all my senses, including that of smell. I became more careful, for the children's sake, to mind whatever I had cooking on the stove. My daughter would eat the burnt rice anyway and wash it down with water quickly after a couple of chews, then compliment my cooking. She understood best; she was an equal. I knew that she had better things in store for her future—a professional career, her own home, a kind, loving husband who would take care of her and give her kisses.

My daughter had been telling me to get divorced since she was eight years old. "Ma, get rid of that man, I don't like him, he hits us too much."

I knew she was right, that I should get rid of him, but how was I supposed to support my kids and pay rent? I would have to leave them at home alone all day while I worked, and I didn't even know how to drive. If I had known then what I know now, I would have figured a way, any way. But now is now and I am free.

After the divorce was final, I needed transportation. I did not have a car, but the "ex" did. As a social worker, my job mainly consisted of being in different places of my community conducting outreach. There was no way I could perform my job without a car, so I used his. That cranberry station wagon was my savior and my crux. With it, I could go from place to place and not have to depend on public transportation, which is reliably unreliable. Without it, I was lost. The "hitch," as I already mentioned, was that it was his car.

I could not afford my own car. I had been working two years already, but the measly paycheck I got, and still get, barely covers rent, food, and utilities. I was trapped by misfortune. The only way for me to get around was in that man's car, or nothing. I chose the former. Hey, why not use him a little after he used me for twenty-three years? It took me another two years to realize that he was manipulating me through the use of his car.

He would come to my apartment and make himself something to eat, while I was out making a living, with his car. I guess this was the "trade-off." I used his car; he ate my food. The lousy bum had no job of his own and was leeching off of me. I hated it, but I put up with it because I absolutely positively needed that damned car. I got so frustrated that I told the pastor of my church about my situation.

He and the congregation prayed for me; prayed that God would help solve my problem. He told me that the car was being purposely utilized by my ex to keep his foot on me. My ex still knew everywhere I went and in a way, he was still driving because I could not get behind the wheel without him knowing about it.

When I got home one day, I had had enough. It took my pastor, my son, and my psychiatrist to bring me to my senses. I found my ex-husband seated on my couch, in my living room, with his repugnant feet on my new rug, eating my food! The dialogue that ensued went something like this: "Get out. Give me my key. Take your car. Here are your car keys. Never again do I want to see your face in my home. Now!"

At last the coward left, without saying a word. And to think that I had to go through all that hardship over a car.

The next day I woke up earlier, got to work later, and ate dinner happier. I phoned my daughter at college and told her what I had done. She congratulated me on a job long overdue. It amazes me that at eight years of age, she was giving me advice that I ended up taking thirteen years later. But this time it was different. I had three men whom I trusted give me the counsel I needed. I'm glad I listened, but now I had another problem.

How was I supposed to get around town without a car? Well, my prayers were answered. I received a phone call from a distant friend who had heard about my problem from my pastor. This friend of mine had connections with a woman who owned a used car dealership and who was known to be sympathetic to a woman's needs. The next day I met her.

She showed me many lovely cars. I sat in some just to feel what it would be like to drive them. The beige Toyota felt so comfortable. They probably thought I wanted that car because I had adjusted the seat, mirror, had my hands on the wheel, and played with the controls. I sat there for a moment and took a deep breath.

It was enough for me just to sit in that beautiful car and let my lungs fill with that "new car smell," which I had never known, since the man I once called "husband" only bought used cars in disrepair. I imagined myself speeding down a freeway, shifting gears like a race car driver, going faster and faster on a smooth road, taking dangerously sharp turns, beeping the horn just for the fun of it. I saw myself stopping at a gas station and pumping my own gas without asking for assistance while winking at a young handsome attendant. I could hear someone calling me and I stopped daydreaming. "Mrs. Cabrera, I asked if you'd like to drive the vehicle," said the dealer.

"Miss Cabrera, and no, I wish to see something much cheaper please," I replied. After touring the entire lot and back lot, I had seen great cars that were way out of my financial reach. By this time the dealer knew my story in its entirety and offered to show me her son's car.

He wanted to sell it and had entrusted this to his mother. It was a cute four-door black Mazda Protégé. I liked it immediately. It was basically everything I needed, small and economical. We cut a deal that was so unbelievable I can only attribute it to the prayers and the fact that this woman's life and mine had similarities.

I finally did it, after all those years. I wash my car, inside and out. I always remove the radio when I park it. I make sure the lights are off when I get out, and I lock the doors. I pump the gasoline, and sometimes beep the horn for no reason at all. People giggle and call me crazy when I drive around beeping and beeping. Yes, my kids like my car, and most importantly, so do I. This is my car. This is my car.

In Search of the Goddess

LILLIAN COMAS-DIAZ

The monkey's cry pierced our hearts. The man in front of me screamed and lost his balance. Jumping at him, tearing his shirt and opening his bag, the monkey knew what he was looking for. In slow motion, the victim's reaction went from terror to embarrassment to awkward laugh.

"It searched for my candy offerings to Kali," the man said, wiping his wounds.

I got dizzy staring at the bloodstained floor.

"Human blood is Kali's favorite libation," our Indian guide said, "but we can't sacrifice people anymore. The government prohibited this practice, and Kali's statue tilted her head."

"Is the goddess angry?" I asked, gasping for air.

"Of course. Today she only drinks animal blood."

Kali possesses.

Originally, Kali's priests used human blood for the bindi—the red dot that Hindus wear on their foreheads. Women offered their menstrual fluid for painting a bindi and opening their third eye. Listening to the guide, my blood began to flow. The uterine sanguine stream renewed my dread of female blood. First, menstruation at age 10, then menopause—so ridiculously premature—that I feared being pregnant. At 50, my uterine fibroids feed a daily bloodshed.

"You need a hysterectomy," condemned my physician, in the same dispassionate voice policemen use when they stop Black drivers on the New Jersey Turnpike.

Before meeting Kali, my blood flow mysteriously stopped at the Jain temple, which prohibited entrance to menstruating women.

"How do they know when we're bleeding?" May, a member of our delegation, asked with feminist fervor.

"They smell you," I joked, and every female in our group laughed in conspiracy. We then took our photographs in front of the sign that admonished menstruating women not to enter the temple.

Adorned for a wedding, the Jain temple screamed female. Flower petals sparkled like rubies glistening on the floor. The aroma from brewing stews awakened our appetites for exotic sustenance. Voluptuous female idols dressed in red, magenta, and crimson garments engulfed the shrine.

The Black one—Kali—is bloodthirsty. My blood flow returned in her presence. Meanwhile, monkeys feasted on candy while a scarlet aura impregnated the air. Entering the shrine, I encountered her face. Kali's tilted expression oscillated between fury and love. I requested to be consecrated. Her priest blessed me and opened my third eye with a bindi. I traveled to Asia to study Eastern healing, but ended up being possessed. As I left the temple, I felt a burning on my back. When I found the heat source, Kali stared back at me.

India was home.

"She's Yemayá," Maria, another member of our delegation, remarked.

Combining our Caribbean heritages, hers Cuban, mine Puerto Rican, we searched for our ancestral Black Madonna. I visualized my Virgen de Monserrat statue, cradling her son while balancing the world on her hand. My brother David regaled her to me, a gift from his Haitian ex-lover.

"You never own the Black Madonna," he shuddered. "She owns you."

Kali destroys.

My mother's death was vivid during my journey. In the midst of soporific grief, Kali gave me solace. Like an orphan, I didn't know I was searching for Mother. Kali—terrifying and enigmatic—is conceived as a kind and beautiful mother in Bengal.

Dreaming in flamenco, I found my maternal line in Andalusia. Santiago Carbonell, a Catalan painter, once told me that he collects vials of local perfumes while traveling. He then conjures up the places with their scents, capturing their essence on canvas. Seville is oranges. I can still smell their fragrance when I see Andalusian images. Competing with the smell is the heat—balming the morning and flaming the afternoon.

The Sevillana streets summoned familiar faces, evoking reciprocal nostalgia. People treated me like blood—using the endearing interpersonal style reserved only for relatives. During my first night in Granada I ate dinner in front of a mirror, or so I thought, until Fred, my husband, told me that the woman in the 19th-century painting in front of us looked just like me.

Andalusia was home.

Raised by maternal grandparents, I etched my identity into theirs. Watching a daily gitana movie, I longed to become a flamenco dancer. One of my favorite movies, *Blood Wedding*, based on Federico Garcia Lorca's play, depicts the central role of blood in gypsy life. Each dance is a blood wedding between human and goddess, between man and bull.

Ese toro enamorao' de la luna…

Singing this melody, I went to visit Virgen de la Macarena. During Holy Week, her acolytes parade her statue, following the path of Jesus' blood through the streets of Seville. The patroness of the bullfighters, Macarena rules over swords, blood, and death. Although she is not Black, she is the Madonna de los morenos—the dark-skinned gitanos. Centuries ago, the gypsies brought Kali from India, transforming her into Macarena.

On an Andalusian afternoon, I invited myself to a gypsy wedding. The best maids marched like vestal attendants—smiling through black mantillas—and flirting with every male. Suddenly, music erupted and the bride appeared in a red dress. She danced down the aisle in the midst of Ole mi maja. Her stomping feet and sinuous arms directed the guitar's cadence.

"La novia dances for Her," the woman next to me said.

The groom waited at the altar, watching his bride's movements with the intensity of a toreador about to kill the bull. When his novia reached him, she pulled out a knife from between her breasts. Taking his hand, the bride cut his palm. She then pierced her own hand and blended their blood, joining their hands in a flamenco clap. Afterwards, the bride threw the bloodstained blade at the Madonna's feet. Macarena smiled at the offering. Later on, the fiesta evoked a corrida de toros—its pathos equally reminiscent of a baptism and a funeral.

During the final adiós to my mother, I recounted Mami's ancestors' journey while she lay on her deathbed.

"I saw your face many times in Andalusia," I said.

Hurt by my decision not to have children, Mami struggled to stay alive in order to greet the birth of her only grandchild. Naming his unborn daughter Antonia (after our grandmother), my brother David sent Mami an ultrasound picture.

"I've seen little Antonia playing in our garden," Mami said, looking at the picture. "She has Asian eyes."

As in a Latin American novella, she did not make it. Mami only met Antonia in her dreams.

"I found my child in Córdoba," I told her.

"She looks like our daughter," Fred said, watching our guide describe the Mezquita.

Praising the co-existence of placid, Moorish, intricate Mozárabe and rabid Spanish styles, she described what used to be the greatest mosque in the world as an allegory for multiculturalism. Standing next to her, I noticed members of our delegation intensely looking at her, then at me.

Her face and mine continued one in the other, jointly drawing the maps of southern Spain and northern Africa.

"Do you have relatives in Córdoba?" a colleague asked me with a perplexed expression, the look I was to witness in Morocco while people stared at me.

The same number of times I saw my mother's face in Andalusia, I saw mine in Morocco.

"Welcome back," the Moroccan woman greeted me as I entered her shop.

Africa was home.

A month after our conversation, Mami died asphyxiated in a blood vomit. She was too old to qualify for a liver transplant; the illness placed its victorious flag over Mami's body. Announcing death, Kali brandishes a blood-stained sword, holds a dripping human head, wears a necklace of human heads, and places her foot like a flag on her husband Shiva, who lies like a corpse. Such a terrifying image wards off evil spirits. Obsessing about my mother's final combat, I invoked Kali to exorcise my pain.

The Tamils know her as Kattavei, the goddess of war who feeds on carnage. Naked on top of a corpse, she devours its intestines. Such a ghastly image comforts and heals.

Losing my mortal mother, I found a divine one. I held this thought during my peregrination to Monserrat.

"Comas, that's a Catalan name," our taxi driver declared in Barcelona.

"I came back after 500 years," I said, paraphrasing every Latino visiting Spain.

Indeed, part of my paternal line was Catalan. In less than a year I traced my roots from Andalusia, to Africa, to Catalonia.

After a train ride, I jumped into a funicular full of Filipino pilgrims. The penitents engaged in a mesmerizing incantation. Moving with the chanting, the funicular swung back and forth between rocks and the sky. The hypnotic journey landed me in front of a basilica carved out of steep peaks.

"Two lines, one for the Mass and the other for the Madonna," a man shouted.

In collective supplication, the interminable line at Monserrat's shrine was welcoming. Like a tourist from the first world, I filmed the occasion with my video camera. When I arrived at La Moreneta—"the Dark One"—she was nesting her black son on her lap and holding the world-sphere in her hand.

Videotaping Monserrat, Kali stared back at me. Amazed, I did not know what to do, except to continue filming. So surprised was I that I forgot to perform the ritual of touching Monserrat's sphere.

Catalonia was home.

I returned and caressed the world.

Kali enraptures.

The day after our visit to Kali's shrine, we left India for Kathmandu. During the trip, Fred noticed my bindi. We tried to explain how it survived strenuous showers.

"Is the bindi painted on your sunglasses?" Fred asked.

"It's a stigmata." I answered. "Kali claimed me."

"Nepal's first tourist attraction is Mount Everest, and its second is Kumari—the living goddess," our guide explained. "The priests select the most perfect and beautiful girl to become Devi's incarnation. Some say she's Parvati, others declare she's Durga, but Kumari is Kali," our guide insisted.

The priests select Kumari from a special caste between the ages of four and puberty. Kumari must meet 32 strict physical and mystical requirements. Her horoscope has to complement Nepal's king's, because he is believed to be Shiva's incarnation. Once the candidates are chosen, they are gathered into the temple hall for the final selection. The girls stay the entire night with carcasses of slaughtered animals. The candidate who withstands these offerings with regal composure becomes Kumari.

Blood is the goddess's line. When Kumari begins to menstruate or accidentally loses great amounts of blood, she ceases to be a living goddess. The selection ritual is reenacted, and another girl becomes Kumari.

"Can we see her?" I asked.

"Not likely. Kumari only comes out of her temple six times a year," our guide replied.

I went to a Buddhist temple and prayed for my dead. A vision of painted eyes on the top of the stupa appeared during my meditation. Encircled with kohl, Asian eyes followed me everywhere, the same painted eyes shown in Kumari postcards. Nepalese children also sported this fashion.

Outside the temple, the guide explained: "The kohl wards off evil spirits and protects children."

A bacchanalia of images, sounds, and fragrances assaulted my senses. The mix of spiritual fervor with tourist materialism did not deter me. Instead, I concentrated on the orange-clad monks, the prayer bells, the soothing music, and the wandering dogs. Suddenly, I heard a commotion.

A caravan—horns blowing, music playing, cries ripping the air—carried a throne. Instinctively, I chased the parade. Fastening my video camera, hastened by fear, and conceiving Kumari, I recorded everything. A beautiful girl with painted Asian eyes emerged from the royal seat. The human mass magically opened for this tourist attached to a camera.

I filmed the living goddess as her attendants lifted her from the chariot—she must not touch the ground with her feet.

Videotaping Kumari, she stared back at me. Her acolytes then carried her into the temple. I continued filming, keeping Kumari prisoner with my camera. At the exact moment I entered the temple, a guard stopped me: "No foreigners allowed."

"You're blessed," the guide told me later. "On your first day you find the living goddess."

Nepal was home.

You die in India and are reborn in Nepal. Soothing the chaos brought by our sojourn, Nepalese sculptures depicted unabashed scenes of Tantric sex. Kali is the sexual sorceress. Her images portray her performing the cosmic dance, mounting her husband's erect penis.

Kali creates.

The heads in Kali's necklace represent the false personalities we assume, vestiges of weakness and attachment, which she must brutally remove, one by one, so we may find our divine selves. The goddess of transformation, Kali erases the line between life and death. She transmutes death into rebirth.

Antonia, my niece and godchild, was to be born after my Asian journey. During the trip's first week, I had a disturbing dream: my brother David was dead. Terrified, I realized that my mourning was also taking place during sleep. However, the following night I witnessed the same lucid vision. Fred reminded me that in espiritismo, dreaming about a death signifies a birth. He was correct; Antonia was born prematurely. My opened third eye had witnessed her arrival.

Our trip to Atlanta was pregnant with excitement and distress. A joyous occasion, meeting Antonia was blackened by my mother's death. David and his wife Holly had asked me to be the godmother. I accepted, but with the condition of not having to take Catholic classes. I was weary of dogmatic impositions.

David could not find a priest who agreed with my request.

"The godparents need to follow Church doctrines. We cannot offer a waiver," condemned the priest.

"He meant he can't commute the sentence," I said. "Who will protect Antonia?" I worried while Fred tried to comfort me. "She'll go to limbo if she dies unbaptized."

The first time I saw my niece, I searched for my mother's face. Antonia's line will be different from my mother's. The carrier of Puerto Rican, Filipino, African, Spanish, Hawaiian, Chinese, British, German, and Taino genes, Antonia looked like a poster for multiculturalism.

I was home.

Videotaping my niece, Kumari stared back at me.

Overweight and
Related Conversations

S. BRANDI BARNES

*"When I look back over my life and I think things over, I can truly say
that I've been blessed, I've got a testimony…"*
As sung by Cosmopolitan Church of Prayer Holiness, Chicago, IL

The pressure to be a size 5 to no-size-at-all was always a topic of conversation in my family among my aunts, sister, and a few so-called friends as I grew from young adulthood to full-figured, blossoming womanhood. It still is a topic among some, even now that I'm middle-aged, self-confident, and totally self-accepting.

With the exception of my two grandmothers, all the women in my family are petite, obsessed with dieting, and therapy candidates for future anorexia…as were seven of my eight former sister-in-laws, ranging in size from 7 to 12.

An overweight child or adult is subjected to assaults on her self-image and dignity from every sector of her being. And a child being repeatedly teased about being chubby or fat will learn to fight on the playground. The innocent cruelty of their playmates is usually the starting point.

It takes courage to rebel against being thin…to stand up to terms of endearment such as fat slob, fat pig, biggie wanting to be small, fat girl, fat, black, and ugly, truckmobile, tub of lard, and the ominous Fat Ass. It takes courage and strength for a child not to cry immediately, and for an adult to maintain his or her dignity when responding to these attempts at humiliation or unprovoked, belittling put-downs.

Of course, adults who commit this type of cruelty would never have the nerve to direct their remarks to Aretha Franklin, if they had the chance, or to Monique, Ella Fitzgerald, or Oprah when she was making her millions when she was overweight. And of course Oprah would never have an overweight and famous person on her show to talk about being fat, or how ashamed they are, or how bad they feel about being overweight.

Over the span of my life, I've ranged from being a little girl who shed her baby fat by age 14, to having real curves, average-sized breasts, and the "pear-shaped" figure in a size 14/16. In later years I went from 14 to 20 and back—stopping at all sizes between. I've been subjected to teasing by well-meaning family and friends, and by the world. I've watched the Oprah and Dr. Phil "fat shows." And let's not forget the Carnie Wilson laparoscopic surgery commercials running on a TV station near you.

I have never had any weight-related medical problems...not even when pregnant. I am therefore a witness to one's supposed health being a springboard to open a discussion or to comment on someone's weight...and usually this "friendly fire" is from a non-medical person—not a doctor, nurse, or other health practitioner. People with genuine health-related issues connected to weight should care for them in medical ways, as should those who love them. There's no excuse not to.

But trust me when I say that those outside of that realm, however, are jive talking. The talk is usually by criticizers desperately trying to cover up their own inadequacies, at the obese person's expense, but the fat or obese person has to give their consent for the belittler to be successful.

America's obsession with "weight" and fantasy ideals is only equaled by its obsession with sex. Indulge me for a moment and take into account the financial success of the diet and fitness industries, with special drinks or weight-loss programs such as Slim Fast, Jenny Craig, or even the Atkins diet.

Consider a Philadelphia newspaper headline in 2002 that read: "Philly We've Got a Problem— a Big Fat Problem." Finally, consider the number of talk shows with fat people as the topic: pathetically paraded on stage to tell what childhood trauma caused them to become fat, or what part of their genetic make-up made them fat, or what adult incident caused them to gorge into their present state. Enough already!

It's as if the hosts are oblivious to their own input in "fattening America." How does one overcome these assaults and attacks on her self image, when it comes from more personal family, friends, or enemies? Does she refuse to take ownership of the other person's problem and come back with a few verbal barbs of her own, such as, "It's more your problem than mine?"

And what imagery options are available to the overweight public, specifically those African-American females, who are not geared for the quick comeback—or choose not to respond in kind?

How does one offset the effects of centuries of a biased, exploitive society when successful methods used by one person may not work for another?

Personally, I think anyone experiencing challenges to their self image based on size or weight should definitely "get toxic people out of their lives" and surround themselves with supportive, positive, non-hypercritical friends and lovers. Then sing, "I've gotten toxic people out of my life." (At least until they know how to talk to you.) Reward yourself every time you do it.

There's little you can do about your family, except distance yourself or be very assertive regarding comments and behavior you will not accept from them, from friends, and from lovers who do not support your self image. My tongue is in my cheek when I say, "Smile civilly when you give them a slice of cake, pie, or poisoned apple."

The good news, if you haven't heard, is that there is a movement afoot—however slowly and subtly in our society—to balance off the negativity of "fat attacks" and the perceptions of chubby-to-obese people. There are more clothing boutiques or shops specializing in women's queen sizes, and the panty-hose companies have now acknowledged larger derrieres. Even some media have taken on the larger females through their commercials, print advertisements, and magazines featuring attractive African-American women. There are television shows now that promote the talents of our particular group. And there appears to be an increase in males choosing "a thick girl," as one of my slender and beautiful high school students cried—when not getting the boy she wanted. Why, even Aunt Jemima is looking better these days.

In addition to surrounding oneself with supportive friends and images, a steady diet of affirming spiritual information can lift one up and indeed "turn you 'round."

Women who don't feel good about their weight, who listen to and feed themselves negative messages, who believe it is a problem, should remember that they didn't get there all alone; some stress, some genes, some media, and some others helped them get to what they're perceiving as undesirable. If they think it's a problem, then they must take ownership of the problem and get busy—that is, if it really is a weight problem and not an image problem. Either way, one must get busy. For what one believes inside must manifest itself outside.

Some of us are better endowed than others, and indeed for some it's a blessing and for others a curse, but if we all looked alike or were the same size, there would be little yin/yang, least of all diversity and choice.

Have a Tina Turner at 50 and 60 moment—and believe how very good you look or can at any time if that's your goal. Give yourself a treat just for contemplating and creating your reinvention, whether it includes losing weight, boosting your self image, or correcting assertively those who need correction regarding you.

Sometimes, that may even be.

Go for That Dream

GILDA HERRERA

"**D**id you see that ad in the newspaper?" I had just entered the dining room and had the immediate impression that my father had been anxiously sitting in wait with that question. "Which ad?" I asked, sitting down, noticing he showed all the signs of a tiger ready to pounce on his prey. I waited patiently; though knowing my garrulous parent could hardly hold this information in much longer.

"They are looking for writers," he said simply.

I was more surprised at his getting to the point so quickly than at the information he imparted. Before I could respond, he continued in somewhat mild rebuke, "The newspaper's been running those ads for over a week."

Knowing my father read the daily newspaper from front to back, including most of the classifieds, I did not doubt his word.

"I haven't seen it," I answered, then belied my seemingly casual interest with my next questions: "Is it the newspaper itself that is looking for writers? Did you keep the paper or the ad? May I see it?"

"Thought you had seen 'em," he said smugly, "so didn't cut one out. Maybe you should get a hold of the paper and look at it."

I reached for the paper he had conveniently left sitting on the table and turned the pages quickly. There it was. The newspaper was seeking writers, which they referred to as "correspondents," to cover local school board meetings. I tore out the advertisement and said I would call and find out what it was all about.

I was in my early forties. I had earned a degree in journalism when I was twenty-four, but life and circumstances had led my job choices to other avenues. As a young girl I had dreamt of being a writer, a writer of fiction. As I got older, my ambitions turned to writing non-fiction. I had this overwhelming curiosity to know everything that was going on in the world and somehow witness it. In my mind, that meant through the newspaper business. I loved newspapers. From junior high school through attendance at the university, I volunteered for every writing assignment I could get. I wrote news stories on events, people making news, meetings. I wrote poetry, editorials, and features. You name it, and I wrote about it. In fact, I did everything but sports. In those days girls didn't cover sports, though growing up in Texas, I was an avid football fan.

My greatest love affair, since I was old enough to think, was with words. I loved reading them, understanding them, but most of all, using them. I have an old memory from high school study hall, where other students sat and did homework. The very tall, very big, hugely intimidating study hall teacher stood beside me and whacked a ruler on the opened book in front of me. I looked up at him, as he had brought me roughly out of my deep concentration into the harsh reality of his presence and the unwelcome focus of the other students' curiosity.

"What are you reading?" he demanded.

I swallowed hard. "He'll never believe me" flashed wearily through my mind. "The dictionary," I said timidly.

He laughed loudly. "Sure you are," he ridiculed. "That's what everybody does for light reading!" He slammed the book shut. "Quit wasting time and study."

After he walked away, the boy sitting across from me snickered, "Couldn't you come up with something better than that?"

I smiled and whispered, "I guess not." No one, unless they loved words, too, would have understood the magic I found in reading about words for their very own special sake.

I called the number listed in the advertisement and spoke to a man at the newspaper office. His title was "neighbors editor." He seemed impressed by my educational credentials, took my name, and invited me to a meeting to explain what the work entailed.

I felt comforted by seeing that most of the other attendees were close to my age, though after listening to their comments, most seemed to be looking for part-time work for additional income. I had not even asked about the pay for the work. I'd never been paid once for all the writing I had ever done.

The correspondents were to attend school board meetings and have a 10 p.m. deadline to call in stories with significant information on what occurred at the meetings. The information we called in had to be in news story form, even though it would be given orally by phone to a reporter at the office. I volunteered to attend the school board meetings at the district where I lived. It would be close to home, demanding limited night driving, and I knew it was a lively district. This school district had almost lost its accreditation. There were factions of cultural and economic extremes in this area of town.

I worked for over two years on this education beat. I interacted with educators, administrators, students, and the community. I did my best at providing fair and unbiased coverage; being loyal to my employer and truthful to the people I met. There was the pressure of deadlines, the overcoming of my limited knowledge of the academic world, the issues of getting along with newspaper people, some fair, others with their own agendas. Plus, I was working full time at a different job. Sometimes the nighttime work went into the dead of morning. The school board, especially when dealing with hot topics, would go into executive session and stay there for hours. They had to come back and face the public with their decisions, but would stay out in executive session so long, many people would give up and go home as the hours dragged on.

At one such meeting the reporter from the rival newspaper, as the clock approached midnight, begged me to leave so he could leave. I smiled at my competitor while declining his suggestion.

"I'm not leaving," I said simply.

He smiled back. "Then I'm not leaving," he answered with no malice. It was two o' clock in the morning when the board returned to announce their decision on a controversial issue. They were not pleased to see the two of us still in attendance. I missed the deadline for the morning edition, but made the next day's afternoon editions.

As someone much wiser than me has said, when you open your heart to what you really want, life has a way of bringing it to you. I loved seeing my name on a byline. I worked hard on the meeting reporting, and a year later my editor allowed me to do features. I wrote on principals, students, new policies, and new programs—all in the field of education. Then my editor asked me to do features on people in other walks of life. I didn't leave this work until the sad day this wonderful newspaper folded.

But my writing pursuits broadened. For a year I wrote and edited a monthly newsletter for a non-profit Hispanic organization. I began to write magazine articles for a local publication and began to write feature stories for a public relations man. Even my full-time employment miraculously changed. I entered as a trainee in government public affairs, and after eighteen months I was placed on the staff of a weekly newspaper in Washington, D.C. Not only had I received payment for my writing, now I was earning my living doing it. My father was kept busy happily cutting out clippings of my efforts.

After three years in D.C., I returned to my hometown San Antonio, where I did a few articles for my old rival daily newspaper, but my heart had returned to the writing of fiction. In one year I wrote three novel-length manuscripts—a mystery, a children's story, and a romance—plus a short story. Late in 2003, a publisher accepted the mystery, and my book *Four Dogs with a Bone* came out in spring 2004. After 2004, I've already completed the sequel to this novel. And the same publisher accepted the romance entitled *The Trip of the Eight Escapades*, which will be released in 2005.

My success in writing has come late in life, but that makes it no less real or special or fun. Writing is more than a dream to me. It is not an eternal flame of creativity, but rather a consistently reigniting spark from deep in the heart of me.

Writing is hard work; it requires dedication, skill, enthusiasm, reliability, a testing of your beliefs and morals, and, if you love it, it is a true labor of love. I am lucky in that writing ideas are always swimming around in my head. I am more fortunate in recognizing that while good writing encompasses inspiration and creativity, it also entails a lot of sweat, rewriting, pick-and-shovel editing, good reviews, and poor ones. I welcome, accept, and work at all of it.

I believe that no matter what your dream is, in whatever field of endeavor, you can't squander time with recriminations about lost time and wasted opportunities. Reviving an old dream or discovering a new one is mostly a matter of choice—a conscious decision. It isn't complicated. It is simple and obtainable. Whatever your age, you can always start again and, most of all, succeed. It takes perseverance, patience, forgiving yourself for silly mistakes, brushing yourself off and starting again when you fail, and enjoying each and every good thing that comes to you in the pursuit of that dream.

I promise you, there will be a whole lot more good things than failures. Success cannot be measured in the amount of money you generate, although the monetary rewards help to validate that success. As I grew older and grew up, I learned that success to me is not only striking when the iron is hot, but also, striking and making it hot. Success is in the process and the challenge. It is the attitude of risking failure and not worrying about failure. It is in the much saner attitude of "I'll just try and see what happens," and in enjoying the journey that follows.

Enough said. Time for me to look up a few golden words in the dictionary.

Toward a Journey of Truth, Love, and Healing

ROCHELLE ROBINSON

One of my favorite writers is bell hooks. Not long ago I read an essay from her book *Sisters of the Yam: Black Women and Self-Recovery* that touched me deeply. Her essay "Seeking After Truth" opens with a quote by our sister-ancestor Audre Lorde, also one of my favorites, which in part reads:

"As we arm ourselves and each other, we can stand toe to toe inside that rigorous loving and begin to speak the impossible—or what has always seemed like the impossible—to one another. This is the first step toward genuine change. Eventually, if we speak the truth to each other, it will become unavoidable to ourselves."

These wise words from Lorde speak to me as a Black woman. Why? Because so much of who I am, and who my sisters are, has not been about truth. In a hyper-capitalist, racist, sexist, homophobic society, who I am— Black, female—has been based on myths, stereotypes, distortion, and mis-representation. My Black sisters and I have historically been mammy-fied, sexualized, and racialized.

We are sexual deviants (as in promiscuous), emasculating (as in the myth of the Black matriarch), lazy and dishonest (as in welfare queen). There are more of these negative tropes masking as truth, but you get the idea. My response is, "This is not who I am, who we are," and I ask myself, "Where is my truth? Where do I go to find myself? Where do I go to find others like me? And why is seeking after truth often painful?"

I realize that the pain is not so much in the truth but in the lie, in the very absence of truth. Hooks says as much when, looking to our past, she writes: "Even free black people knew that white supremacist power could so easily be asserted in an oppressive way, that they, too, practiced the art of hiding behind a false appearance in the interest of survival."

Had I been surviving on lies and falsehoods? This really hurts.

Audre Lorde and bell hooks' words resonated within me. I came to understand that the pain I often feel deep down inside—pain that is often shared but not always expressed, pain from living in a white supremacist society—ought to be tended to with truth, and that love must precede it.

To be free of the pain, to begin the healing process, truth and love are the main ingredients. I must blend them carefully, lovingly. One cannot be substituted for the other; they must work in tandem. Seeking after truth means loving self, loving others. It means being proactive, responsible, and practicing what we preach. I cannot begin to find truth if I am unwilling to be honest with myself. None of us can.

Thus, I cannot, we cannot, be comfortable avoiding truth. Certainly Lorde and subsequently hooks have agreed that this kind of practice is bad for our mental, spiritual, and physical health and well being. We must recover from this. Bell hooks speaks to this when she writes: "Healing takes place within us as we speak the truth of our lives." In order to heal, in order to be whole with ourselves, and each other we must engage fully in this process.

Hooks' essay, which I highly recommend, gave relevance and meaning to my life. Her words changed me; they made sense. As I began my journey seeking after truth, a journey that I am still on, I realized that I can and will do this alone or with others. I chose to do both. My writing is my truth. When I write, I am raw and naked. I can be myself, see myself. I can deconstruct the myths and the lies told about me as I reconstruct my truths. I can write my own herstory and indeed I must. But I also want to share this phenomenon of seeking after truth with other sisters so that our herstories can help us in our understanding of each other.

Historically, our survival has depended upon our avoiding truth, because it has been almost impossible to do so under such an oppressive system of racism and sexism. It has been an unloving practice that's done us more harm than good. Black women still experience racism and sexism in our contemporary lives because it is so embedded in our social, economic, cultural, and political structures.

We must move away from avoidance and dare to tell the truth about how these interlocking systems of domination have hurt us in the past, and continue to hurt us, and cause us to hurt each other. Are you ready to heal? Are you ready to begin your journey of seeking after truth?

Our survival now depends upon us letting go of fears of tellin' it like it is—it depends on our taking off the "mask" by calling out our truths and healing from them. It must be our new ritual, our new tradition. It is never too late to heal. Our survival depends on our loving ourselves, and one another.

Until recently I have been unwilling to tell the truth about my desire to be free of the burden of the "strong Black woman." I am often not strong, and that mask of strength has been killing me; it's been killing us. It has been one of those contradictions in my life, in the myth about Black women as strong matriarchs, which I am no longer willing to accept.

Freeing myself of this has been hard but liberating. I can now be vulnerable and accept my vulnerability. I can be afraid and accept my fears. It does not have to mean that I am weak, but if I am, so be it. I am willing to say, "I'm tired of having to carry this heavy, cumbersome luggage around with me. I am not strong enough. I need help. I need love, I need support, and I need to be able to love myself more."

We are bone weary (I know I am) from carrying the heavy banner of the "backbone." I am ready to be well. I am ready for my sisters to be well. I can begin the process of healing by using my pen as a weapon to exorcise the demons of denial and deceit. I believe in the power of writing as a way of healing, as a way of speaking and seeking truth. A year ago, I began and participated in a process of seeking, even longing after truth by organizing a writing collective.

The Sisters Solstice Writing Collective began because there was an urgent need for Black women to tell their stories, to speak their truths, and to have a safe space to come together with each other in a collective healing process. It was born out of a conversation with a sister-friend. One beautiful Sunday afternoon in Oakland's Jack London Square, she and I were discussing the lack of writing by and about Black women that spoke to our experiences.

I was personally frustrated, when as a graduate student working on my master's thesis about Black women in the suffrage movement, I found very little history that made Black women visible. What I did find was a history buried, and beneath the ashes lay a wealth of Black woman herstory that had yet to be told. My friend and I grew tired of reading the same books over and over—books by and about Black women where we could find ourselves, short of fiction, were scarce.

"Our voices are necessary and instrumental to our own struggles and victories," I told my friend. "Girl, we've got to define ourselves for ourselves; someone else's truth is not necessarily our own."

After a lot of "Yeah, girl," "I'm tired of being invisible," "There are too many stories out there that don't get heard," She and I decided to team up and get a writing group started. We have just celebrated our one-year anniversary and have long-term plans to edit an anthology of the writings from the many talented, fierce, and truth-seeking sisters in the collective.

I discovered, with the help of my sisters, that who I am and where I come from is often a painful journey of truth-telling and self-discovery that is not always easy. Sometimes I am still afraid of telling the truth, even when I am writing in a confidential manner. But recently I was able to talk about being raped some twenty-plus years ago.

In seeking truth, I came to some terms with that brutal night. I am no longer ashamed of what happened to me, to say it out loud, to realize that it was not my fault. There was something very powerful, in fact liberating, in the act of telling. The rape had silenced and shamed me, and made me believe that my body was not my own.

There was terror and tyranny in the violation of my body, and it had been buried within me, always haunting me, wounding me. Yet my disclosure brought other sisters to disclose their terrors. I discovered that too many of us have been violated in this way. But the beauty is that we have also survived. I have survived.

After two decades I have come to the realization that this rape was not about me, not about anything I did. It was a brutal act perpetrated by a brutal man who had no regard for my humanity, my right to say no, and my right NOT to be violated. It was not my fault.

I have forgiven myself. I've forgiven my soul and spirit for allowing my perpetrator to wound me, terrorize my body (he took away my right to choose who I love, have sex with, but I'm reclaiming that right!). I've forgiven myself for the blame that I took on. I know better now, I am better now, and I'm breaking my silence because I was able to seek truth.

I now understand why hooks writes about this subject, because we have—I had—become adept at wearing the mask; we have become adept at being masters of deceit because we tell ourselves that it protects us from those things that may do us harm. I have taken off my mask. I am exposed, naked, vulnerable, but my healing has begun.

My spirit is released when I am writing and reflecting upon those injuries that have dampened my sense of self. I know that there is a power within that comforts me and I must not deny that power. I must embrace it fully. I must not be afraid.

To come full-circle with the truth is liberating. It is a love-filled mission. I know that we cannot tap into the spirit if we resist the truth. We must allow freedom and liberation to come by letting go of the lies and myths that have consumed us. We must be mindful of the spirit. We must always nurture it. Writing has been my salvation. It has saved my life. It is my way of embracing and acknowledging truth.

When I write I no longer despair. I hope, I dream, I am. In her book

The Cancer Journals, Audre Lorde asks, "How do I fight despair born of fear and anger and powerlessness which is my greatest internal enemy?" We fight it by speaking the truth.

And finally, I pose the questions so eloquently penned by Lorde: "What are the words you do not yet have? What do you need to say? What are the tyrannies you swallow day by day and attempt to make your own, until you will sicken and die of them, still in silence? Because I am a woman, because I am black, because I am lesbian, because I am myself, a black woman warrior poet doing my work, come to ask you, are you doing yours?"

Well, are you? What fears do you need to let go of? What truths have you got buried beneath your pain? Speak it. Write it. Paint it. Capture it in black/white or color. Sing it. Praise it. Do it with love. The truth is our strength. I know it has become mine.

BREAKIN' BOULDERS WITH MY SHOULDERS

I'm breakin' boulders with my shoulders
My strong, strong shoulders
That carries so many burdens
Both yours and mine
And those burdens, they don't break me
Because my God, He never forsakes me
So, I'm knockin' down obstacles
Clearing a path
Making a way
I'm pushin' on through
Both for me and for you

Yes, I'm breakin' boulders with my shoulders
My lovely, smooth, graceful shoulders
Where the heads of many loved ones have rested
When they thought they'd been bested
By those they've trusted.
I've dried their tears of pain and tears of joy
And my proud and noble shoulders
Still continue to break down boulders
Boulders that shroud the dark and ugly images
That were created just to be
The gnawing fear of uncertainty
Therefore blocking me
From the knowledge that keeps me free

So, I firmly set my shoulders
That keeps shattering those troublesome boulders
And, as my determination grows stronger
My strides get a little longer
I lift my head a little higher
And work harder to inspire
A conscious burning desire—to succeed
In the new breed who follow behind me
I don't allow silly people to get me rattled
With the tall tales they choose to tattle

'Bout who they think I am
And where they think I'm comin' from
'Cause I've already endured every evil under the sun
But, I don't let that spoil my fun
That's why I always set the tone
When I artfully shrug my shoulder bone

And the funky message I send
Is that strong shoulders can bend
Without breaking
I can leave the whole world shaking
With the ability of my boulder-breaking shoulders.
— *Katherine A. Parker*

HOLDING BACK

I don't have the strength:
to shave my legs
be funny and charming
show interest in contact sports
cook
pretend to eat salads ALL the time
shop for sexy lingerie
make sure I don't wear the same outfit twice
agonize over my shapely shortcomings
get a background check
condom shop
do my muscle-tensing exercises—hourly
hide my PMS symptoms
hold my farts
sleep in the wet spot
try not to snore
and
angle our conversations,
so you only see my best side
                              —*Estelle Farley*

FULL COURSE MEAL

I am a generous recipe of a woman
Created long before calories counted
I am two cups of brown sugar
Stir slowly,
Bring to a fast boil, kind of woman
I'm rich,
Thick, and tasty...
Full of mouth-watering sin,
I'm the kind of woman that stays on your mind
From the beginning until the end,
I am a generous recipe of a woman
Made with lots of butter, eggs, and the sweetest of cream
Whipped together all silky smooth,
When I laugh, out come the stars and the moon,
Then I sigh when I see you reaching for your plate,
Knowing we will satiate today's hunger
and tomorrow's needs,
Just keep in mind that there is so much more of me,
I am a generous recipe of a woman.

—*D. L. Harris*

Sistahs Survivin'
and Workin' It Out

Lasting change does not happen overnight.
Lasting change happens in infinitesimal increments;
a day, an hour, a minute,
a heartbeat at a time.
— Sarah Ban Breathnach

Three Cheers for Courage: "No Guts, No Glory!"

JENNIFER BROWN BANKS

We were packed like sardines at the renowned United Center. "Gate 4," the instructions provided. Women from all ages, walks of life, and nationalities came—teachers, office managers, financial analysts, sex therapists, performers, and college students. Married, single, some divorced. Black, White, Asian, and Latino alike.

All vying for a chance to join the prestigious ranks of the Chicago Bulls' dance troupe, the Luvabulls. The competition was fierce, and the screening process detailed and thorough. The application I downloaded from the Internet probed everything from weight, to age, to dress and shoe size, to references and work history, all just to get a foot in the door. A full-length photo was the deal sealer.

As I stood in the lobby, waiting for my turn to register, I was in total awe of all the beauty, poise, youth, and talent assembled. Like a person afflicted with amnesia, I wondered just how I had gotten here. And would I survive? Me, a woman twice as old as most of the participants? Pretty, but not particularly glamorous, with a body less than perfect by comparison.

To make matters worse, notification of my acceptance came only 48 short hours before I was to audition. Certainly not enough time for the preparation someone my age would need. Within this limited time frame, I would have to replenish my supply of cellulite cream, find a girdle with more "control" than Janet Jackson, buy a miracle bra, limber my body, steady my nerves, and come up with some sexy dance moves all in just 48 hours.

Those 48 hours transpired more like 48 minutes, and then, as they say in Hollywood, it was "show time." Shortly after our arrival at the arena, we were assigned numbers reflecting the order we would appear (I was 112) and then placed in a waiting room pending instructions. Much to my surprise, the women were all extremely friendly, supportive, and sweet. We exchanged make-up, advice, aspirations, and words of encouragement.

It felt like a beauty pageant. About an hour into the process, we were greeted by the Luvabulls director and given the rundown. Smile, she told us, smile as much as possible. No tights, no shirts as cover-ups, no skirts, no braless outfits, and make-up is mandatory. No body piercings, no tattoos.

"Remember your turns and don't freak out if you're asked to do something you don't know how to do. We can teach you. And have fun!"

With that, and some rah, rah, rahs, we were presented to the judges in groups of 10. We danced freestyle to random music, vogued, and answered questions from the panel. We were turning, swiveling, and smiling, while anxiously awaiting the announcement of who would advance to the next stage.

Caught up in the excitement of it all, when it came my turn, my memory went AWOL. I forgot to do my turns, gave a lame answer to the question asked, and had trouble pulling myself off the floor after positioning for the requested left-leg split. I didn't even make it past the first cut.

It was the most gratifying disaster I had ever experienced! Friends, family, and co-workers were certain I had gone off the deep end for even trying out. Said it was totally out of character. Called it a midlife crisis. Some teased and even predicted my fate. But for me, it had nothing do with winning, measuring up, or needing the validation of a cheerleading squad to feel worthy.

For me, it was about living out a dream of being a dancer, about being bold and adventurous. About expanding my horizons...having courage. Who says that beauty has to be defined by blonde hair, youth, or a 24-inch waistline? Of course, prestige and the added incentive of meeting some gorgeous, eligible basketball players didn't hurt, either!

Would I do it again? In a heartbeat. Sure, in the "traditional" sense I came home a loser. But sometimes a victory in spirit is equally important.

Full Circle

DEBRA SLEDGE

I continue to feel that I need a starting point or direction: the more I think about it, the more I am unable to define that. I need a theme, yet one escapes me. There are words longing to come forth; they always have. The desire started as a young girl wanting to write children's books, and I guess some dreams don't die. Who do I want to reach? What do I want to say?

I want to talk about life lessons, the school of hard knocks, the things Momma never told me what I learned while becoming a woman. I want to talk about the importance of knowing oneself, being confident and keenly aware of the heavenly spirit within each of us. I want to talk about the longing in our souls for more, so much more than the world can give us.

I want to talk about looking for love in all the wrong places, while finding self-defeat and self-destruction and, finally, the journey back to oneself. I don't know why this needs to be done, but I am learning to follow the inner voice inside me.

I let others define me: I was, at one time or another, John and Mary's daughter; Raymond's girl; the conceited girl; "hoetta" (I was proud of that name because at least everyone knew me); Mark's wife; the lesbian; the nurse; Captain Johnson's wife; the mother to Sharon and Rhonda; and Edward Hall's wife.

I don't have a clue how I was all those different people, yet, I know…I never became me. The journey to self is enlightening but long. Within me I carry pieces of broken dreams, shattered hopes, pain, so much pain, tons of other people's expectations, and, finally, none of me. Where did I get lost?

Perhaps it started with the innocence of exploring my sexuality, or maybe earlier, when I wanted to save Tony from the abuse (at least that's what it's called today). Maybe I was born needing so much and was never given the tools to search…

Thank God life is a never-ending journey, because I should have given up long ago. God has a reason for sparing me, although that, too, escapes me today. My hope is that in writing this story someone will be helped, and I will finally discover God's purpose for my presence here on Earth.

Dear Heavenly Father,

I am following the nudges within my soul. I follow what I perceive as confirmation to begin this journey. I ask You, Father, Your will be done. I ask that You use me as Your vessel; that You direct my thoughts and my fingers. I pray, Father, that You are pleased with this work, for my desire is to please You. I ask for Your blessings on this journey, and may those who are charged with reading this, that they, too, be blessed. In the precious name of Jesus, I pray. Amen.

On good days I wake up and feel loved by others, and myself; on bad days I desperately try to figure out why I am here. Low self-esteem and self-worth issues challenge me, as do a lack of direction, lack of focus, self-destruction, and perfectionism.

It's okay for me to express my needs and desires. It's even better that I can identify them. As I write, it feels like I am talking about someone else. These are not my words. Everyone had such high hopes and dreams for me, and I was supposed to be someone; someone famous, someone the entire world knew.

I was the perfect child, the smart child, the confused child, and the insecure child. I lacked the ability to question (anything). I was so happy someone paid attention to me it didn't matter if they used my body for their own selfish reasons: someone was paying attention to me. I was tired of being put on a pedestal and always having to be perfect. I just wanted to be!

Why couldn't he stop making him angry! Why won't he just stop? He knows the rage that will come, that he loses his senses, and punches and hits with his entire being. Why won't he just stop? Because when they leave, I will be the receiver of his revenge. It is me he will attack, who will feel his rage, and although I fight back I am no match for his anger. When he brings this to my room, he tells me I better not say anything, just open my legs...

The back staircase in junior high school is where I lost my virginity. The day before, he told me to wear a skirt to school. I followed his instructions to the letter. That morning, game day, he gave me the plan: "Meet me on the back staircase by the locked exit door." I cut class and met him as scheduled. He was there. I was scared. There was not much time, only 45 minutes.

After I lay on the cold, hard floor, he entered me. When he was done, I pulled up my panties and looked at the door at the top of the staircase—

there stood his boys, watching every moment. I wasn't angry they were there; in fact, it didn't matter, because now I was in the club of being accepted. I was his girl, and I proved it by giving him the most valuable thing I owned: myself.

That humiliating episode has replayed itself over and over and over again all of my life; settling for less when I deserve the best. It was not until the transformation, which occurred many years later, when I slowly began to understand the treasure that I am; the temple I inherit: I am God's most precious child.

I felt a void inside and would do anything to gain the needed acceptance. I could not (in my own mind) measure up to the white kids I was forced to assimilate with. I could make the grade, that was never a problem, but how could I measure up to their standards of what was supposed to be superior?

At home they were called "crackers," at school I was called "nigger," and in society they were treated as chosen. Any attempt I made to be accepted by them and dress like them didn't work, because I couldn't afford the price. To look like them would not happen; my skin color was not their color, and my hair was short and curly, not long and straight.

It was easier for me to be accepted by folks that looked like me, which meant I had to do the things they did, unless I found an easier way, and I did, so I thought. I lost my virginity to the most popular and sought-after bad boy. The acceptance of my peers made me feel untouchable and seemingly invincible.

The status I gained allowed me to freely walk the halls, take the bus, and not be attacked by the bullies and the wannabes. To my surprise, I could remain smart in my classroom full of white kids and still take the bus back to the 'hood. Apparently, the newfound status and protection were important to me.

I degraded myself many times; simply to keep what I thought was important. I failed to learn how to value myself. I failed to learn how to stand up for myself. What I learned, instead, was how to people-please, which has followed me, along with the need for perfection, most of my life.

I learned how to perform for men. There were things I needed to keep them coming back to me—as long as I was needed and sought after, I thought there was some value in it for me. The degrees of dishonesty, dishonor, and disrespect didn't matter: as long as they came back, I was complete.

What I eventually realized is that in every serious relationship I've ever been in, I searched for the same thing: to be loved, cherished, and honored. To know and to have a relationship with one person who values me as much as I value them; to know and to have a relationship with someone who would not cheat on me; for someone to trust completely.

It hurts not to be able to trust someone you sleep with. It hurts to feel trapped in a relationship that is killing you. It hurts to feel powerless and know that is not who you are. It hurts to know that, once again, you have fallen in the trap, the trap that makes you feel like a caged rabbit: powerful, but cornered. It hurts to give away so much of you and have it disregarded as yesterday's trash. It just hurts. And the pain will not go away…

Nothing prepared me for the transition that started at age 40 and continued into the next two years. However, in retrospect, my whole life prepared me for this transition. Although turning 40 was not the primary cause of the numbing effect, the world, as I knew it, had suddenly been turned upside down.

Without warning I looked at me and did not know who I was. All my life I had sought to please others, which meant becoming whoever I needed to become in order for that relationship to exist. Suddenly, I had no idea what I wanted, what I liked, or what I needed. I felt a void so huge I wanted to die.

In the midst of this inner turmoil, my life partner wanted out: out of a 13-year relationship that I'd (for once in my life) committed to completely, even though I was drowning without a lifeboat. I was determined to endure the pain, not to take any hostages, and pray that I landed with something that resembled life.

Two years later, I realize with great happiness, that it was the turning point in my life. Through much pain, suffering, and finally surrender, I am comfortable with me. As a result, I've found the only thing that could fill the void I sought in alcohol, drugs, and sex: my Higher Power.

I've spent most of my life in church and was accustomed to following various routines, but never was I comfortable enough to surrender myself to something I could not feel, hear, or see. Today I believe, feel, hear, see, and trust my Higher Power.

Also, I have come to understand the true meaning of a "soul mate." My life partner and I are one. We stayed together and rocked and rolled through the hardest times of our relationship. There are days I don't know how I made it through. Often, it was my commitment to others that kept me going.

Pain sometimes forces you to your knees. Many days and nights my prayers were to be released from the life commitment I'd made. Each time I prayed the answer was always the same—just stand. What? Oh, I fought with my Higher Power: "Why do I have to stand? Why do I have to take this? How much of this am I supposed to take? I can't take it anymore. REMOVE HIM!"

The funny thing is, once again, it was not until I got to a point of complete surrender, when I stopped trying to fix it, when I no longer had any more tricks, when I threw up my hands and said it's all yours, did my relationship with my life partner, my soul mate, begin the process of restoration.

Only soul mates will stay and fight. I've been divorced twice: I know how to do that; but what I didn't know was how to stick and stay, how to build and rebuild, how to honor commitments to others and myself, and how to be faithful to myself.

I have come to understand we attract people who represent an unresolved issue in our lives. An issue may go unresolved and the relationship continues as such. Sometimes, one's issue is resolved, and the relationship dance changes. The challenge is to dance when neither party understands what is going on.

Soul mates learn (through divine intervention) to embrace the change and grow on new terms. My marriage is still going through a restoration process, and that is okay. It is being redefined on new and improved terms that value each of us as individuals, and on respect for the sacred covenant of marriage.

Breaking the Silence

JANET MICHELLE ELDER

R A P E. A seemingly innocuous collection of letters, a pairing of consonants and vowels that I never gave much consideration until it happened to me; like a lot of women who have heard stories about rape. I wondered how women let that kind of thing happen to them, and thought I knew what to do to fight back and protect myself.

On January 1, 1981, I found out that rape isn't something that just happens to other people; it happened to me. Even though I am now a survivor and no longer a victim, it's strange how I can still recall every little detail of what happened. Some people think women somehow entice unwanted attention and advances by what they wear or how they act; I wore a long-sleeved, brown velour pullover with a shawl collar, brown corduroy jeans, tan trouser socks, and rust-colored pumps; I had a roll of Certs in my pocket along with four dollars and some assorted change. I was never a flamboyant girl, more on the shy side than anything. I thought I was safe because I got a ride with someone I had known most of my life.

After the rape was over, he took me back to my sister's house and made me promise not to tell anyone, so I sat in my car outside until he drove away before I went into the house and woke her up. We did all the right things, called the police, went to the hospital, and he was arrested, but that's when the silence started. The parents made an agreement that in exchange for paying my medical expenses, the charges would be dropped; no one was to know what happened. I went back to work the next day even though I was too afraid to go outside to my car alone.

I spent most of the day in the bathroom crying, but when anyone asked what was wrong, I just said nothing, I was fine. The real truth is I wasn't fine, far from it. I was afraid to walk to my car alone if it was dark; I slept with the lights on; I was afraid for any man to get too close physically. I became withdrawn from everyone and almost everything. I'm not sure how much I would have lost emotionally if my mother had not insisted I not stay shut up in my room. The first outing with my family was to a high-school basketball game, and my rapist was almost the first person I saw there.

He walked past us and smiled and actually asked how we were doing. I wanted to scream at him, hit him, I wanted people to know how he hurt me, but I didn't do any of that because nice girls don't make scenes in public.

After that I kept a journal to write the things I couldn't say out loud. One of my first journal entries says, "Do you know how much you hurt me? Do you know what you took from me? Probably not, since I'm the one who had to endure the examination with all the plucking and probing and scraping. I'm the one who had to tell strangers what you did to me. I know you don't know, and I'm even surer that you don't care."

At the time I was involved with a young man who was away in the Navy, and during this period in my life we lost touch, even though I wrote to tell him what happened. In my heart I always believed it was because I had let the rape happen to me and he couldn't face being with someone like me. Well, I was wrong. When I saw him years later, he didn't know, but even so, after being apart for 20 years, he apologized for not being there to protect me.

I kept this hurt and anguish inside of me for 12 years before I told anyone else. The breaking point came for me one day at my job as a registered nurse in labor and delivery. I had a young patient who became pregnant as a result of being raped and had decided to keep the baby. She seemed to be coping with the labor quite well and had a birth plan, but when it came time for her to push the baby out, she wouldn't do it. She kept saying she couldn't do it, and she told me at that moment she realized that this was the real thing about to happen. What if the baby looked like the man who raped her?

I became so shook up, I turned her care over to another nurse. I should have been able to deal with her on a professional level, but the flashbacks I was having were real and personal. I called a minister friend of mine that night. I was crying so hard he couldn't understand what I was saying, so he just prayed and played some soft music until I calmed down. I told him what happened to me all those years ago. With his help I forgave myself and realized I didn't do anything wrong. My rapist was the one who was wrong, and by keeping the silence I was letting him have control over me again. I learned rape isn't about sex; it's about power and control.

Refusing to be silent anymore was liberating. I wrote to my two oldest sisters and told them what happened to me. They were astonished that I had never told them and concerned about how I dealt with the situation. Shortly after I told them, I started dating again.

I.C. was very sweet and attentive. Even though I found myself falling in love with him, I was still afraid of physical intimacy. Kissing was no problem, but if he made a move beyond that, I would move away from him, or when he would hold me in his arms, I would just shake uncontrollably. He never pressed me about what was wrong, just showed concern about whether he was rushing me.

Finally, one day I told him to hold me tight because I had something to tell him. I cried, but I managed to tell him the whole story and then tried to pull away from him. He said, "Don't ever pull away from me. I'm sorry he hurt you like that; he is less than a man. I promise I will never touch you unless you want me to."

With his help I rediscovered my sexuality. He taught me things about my body I never knew. I came into my own as a woman with his love, care, and understanding. I slept with the light off for the first time in years, took more care in my personal appearance, and became more outgoing. The more I broke the silence, the better I felt about myself. I spoke to other women about the experiences and consequences of rape, and it is amazing to find out how many women have been victimized by this crime.

My journey through hurt and healing allows me to help other women make the journey to wholeness again. I was truly a survivor when I was able to look at the man who raped me and say I forgive you. Thank God for my journey out of darkness into His marvelous light.

Important Lessons

LARRAINE JOHNSON

Life teaches us lessons very early in our lives if we will stop and listen. Isn't it the cry of the infant, which taught the babe that if it cried then it would get held, diapered, and fed? Recently I remembered what might have been one of the most important lessons I have ever taught to anyone.

The lessons were given to a lady I will call Carrie. Carrie was a middle-aged mother who had raised her family and had thoughts of working outside the "nest" as soon as her children grew up and left. Her problems multiplied when the children returned too quickly with their babies in need of childcare. Being unwilling to say no, Carrie once again felt chained to her home.

Carrie was a strong, generous woman who had raised not only her five children (three boys and two girls) but in addition, a niece. Living on some form of public assistance for most of her life, she and her husband had always struggled to make ends meet. Even when her husband would receive a promotion or a raise in the civil service ranks, the increases in salary just seemed to disappear. After years of sacrifice, Carrie longed for something more.

That something more came in the form of a cook's position at one of the area grade schools. It was likely that Carrie knew of the position being open because of the time she worked in the kitchen in exchange for food stamps for her own household. Carrie saw the job opening as an opportunity for freedom: freedom outside her own home, freedom to her "own" paycheck, and freedom from always "may I please." You see, Carrie was from the old school: her husband disbursed the finances, leaving little left for her on most occasions. But there was one barrier to her working this job outside the home: Carrie had poor math skills, and she knew she would have to pass a math test to qualify for the job.

I was visiting Carrie one afternoon in what I learned was a typical day for her. Her large, four-bedroom split-foyer home was typically congested with family and friends, as the smell of stale smoke hovered over the heads of people talking all over each other usually in a heated debate. On that day, the chrome kitchen table with the yellow Formica top was full of players, and the game was euchre. The sounds of lies and exaggeration filled the kitchen as thick as the cigarette smoke lingering in the room.

I was sitting in the small adjoining living room on the L-shaped sofa with the women folk: daughters, girlfriends, wives, grandbabies, neighbors' kids, and anyone else who would wander through the front door to stay a spell. I watched Carrie come out of her bedroom freshly dressed; ready to greet her visitors and the day. As she descended the small, few steps from the upper level, I could see downright disgust in Carrie's eyes as she viewed her front room full of people.

I followed Carrie's footsteps into the kitchen and positioned myself over the shoulders of her oldest son, my sweetheart at the moment. I watched her as she surveyed the room: the chipped counter-top full of dishes from breakfast, the dirty stove-top, and the smell of old grease from someone who had fried fresh fish and not cleaned up after himself. In the corner stood a large, plastic garbage can, which overflowed, with a diaper box full of trash and other rubbish located on the floor beside it. Since Carrie's entrance into the kitchen, the players at the table had lowered their voices and howls in anticipation of Carrie's remarks and chastisements.

Disappointing her audience with a very calm voice, a resilient Carrie caught my eye and asked me in front of everyone in the house if I would tutor her in math. One son quickly chided, "Momma, why do you want to learn math?"

Carrie answered sternly, "So I can get a job and get out of this house!"

From the quickness of her answer, it was clear Carrie had been home one day too many. I assured Carrie I would be pleased to spend whatever time it took to help her gain the needed math skills.

Carrie and I worked together for several days leading up to the test day. Carrie was serious about her task and was a good student. We busied ourselves multiplying recipes and solving other word problems. We worked on basic fractions until she was confident and secure in the methods. As the day of the test came and went, I remember receiving a telephone call in my office from a very happy Carrie.

"I passed the test! I got the job!" Carrie exclaimed on the other end.

With the first paychecks, Carrie took her examination for a driver's license. Her sons helped her get a used automobile so she would not have to walk to work on rainy and snowy days. One son faithfully made sure the oil was changed and provided occasional repairs if necessary.

Immediately, all the grandbabies and their mothers found other caregivers, leaving her home much quieter and cleaner when she came home from work. Eventually, the one adult son who had been living with her and her husband found another place to live, as the evening meals were planned to exclude him so that the couple would be able to dine out together in peace. Within a year, Carrie and her husband moved out of their old community into a new, smaller home of their own, which was part of Carrie's original dream.

While the lessons I taught Carrie gave her the skills to obtain a job, the lesson she taught me was about empowerment. Carrie never lacked the drive; she lacked the skills. When she saw the opportunity to be tutored one-on-one, she grasped the chance she had been waiting for, and it made all the difference.

Those lessons were taught over twenty-five years ago. It has been at least ten years since I last saw Carrie. When we met in a chance meeting, I observed a woman transformed by her choices. Still married, she was a happy and well-adjusted woman in her late fifties/early sixties, living a Christian lifestyle, surrounded by friends and family. Her occupation as a cook for the local school system gave her enough income to be comfortable. Her long summer vacation gave her time to enjoy her grandchildren and pursue her own recreational interests with or without her husband if she wanted. Her life was transformed because of the power of knowledge from the lessons learned.

It took years for me to fully recognize and appreciate the meaning of empowerment in my own life. Today, as a middle-aged woman, I have found myself in Carrie's shoes; life has been less than perfect, leaving me twice divorced, having to raise my three children on my own. As I have turned my back on the past and focused on my future, I have been greeted by a whole world of possibilities. Once I could see the possibilities just like Carrie, I have been able to discover guides, friends, and mentors along the path to assist me on my journey.

In 1991, I started my college career, working toward my Bachelor's degree. While it has taken me years with many stops and starts, in June 2004, I will graduate with my Bachelor's degree in Leadership and Liberal Arts. I have applied to a major university for their Master's program in Social Work, with hopes of being able to complete the degree to allow me to become licensed as a private counselor. I want to be able to provide assistance for families in crisis.

Today, I can see the power of the learning process as I attempt to observe and squeeze every ounce of instruction from those lessons of life. At this moment, I have no clear view of the map or the look of the journey ahead. I simply believe in myself, and the power of God that lies within me just like Carrie did. When I saw Carrie, she stated she was better for the important lessons she learned. In the end so will I.

TRANSFORMATION

I need to forgive the men
who walked out of my life,
my dad, my son, my brother.

I need to forgive the women
who walked out of my life,
my mom, my wife, my sister.

I need to ask for forgiveness
for the hurt I have caused,
for the wrong I have done.

I need to forgive the pain I have inside.
I need to do the hardest thing,
I need to forgive myself.

Only then...
will I be able to make a change.

— *Evelyn Hall*

Death Can Be an Awakening

As women we want to know we are important and that we have a significant place in our worlds. We need to know that we matter to someone, that our lives are making a difference in the lives of other people, that we are able to touch their souls.
— Beverly LaHaye

Until Jesus Comes Back

LA RHONDA CROSBY-JOHNSON

I sat as still as possible, focusing on something I rarely paid much attention to: breathing. In and out. The church was warm despite the coolness of the winter morning. My eyes came to rest on the church fan, a cardboard square advertising the nearest mortuary stapled to the wooden handle. Those handles always reminded me of the wooden spoons we used as children to eat the ice cream we bought at the corner store, only bigger. That thought made me smile.

Reaching for the fan would take energy, and I needed all my energy to breathe normally. I was here to celebrate the life of a woman who, because of our sons' friendship, had come into my life and become a member of our family. Now, in death, she was my new model for courage. I was determined to remain present in the beautiful sanctuary, filled with her family and friends, not to focus on the "what ifs" or "how comes."

As her daughter, a high school junior walked toward the podium to share thoughts of her mother, I felt the warm tears sliding onto my face. I breathed deeply. Stay here, something whispered inside of me. Don't go back. Don't relive that day...the day I was the daughter.

It was February first. Mama was still dead. It had been two days now, and she still hadn't returned. I was seventeen years old and certainly old enough to know that "dead" meant you wouldn't be returning, at least "until Jesus comes back," as they told us in Sunday School. Mama had never stayed away this long, and somehow I thought her "dead" would be different.

Instead of Mama coming home, more and more relatives filled the house. I willed myself not to gag as they marched in with tear-reddened eyes and sorrowful looks. Food was everywhere, and my army of aunties (some blood, some not) busied themselves putting out bowls of potato salad, platters of fried chicken, and cakes of all kinds. Where there wasn't food, there were flowers. Mama loved flowers, so that seemed okay. Maybe she'd see them all and come back.

Jesus rose on the third day, and so I awoke the next day knowing I'd see Mama sitting at the breakfast room table, drinking coffee from her favorite mint-green mug and smiling her "good morning" smile as I stumbled through the kitchen in search of my chocolate Instant Breakfast.

"Good mornin', baby, how you feelin'?"

"Come on and get some of these fried potatoes and sausages."

"I'll have these pancakes ready in just a minute. Get you some juice."

"Where's your house shoes, girl? This floor is freezing. Your mama never could keep no shoes on your feet."

My aunties' words swam together as I wondered why Mama had never told them that we didn't talk like this so early. The fact that they were all crowded into our kitchen was a clear indicator that Mama wouldn't be coming back. Not on the third day. Not on any day.

Instead, cards started arriving. Cards with flowers and angels and sea shells and green pastures and Praying Hands. Cards that said "In Sympathy" and "In the Loss of Your Mother" and "She's Away." Cards sent with love, some filled with money by folks who wanted me to feel better, somehow made me feel worse. One of my aunties took on the task of displaying every card.

She said that way people would know we appreciated their thoughtfulness. There were cards everywhere: on the mantle, on the buffet, on the TV and the end tables. When she started taping them to the walls, I'd had enough.

"Please don't put up another card," I'd said in a voice that sounded strange to my ears. Since I hadn't spoken much in the last few days, everybody stopped to listen.

My auntie's right hand clutched the tape dispenser as a card with a big, white lily on the front dangled from her left hand.

"Okay, baby. Looks like we got enough up anyway," she answered, forcing a smile through her lips as they began to quiver and new tears fell fresh on her cheeks.

The buzz of mourning that had filled our house the last few days returned. I caught a glimpse of my daddy's face as I left the room. He looked as if he'd just been rescued from some terrible ordeal. As I closed my bedroom door and closed out the sounds of voices that were not my mother's, I wondered if my daddy had looked that old when I went to bed the night before.

"You gonna be all right," my cousin stated, as she sat down on the end of my twin bed. I believed her, not because she sounded or looked convinced, but because she never lied to me.

"Yeah. I gotta be. She's not coming back," I responded.

There. I'd said it out loud. The words had been screaming inside my head and taking up room in my stomach for days. Mama wouldn't be back. Not anytime soon anyway. As the words began to sink in, a hole big enough to jump into opened up inside me. Maybe I could stay there until Mama came back?

"We're only a phone call away." My army of aunties had hugged their goodbyes as the buzz of mourning left the house and living without Mama began. Just as they had come, they were now gone.

The days turned into weeks, which, as weeks do, turned into months. The calls to my aunties were fewer now. Instead, I decided to call God. He answered. Mama had taught me everything I needed to know. Our seventeen years together would have to serve me a lifetime. Most days, strength took the place of pain. I realized our time together had been enough. Mama had completed her work in me.

One day I stood in the kitchen cooking dinner and giving my little sister a spelling test, wondering how Mama had made it all look so easy. And then it happened. I started to feel her. It had taken longer than three days, but here she was. I heard her laughter in the sizzling of the hot grease as I eased a fat, floured chicken drumstick into the black, cast-iron skillet without burning my fingers.

I felt her warm, soft hand on my shoulder as I buttered the biscuits. I could see her smile as my sister set the table and rattled on about something that had happened to her during recess. I felt her arms around me, gently rocking me at night, as I cried into my pillow because I missed her so much.

"Shush. Mama's here," I heard her whispering gently in my ear.

I dried my tears and reached for the fan. A smile came easily to my face as I watched my friend's daughter walk back to her seat, her tribute completed.

Twenty-six years have passed and I know I'll have to wait "until Jesus comes back" to see Mama again. But, I also know that I can close my eyes and feel her any time I want or need. And for me that's enough. In the days to come, I'll share those thoughts with my friend's daughter, to trust God, and know that it will be enough for her, too.

A Mother's Love

JUANITA J. CARR

We were celebrating my granddaughter Olivia's fourth birthday. The room was filled with chattering, excited children, their parents, and of course Olivia's own adoring parents, my daughter and her husband. Doting paternal and maternal grandparents watched from the sidelines as my daughter lovingly chided Olivia to be patient and began the suspenseful task of unwrapping her colorful presents.

I watched the magic unfold for my granddaughter and felt the love flow within the room. My thoughts returned to another place and time, when my life was touched and nourished by a selfless love. Over the years, that moment in time has filled my life with the knowledge that nothing surpasses the expression of love.

It was 1943, and unknown forces called the Axis had disrupted my world. Our country was at war, and my oldest brother was somewhere on the other side of the world fighting a strange enemy so our world would remain free. I saw how this worried my mother, but unknown to me, she was fighting an unseen enemy of her own. In early spring she had undergone a mysterious surgery, followed by a strange treatment called radiation. I overheard whispers about it from my father and my aunt, and it was very puzzling for a ten-year-old.

Our Midwest spring arrived, and the last of the melting snow brought warm days filled with sunshine and white blossoms on our snowball bush. My mother was an ardent Baptist and sang in the choir every Sunday. I was expected to attend Sunday school services at nine-thirty, and remain through the eleven o'clock worship service, which my mother faithfully attended. From the choir stand she kept a vigilant eye on me, but I usually managed to sneak a few giggles with my friends. It was difficult to suppress our irreverent laughter when some of the female members, overcome by the Holy Spirit, would jump up and give joyous "shouts." It was our way of releasing the pent-up energy that filled our young bodies during the endless hours of inactivity.

One Sunday in early summer after school had ended, my mother called me to her side and announced that we weren't going to church. I knew something terrible had to have happened for us to miss church, and

I held very still, waiting for the bad news.

She must have seen how rigid I had become, because she gave me a warm hug and smiled. "Today we're going to do whatever you'd like. Would you like to see a movie?"

I couldn't believe my ears, but I had the good sense not to question the unexpected change in our routine. My mother knew all too well that I loved movies. We had to ride a bus downtown, because our small community had no theater, and this only increased my excitement. Sundays became our special day. We never missed any episodes of the cliffhanger serials, especially Buck Rogers.

My mother and I developed a close bond, and I dared to reveal some of the childhood fears that often confront ten-year-old girls. She listened and encouraged me with sensitive understanding, and I wondered at the sadness that often filled her eyes.

Summer passed all too swiftly, and we stopped going to the movies on a regular basis. Momma seemed to tire easily and spent more time in bed. My father worked the graveyard shift, and once school began, I noticed he frequently prepared our meals. Aunt Anna, my mother's sister, lived next door, and she made lots of pop-in calls. There were quiet whispers between other grown-ups in the family. I listened and kept my eyes open, but understood nothing.

October came, and the fall air was filled with the pungent smell of burning leaves. I loved school and was caught up in my studies and the company of my small circle of friends. Encompassed by my little world, I wasn't too attuned to the gradual changes that were occurring around me. A week before my birthday, my mother asked for the names of friends I'd like to invite to my birthday party. I was speechless, because I had never had a formal birthday party. I managed to give her a list of my best friends and felt like I was awake in a dream.

My mother bought nice, colorful invitations, and I gave them to my friends. I lived in a state of high anxiety, wondering if anyone would come, and if they did, would they be impressed or disappointed. This was a totally new social occasion for me, but I knew my mother wouldn't let me down.

My doubts and worries proved to be unfounded. Everyone I had invited came to my celebration, and we eagerly joined in the games my mother had organized. We tried hard not to ruin our party dresses as we played pin-the-tail-on-the-donkey, hide-and-seek, and blind man's bluff. When Momma called us in for the important part, we were delighted with the delicious potted meat sandwiches and strawberry punch. Then, it was on to the best part. Momma had spent most of the day baking a three-layered cake, which she had frosted with white meringue icing.

My eyes bugged out over the eleven candles she carefully lit, and which I extinguished with one powerful puff. Everyone clapped and yelled, "Happy birthday." Then they called for the presents. I eagerly unwrapped colorful hair ribbons, barrettes, ankle socks, games, crayons, and storybooks. We were all caught up in the fun, giggling inanely, eating our fill of food, and it was some while before I missed my mother.

I quietly left my friends and crept into her darkened bedroom. She was lying on her bed, smiling. "It's not polite to leave your company. Go and enjoy your party. Today is your day. I'll just lie here and listen to the happiness."

I never told my mother how happy she had made me, but I'm sure she knew. Only hindsight has made me realize the tremendous effort she made to ensure my eleventh birthday was one I'd never forget. I also realize how much she loved me to sacrifice her inherent need to worship God each Sunday, so that she could spend that time with me.

To this day, I can never attend a birthday party without fond memories of what it means to be loved by those we hold close. As I watched my mother's namesake, Olivia, smile gleefully with happiness, it all came full circle. My mother died in November, only a few weeks after my party. It was only then that I learned my mother had been a victim of breast cancer. That she had surmounted her own pain and knowledge of her impending death further confirms for me that nothing compares to the depth of a mother's love.

Inspired by His Band

STRELLA JASPER

I was holding his hand when he passed away. I held his left hand, the hand where his wedding band had for 43 years announced to the world his pride in our union. We let him go naturally. It was the way he had lived every day. Naturally. No pretenses. Naturally.

The funeral arrangements had been made long in advance, as we knew that the inoperable cancer, which had begun in his back, had spread to his entire body, so that his every heartbeat sent cancer cells pulsing through-out his body, which then drew even more life from his organs.

It, too, had been a natural process. Ravaging, but natural. Dr. Sanderson diagnosed Less with a rare carcinoma after pain persistent in his tailbone area wouldn't go away. We went in for a checkup, hoping that chiropractics would be the remedy. We learned, however, after a complete physical and several blood tests, there was cancer in the tissue around his lower back and in his bloodstream. From there, it was only a matter of time.

After four months of treatment, there was no remission. We began to plan for the end. For the past few weeks the children, Brian and Maggie, and the grandchildren, Cyndi, Porter, and Amber, had come to visit as much as possible, but I spent almost every waking moment by Less's side. It was natural for me. We had barely ever been apart, flagstaffs of security for each other during a long and good marriage.

When I heard the slow, soft gasp, I knew. I looked at the heart moni-tor and watched it slow down until the line went flat. I sat for a few moments with him. I heard the sound of hurried steps as the nurse rushed down the hall and floated into the room. I didn't move. She took his hand, looked up at the monitors, and looked back at me. It was over.

The children took care of the last details while I got some rest. Condolences came in from his company and our friends. Relatives were planning to fly in from three states. There was no real shock. I simply needed to change gears. I wandered through the house, letting it sink in. He would never stand and watch me walk by again. Less had always been proud of how I'd kept my figure, even after two children, and so close together.

Brian Jerome was born when Margaret Helene was 18 months old.

She was just starting to talk and had learned to tear down and break as much as she could reach while I grew ever larger with the new baby. Less was so excited. We knew the baby was to be a boy.

Over the years I had kept up with my sculpting and painting in a studio built on the back of our property. With two young children and my art, I had managed to keep plenty busy. Less and I had taken up several sports that we could play together. I sometimes joined him in golf while he played tennis with me every weekend. We had taught the children to swim early, and our family enjoyed swimming together. Our vacations were always full of lots of physical activity.

We always made time for each other and the children. It all seemed so natural. Less would watch me and compliment me as I rushed around the house, here and there, in and out, up and down. There always seemed to be a project in the works, either with the children or preparing for an art show of some kind.

My pieces got larger as the children grew. My most recent life-size painting was sold to the golf club where we belonged. It was placed in the conference center of the new addition. It is a picture of a family golfing. The golf club also purchased several smaller sculptures over the years.

The pieces were placed in the foyer, one in the formal restaurant, and one in the women's restroom. Less had always been wonderfully supportive and promoted me in every way he could.

At the funeral, we passed by the coffin, surrounded by gorgeous flowers from the many friends and organizations that we both were associated with. Less looked as if he were asleep. The cancer had never ravaged him until the last few weeks, so he simply looked slim and rather fit. His tanned hands were crossed. His wedding band beckoned to me. I had last held that hand just three days ago.

After the internment ceremony, a memorial representative handed me an envelope with a bulge in it. On the way back home in the limousine with Brian, I took the envelope out of my black dress-coat pocket. I ran my fingers over the handwritten lines.

"Mrs. Lesster Joseph Mitland," was stretched over the bulge in the paper. I opened the envelope slowly, wondering if it was a bill or forgotten paperwork. There was a tissue wrapped around something. It was Less's wedding band. I turned it with my fingers and looked at it closely. Scratched and worn, it still had luster.

The funeral home staff had polished it. I held onto it and remembered the day I first picked it out for our wedding. I learned later that Maggie had asked that the band be given to me. I had never thought of that when we made the arrangements. A mother can only be proud of a child who knows how devoted her parents were to each other.

I wanted to find a place to keep the wedding band where I could continue to see it every day. I was used to seeing it on his hand and feeling it when he held my hands. After a few weeks I was prompted to create a sculpted piece for my dressing room, a piece in which I could place the wedding band as a part of the surface. The concept came to me as I was dressing one morning, the usual time when Less would watch me and compliment me on my figure.

In my studio I fashioned a piece that took on the colors of the bedroom suite decor, and that had a multiplicity of textures and transitions. It turned out to be a mélange, a boxy shape of fabric, mirrors, tiles, and earth, almost two feet high. The wedding band, the only metal in the piece, was embedded in the plaster but stood out from one of the outcropped areas, with a gold glistening, which caught the light.

I placed the piece on the counter by the door. That's where Less used to stand with his arms folded after he was dressed and I was still searching for a pair of shoes, or a scarf, or just the right earrings. Every time I turn the corner, I feel he is still watching me. I promise to keep my figure until I see him again.

My Nomsa

DONNA KINSLER

December 9, 2001, is a date etched in every cell of my body. For that is the day I discovered my Nomsa. I was at my desk and packing my bags as usual with reading material to review at home. An AP news photo caught my eye as I perused the Los Angeles Sentinel. I saw the most poignant photo of a four-year-old South African girl stricken with AIDS.

According to the caption, her name was Nomsa, and she was found clinging to her dead mother's body as she had been for three days. She was taken to an AIDS hospice village called Sparrow's Ministries. I clutched the paper to my heart and prayed for her safety and health. I couldn't get her out of my mind, for she looked so sad and full of despair.

The next day I researched Sparrow's Ministries and found contact information via the Internet. I called and spoke to one of the caretakers. She told me that they did have a child named Nomsa at the facility and she was gravely ill. I spoke to the director and clinical psychologist, Lynn Nel. Lynn gave me insightful information about Sparrow's Ministries, the CEO and founder Rev. Corinne McClintock, Nomsa, and the other precious children and adults who are fondly called Sparrows.

I asked how I could assist with Nomsa's care. Lynn told me that Nomsa was in need of antiretroviral medication, but there was no guarantee that she would be receptive, for she had irreparable damage to her heart, liver, and lungs. I immediately looked at my finances and sacrificed a few items to support Nomsa at $60.00 U.S. per month.

Her body accepted the antiretroviral meds, and she began to show signs of healing. My first conversation with Nomsa was on my second call to Sparrow's. She was on oxygen and would gasp between words. I told her that I loved her and she responded, "Yes, yes, I love you, too."

Our connection was solid, and I felt we were bonded for life. Lynn was an excellent liaison, for she would upload pictures of Nomsa via email and synchronize the time for my phone chats with Nomsa. I felt as though I were her mother. I also would send boxes every month of clothes, books, and toys.

I became anxious and wanted to visit Nomsa. My funds were limited, and the price of a round-trip ticket was out of my league. With the help of some friends and my savings, my dream became a reality. On March 15, 2003, I was blessed to visit South Africa. Nomsa and three of the children greeted me at the airport with Corinne and a friend of Sparrow's, Yvonne. Nomsa was holding a bouquet of flowers with a Nelson Mandela spoon. Our eyes focused on one another, then we hugged for ten minutes. It was one of the happiest moments in my life. I spent two of the most glorious weeks with Nomsa and the other children.

Although Nomsa had many close calls during the almost two years that we were connected, she had more vim and vigor than ever during our two weeks together. When it was time for my departure, Nomsa came to the airport. She told me that she was strong and would be coming to America.

I was filled with sadness and tears, but also overflowing with joy simultaneously. Sixteen days after my return, I received a phone call that my Nomsa had passed. I had spoken to her four days prior, and we had laughed and shared moments of my visit. I am blessed and honored to know such a special, a precious six-year-old angel. I will continue the work in honor of my Nomsa and continue to love and support the Sparrows.

Nevertheless, a Writer

DORIS HOUSE RICE

The divine gift of writing is in earthen vessels, imparted by the supreme author to serve many purposes. When my only son, a rookie police officer, was murdered at age twenty-nine, writing proved therapeutic and healing for me.

I was doubtful I would be composed enough to walk down the aisle of the church packed with police officers, church members, family, and friends. There I was, the head zombie leading the procession of grieving relatives. My front-row seat put me in reaching distance of the blue casket entombing my oldest child.

Is it fair taking a beloved son who has not lived the promised portion of the three score and ten years, I had the audacity to ask God. In my state of delirium, my deity was challenged to condescend to my level of thinking. Well-meaning friends read their eloquently written expressions to edify attendants of my beloved legacy. Impressive words could not give back life, no matter how inspiring.

Just as sadness took me to the peak of my misery, my eyes were drawn to a yellow potted plant sitting beside the pulpit. Seemingly, the rose petals floated up and spiraled down as though someone was blowing them softly. I pointed out the miracle to my husband. He went and picked up the fallen petals and watched periodically, trying to witness what I had told him. To his amazement, he never saw other petals fall and drape around the flowerpot during the service. Later, after inquiring, he discovered God only allowed me, my two daughters, and my children's biological father the pleasure of seeing Him do His work.

That was what I had prayed for, a sign to let me know my child was all right. It sustained me for a while. But when friends and family stopped calling and things returned to business as usual, grief overcame me, stripping my faith bare like a shucked ear of corn. I was miserable in the company of others and worse when I was alone. Returning to work was my chosen option.

The constant talk of my loss was contagious, draining the joy from those around me. Being reassigned to work in the basement, the dark film-processing room allowed me space to engage in constant thought. Self-pity caused tears to flow until my eyes were swollen like those of a battered, defeated boxer.

No argument, I was at the lowest point of my life. While on my knees begging God to take my life in exchange for my son's, a still small voice got my attention. "Write!" the voice commanded.

Write? I asked for clarity. There was reason for the doubt. In addition to being omnipotent, omniscient, and omnipresent, God also had a sense of humor, I knew. Understand, my primary language was greatly influenced by Ebonics, and my attempts to spell created a new language altogether. Yes, I'd written skits and poems for teenagers to perform in the Sunday school class I taught, but my writing ability at best was still closet rated.

Pencil in hand, scribbling on a torn piece of paper, I felt my thoughts begin processing, and the incident of the time my son was ridiculed in a classroom inspired a poem.

Little black child with tear-stained eyes, why do you cry?
Oh, someone in the classroom called you a coon.
You wanted to run and hide from the laughter of the children on the other side.
Little black child, broken heart won't let you smile.
Your skin color is different. That's what ignorance sees.
Let the minds of the so-called powerful be shackled, but set yours free.
Adore yourself; let your being speak loud; hold your head up high.
You are a wonder of the universe, little black child
A descendant of kings and queens, origin of the earth
A child of great inventors
Of a race willing to die for freedom's birth.
From slaves who survived a planned genocide
Little black child conceived from a black nation's pride,
Let the laughter ring. Ignorance will never cease to be a fool
It's a perpetual thing. Learn, you're being schooled.

During those sleepless nights and weary days, writing fulfilled its purpose, sustaining me, precipitating healing with the aid of pen and paper.

No, I can't throw words against the wall and make them dance like my mentor Maya Angelou, or use the power of the pen to write with the same elegance as many other great sistahs. Nevertheless, a writer. My work isn't Nobel Prize in Literature standard. Nevertheless, a writer. Perhaps none of what I write until my fingers cramp is agent quality. Nevertheless, a writer. Most important, the gift of writing has been imparted to me to heal, reach out, touch, and uplift. I count myself blessed beyond measure because I am, nevertheless, a writer.

Transitions

DR. NORMA D. THOMAS

My mother's name is Queen. You should give your children a name they can grow into and that gives them a story to tell. My mother was royalty. She should have been a famous gospel singer, but she had seven children instead, giving us her life and dying too young, at the age of 53.

My father, received his first name from his grandfather and his middle name from his grandmother's brother. I did not know that when he was alive, and I struggle to know more about him now that he has gone at the age of 66. My sister, who was always the "different" one, burned the candle too fast and the flame could not be sustained past age 39.

There is a saying, "What doesn't kill you makes you stronger." I would add that it also changes you in profound ways. I became an expert in cross-cultural issues in end-of-life care because of my own personal experiences when my mother, father, and sister transitioned from this life to the next at very young ages.

I learned very clearly that with all of this technology to prolong life, we sometimes forget to teach basic good communication skills to medical staff, who are often focused on cure, versus quality of life. When they can't cure, they sometimes wish it away.

My mother had a series of cancer surgeries, from which she bounced back each time. She completed her bachelor's degree in social work after her stomach cancer surgery and was applying to graduate school when she became ill the last time. When she was hospitalized for the next-to-last time, my older sister and I walked into the hospital expecting to be told that, although yet another surgery was needed, my mother would surely recover again. To our shock, before the physician even said hello, he stated literally, "Oh, you are the family. We have to talk about a do-not-resuscitate order."

We did not give him that power at that time because we were convinced that she was invincible. This was in 1985. When she was hospitalized for the last time, it was she who told the physician that she was tired. Her invincibility had run its course. She had run the race, fought the good fight, and it was time to meet the Savior that she served all her life. She died on June 23, 1986. "Yea, though I walk through the valley of the shadow of death, I will fear no evil..." Just cry a lot.

My sister died a decade later. My surviving sisters and I walked into a hospital where it was déjà vu all over again. The female resident stated without even saying hello, "I am glad the family is here. You need to authorize a DNR order." In both cases we were confronted with signing to end the lives of family members before we had been briefed on their medical situation.

After requesting to review the chart, something I could still do in those days, I found that my sister had stated specifically that she wanted them to do everything to keep her alive. We could not sign a DNR order even if we wanted to, and in my sister's case, given the subsequent medical procedures instituted to keep her alive, we would have gladly ended her misery. Even though my sister tried desperately to live, she lost the battle on June 2, 1996.

I have never forgotten the sense of disrespect and insensitivity I received at two different hospitals from two different physicians toward my African-American family and me. Without saying the words, they wanted us to just do what they thought was right, whether we understood their reasoning or not. No discussion. I have never forgotten those persons who showed kindness and compassion, and cared for us in those difficult times. There were people who got it right, and I made sure to praise them both verbally and in writing.

As the Creator would have it, my father went into intensive care and was dead less than 24 hours after my sister. It was as if the role he played in life, protector of a lost sheep, he needed to carry over into death. He did not want her to be alone. Each of their terminal diagnoses, one from cancer, one from AIDS, was made almost at the same time. Each one lived only two months after being diagnosed. My mother lived three weeks after they pronounced her terminal.

While we raced from New York to Pennsylvania, the hospital kept my father alive until we arrived so that we could say our farewell. He had a fourth heart attack soon after we had the opportunity to see him, and he was gone from this life. He died on June 3, 1996. "Yea, though I walk through the valley of the shadow of death, thou art with me..." But I still cry a lot.

For a while I thought that I could not survive. How do you lose your mother when you are only 33 and your father and younger sister a decade later? My field is gerontology. I had great visions of hanging out with my father playing cards, traveling the world with my mother, laughing with my sister, and sharing them all with my children. Well, I am still here; I can attest that you can survive, but it does not mean that you do not grieve.

I am searching into my roots so that I have a better understanding of who they are and who I am. I have decided to celebrate their birthdays versus mourn their deaths. People who know my story have asked me to talk to others in the medical profession about how to approach the end of life with families, so that more assaults are not added to already-difficult situations. I also encourage my audience to put their end-of-life wishes in writing.

I speak of my mother, father, and sister as if they are still visible in this world because I know their spirits do surround me from the beyond. I am now an orphan. It is not lost on me that my mother died on June 23, my sister died on June 2, and my father left this world on June 3. The year 2006 is approaching, and I come from superstitious people. I will face the month of June 2006 in intensive prayer.

A New Dancer

LEVONNE GADDY

I leave the circle of my mother's eight sisters and brothers to go into the funeral parlor. It will be the first time that I see my mother dead. My half-brother, his girlfriend, and a sister-in-law are already inside.

John, my husband (who is Canadian), walks beside me toward the front door of Troy Memorial Funeral Home. I cannot wait to see Mama. It has been over two years. Dale, my younger brother, had found her dead two days earlier on the ground in her front yard.

"I stopped by to check on Mama like I do most every day on my way home from work. I parked my work truck out on the road in front of her house, then walked all the way through her house calling, 'Mama, where you at?' I couldn't find her. So I went back outside and stood on the front porch. She must be out back, I thought. Just as I started down the steps, I saw something from the corner of my eye. Well, I looked over towards Mama's flowerbed, and there she was lying curled up in a patch of purple lilies. She'd just been to my house the night before, having supper with us."

Dale's wife, Margo, helped groom and dress my mother for this most special occasion of her last few days in view of others before being placed in the ground. Margo is inside the funeral home.

I know exactly what everyone will say. Someone will say, "She looks as though she is sleeping peacefully." Another will say, "Isn't she beautiful?" There will be comments about her hair, her make-up, the expression on her face, her clothes. I am ready for this. I have traveled from Arizona to North Carolina over several days to see her. I need to see her. My husband does not understand this need. I cannot explain it to him.

We go inside and learn that Mama is in the West Room. We approach the door where the funeral director stands straight, looking serious, hands folded in front of him. He is guarding the closed door. I reach for the door's handle, eager to enter. At the same moment of my reaching, the funeral director blocks our way.

"Family only," he says, as though he is protecting a queen's tomb from grave looters.

I know exactly what he is saying. I am angry in a flash. I know that what he means is that the family members of the woman in this room are Black people and you two are White. I snap back, "That's my mother in there!"

The funeral director apologizes and moves quickly aside.

I am angry and tremble all over. I hate that at this most personal moment, the old issue of race surfaces. I grumble to my tanned-skinned husband that if the man had used half his brain he would have realized that not only is my mother's skin nearly as light as his own, but so is the skin of half our family. I am hurt that White people can be so dumb about the Black people in their midst.

We enter the room where my youngest brother, Lewis, who is my half-brother, stands crying and talking out loud. He is saying that he cannot believe that our mother, his last full-blooded relative on this earth, is gone. He seems exaggerated to me; his response so emotionally big, his tears and words so unrestrained.

Lewis calls out my name from his standing, bent-over-at-the-waist mourning position, "Levonne. Levonne. Can you believe it?" His tears flow so hard that I wonder how he can see. "Mama is gone." His words wash over me like a lone wolf's howl on the desert. "Mama is gone."

Lewis paces back and forth from one spot to the next, talking louder and louder. My eyes leave Lewis' circus crying. I turn towards my mother's casket and am greeted with long, quiet hugs from Margo and from Lewis' girlfriend.

I am allowed some moments alone to look at my mother, to touch her, to examine her in a way as one might examine a new baby for the first time. How do her hands look? Her lips? Her closed eyes? What does the expression on her face tell about her last moments on this earth as a living person? She seems small. I cannot take my eyes or my hands away from her. I know that there will not be enough time for me with her. I know it and, as I have my entire life, hope for it in the same instance.

The questions begin: "Isn't she beautiful?"

"Do you like her hair?"

I want to say in response that she is dead! How can she be beautiful? But I do not make known this incongruence between their words and my thoughts. I know that they need for me to approve of how they have cared for Mama in these final days. I know this, so I say, "Yes, yes, she looks wonderful. You've done great. Thank you."

Lewis' girlfriend and Margo hug me again. I feel envious that Margo has spent hours with my mother's body. I ache for those hours.

I want most to be alone with Mama, but others come into the room.

I am flooded with their expressions of caring, with comforting touches, words of love and astonishment that Mama seemed healthy one day and was gone the next. In the midst of my own yearning, and everyone else's needs, I realize that the holder of the memories of me as an infant is gone forever. I feel alone even with everyone around me. Pieces of my past and my future have, in an instant, slipped irretrievably and irrevocably away. I plunge deeper into feelings of guilt, humility, and despair.

In the solitude and quiet on the drive with John from the funeral home to Mama's house, I notice the white clouds against the bluest June sky. I feel the warmth from the sun that has been shining into the car. My thoughts are moist and heavy with vivid pictures.

I see myself at five. It is the summer before I begin school in the fall. The ground that I stand on is soft and dark and covered with grass that has grown nearly to my calves. I have placed a sheet of plastic from my father's construction job on the ground, over the grass, to create a living room floor where I play with my two dolls. It is a day with a turquoise blue sky and white clouds, and it is warm already though it is still morning. The moisture in the air sticks to my skin and makes sluggish flies slow to leave my arms and naked back. I have learned by the time that I am five that damp air and sticky flies mean an evening thunderstorm.

I stop my play to watch Mama as she stands on our porch smoking her Salem. She has paused from washing clothes and is looking out into the woods that surround the property where we live. She seems further away than the hills and valleys with pines and oaks and maples that fill her eyes. She stands in her bra and shorts, no shoes, black hair braided and coiled like snakes, pinned at each side of her head.

Could she have been thinking about her life before she met our father, before she had three children and moved to an isolated shack to live without a car, money, or an automatic washing machine, and with only a radio that picked up one station to keep her adult self company?

On that wash day, when I was five, did Mama wonder what life might have been for her if she had not married the man who charmed her into a life with him, then later smothered her with his heavy, booze-infested rages? Did Mama remember the violet satin dress that hugged her waist and the high-heeled shoes that made her feet and legs look like those of a Hollywood movie star?

The last time she had worn the dress and shoes was before I was born. She and my father had visited people that lived in Candor amongst the peach trees of a sandy Piedmont, North Carolina, orchard. I know this because a picture was taken of them that day. Daddy sits in a straight-backed, cane-bottomed chair, smiling. Mama stands beside him, not smiling, in those shoes and that dress.

They are courting. She is eighteen. He is thirty-five. If you look close, beneath the prettiness of her face, you can see the sadness already forming, before they even say, "I do." By the day that I am watching Mama stand half-dressed on our porch, her pretty shoes and satin dress have long been worn out from people borrowing them for weddings and funerals and from a little girl's grownup games.

During those days Mama was having recurring dreams about her teeth falling out. "They crumble," she'd told us. "I sure hope that dream does not come true," she'd said. "I need my teeth."

The dream seemed odd to me. Mama faithfully brushed her teeth every single morning without fail. First, she'd make a cup of Sanka and, while sipping it, prepare breakfast meat and eggs for three children. After her last sip of coffee, while I chewed on my last piece of fatback rind, Mama washed her face with a rag she'd wet and soaped in the dented aluminum pan. Next she washed her hands, paying close attention to scraping beneath each fingernail on each hand with the thumbnail from the other hand. Finally Mama brushed her teeth. Every day was the same. She had good teeth.

I am sure that if someone had told Mama to make a wish back then, she would have wished for never having met my father. She would have wished that she had met a man with money and kindness in his everyday actions towards her. She would secondly have wished for an automatic washing machine and dryer set.

I recall Mama turning away from her dream position on the porch and going back to the chore that always took an entire day. More soap into the wringer washer that no longer wrings. She squeezes water by hand from every single garment of a five-person family. My father's blue overalls are the hardest for Mama to wring. He is almost twice her size. The overalls are filled with sweat and oil and sawdust from the construction site where he works. The overalls are too big for her hands. She can barely hold them tightly enough to get a decent amount of water wrung out before putting them into the galvanized metal rinse tub that doubles as our bathtub.

"Lee," Mama calls to my older brother. "I need another bucket of water."

His seven-year-old, grownup-acting self zips from horsing with our younger brother Dale to the well where he lowers the bucket on a soggy rope already lowered and raised twenty times the same day. Thump, crack, thud. The bucket hits against the sides of the well on its way down. He pauses for a minute to allow the bucket to sink beneath the water's surface and fill. Then up, the bucket is cranked. Creak, moan, splash. The bucket is hauled to the top of the well with a rusty pulley fastened to an old, wood frame.

Lee pours the water quickly into another bucket of the same size and then speeds to the porch and Mama, barely splashing a drop along the way. She doesn't say she is glad for his help, but I know that she is. She looks at him, not smiling, but peacefully anoints him with her eyes. He goes back to playing with Dale and she continues her job.

I go back to playing with my dolls. I say to them, "I am tired of all your noise and nonsense. You children go outside and play. Now. I want some peace and quiet around here." I shoo at their plastic bodies, to make them go out of the make-believe living room to the outdoors so that I can breathe.

My mother's death was sudden, shocking, confounding. It shook me out of my complacency as a daughter who was always wanting from her mother. It shook me out of the dance in which I was engaged my entire life with her. The dance was one of trying to get her attention. Along with that attention, I longed for her approval. She died while I was in a final phase of my dance, but before I had finished.

Two years before my mother's death, I had retreated from her life, much like a wild, frightened rabbit retreats from the sight of a hunter and his dog, with only the white cottontail back in view on leaving. I sent no letters, made no phone calls, and did not visit. The last visit with her had frightened me to no end.

Her house was smoke filled. Her teeth were browned by nicotine. Her face had turned square. The squareness I am certain was related in some way to the poison she was, and had been absorbing into her body for her entire life as an adult—over fifty years of continuous smoking. The worst was the cough that sounded to me as though she had a bucket of gravel in her chest, rattling and popping off the insides of her lungs. I was terrified by what I saw in my mother's face and in her home and by the noise that I heard coming from her body. As clear a thought as any I had ever had was the awareness that my mother was dying before my eyes. And that she was killing herself.

I stopped writing, stopped calling, and did not return after that last visit. I thought I had endless time for this portion of the dance. Though her death scene terrified me in my head, I did not register the fact that if my mother was killing herself, she would actually have to die. I did not register that if she died before I reconnected with her that all that was unfinished between us would remain unfinished. I did not register that there was a time limit on how long I would have to know my questions and to ask them of her. If I had truly known, I would have chosen another dance.

But I did not choose another dance. I did not choose to walk a brave walk. I chose to hide from her and from my feelings about losing her to something over which I had no control. Those two years between seeing my mother's suffocation of herself and her sudden death seem barren now. Those two years were desert times. I was in suspension from life, from my family of origin.

I find some comfort in that I was recovering from my own demons during that time, yet I also mourn over the lost nurturance that could have come from the pride of accomplishment in walking tall and strong and looking death in the face without a shudder. In my present and future, I am and will be bolder, stronger, and more courageous when it comes to the people that I love and that love me. I have become a new dancer.

The Spirit...
Always Present

*Faith is knowing that after we have done what we can,
there is a turning over, a letting go, a trusting beyond
our knowing that relieves us.*
— Anne Wilson Schaef

SHACKLES ON MY SOUL

I had heard of many stories
Of shackles on the feet of a slave,
And the history of the awful bondage
Sometimes suffered to the grave.

I had even seen pictures
In books and on the screen,
Of the way slaves were bound
And confined by those horrible things.

Pictures could not impart the actual affliction
Nor could anything else that was foretold,
When one day I personally encountered
The shackles on my soul.
I can recall a multitude of wrongs
That branded me as a slave to sin;
I did precisely as I chose to do
And so discovered my soul shackled within.

"Have mercy, Jesus!" I sincerely pleaded
"These weights are too heavy for me;
Please take these shackles away
And set my soul free."

I cried, and I cried, and I cried
God is so good that he heard my plea;
He delivered me from sin and shame
And cut those shackles completely off of me.

I rejoice with the reflection of freedom
Much like the Negro slave of old,
And I shall forever praise the Lord
For he lifted the shackles on my soul.
                              —*Saundra Kay Mock*

Grace

Black, single, female,
head of household,
state penitentiary—
mail order bride.

She rents two rooms in the
bowels of a city.
Three kids, two beds,
a crib, her mother.
Eight loads of laundry.
One washer/dryer,
down three flights of stairs.
Two brown books of
food stamps,
twenty-one days remain.

Grace irons last-last year's
Sunday best, dresses for church.
Presses pancake powder over
bags filled with pails of tears.

She rocks in her pew.
What is written to the devil
on soles of her shoes,
cannot move her to
shouts of hallelujah!

Her body drunk on
melancholy, too weary to rise;
sing one verse of
Amazing Grace.
One note could ignite this
pressed powder keg
into splinters of despair.

It's His touch that
crystallizes tears,
slips her into charismania;
dancing her out of her shoes,
clean out of her mind.
Sealing off the sorrow.

—Oktavi

A Timely Messenger

META JONES

I dragged myself into the bathroom, feeling more weighed down than ever before. My shoulders sagged; my legs so anchored in depression I could hardly move. Lowering myself onto the edge of the tub, I watched for a moment the steam rise, fogging up mirrors and covering the floor and fixtures with slick, dangerous condensation. I imagined the same thing was going on inside of me. My brain foggy with a job I hated; my peace of mind smothered by my husband's cheating. I had fifteen minutes to bathe, dress, and get to work on time, but I just sat there, in tears and despair.

Nothing seemed important. There were no bubbles in the tub, no nice softening oils as usual. Those were soothing things for deserving people. I had run only hot water, and although I recoiled at first from the steaming liquid, I immersed my body in the tub and yelped with pain as my flesh heated and turned bright red. It was what I deserved to feel. I wanted every part of me to hurt as much as my heart. I needed punishment for being so unhappy.

I sat in the water until it cooled, absently dabbing at my skin with a soap-filled cloth. All my motions were mechanical, a mindless revival of the day before. Looking up at the ceiling, I sobbed even more, blubbering recollections of an uncaring father, an abusive grandfather, a childhood lacking in all the accoutrements of Donna Reed and *Father Knows Best*.

As those memories flooded my thoughts, I climbed out onto the floor and fell in a heap, heaving and cursing God for letting so many bad things happen to me. For a few minutes I lay there, still convulsing, but with new resolve. I had decided my fate. I would finally do what I threatened myself with for so many years. I would end all my hurt and pain.

Pools of water gathered around my feet as I searched the medicine cabinet for something lethal. I pushed aspirin and Pepto Bismol aside, sent them crashing to the floor, in a quest for a bottle of Valium I'd been prescribed years before but had never taken. Unable to find it, I collapsed on the toilet seat, head in hand, bawling, screaming, rifling through my mind's catalogue for an acceptable means of suicide. I was too afraid of guns to shoot myself. I wasn't brave enough to cut my wrists or drop an electrical appliance in the bathwater, and I was scared that an overdose of Motrin or Benedryl would leave me only crippled or brain impaired—not dead.

It was the lowest point I'd ever reached. And I had had bad times. I had struggled through my first marriage; a series of unfulfilling, underpaid jobs; three ungrateful children; bouts of abject poverty; eviction—a multitude of life-shattering events. Never before had I been as certain there was no point in tomorrow. I couldn't grab hold of one thing that was all right in my life. Everything was wrong and I was tired.

I cursed God for not loving me, for not rescuing me, for not making my childhood better, and for not giving me the courage to get a butcher knife and cut my throat. I looked up at the ceiling and said aloud, "God, you don't love me. You couldn't. You wouldn't let anybody you loved feel this bad. I hate you! Just like you hate me!"

The instant I finished my blasphemy, the phone rang. I continued crying, cursing, and screaming louder. Tears streamed down my face, mucous poured from my nostrils. The phone kept ringing. For a fleeting moment, I wondered why the voice mail hadn't picked up. After two straight minutes of ringing, I answered.

"Mona?" the voice asked.

"Yes. Who is this?" I said with as much venom as I could spew. I didn't recognize the man's voice, and silently I vowed to hang up on whoever it was.

"This is Reverend Raymond. Do you remember me? I head the Veteran's Ministry your son attended a few years ago."

"Yes. What do you want? Kalvin doesn't live here anymore."

"No, no. I was calling you. God told me to call you today."

"What? Are you crazy? How did you know I was here? What do you want?" I shouted, sniffing and wiping the tears from my face.

"God told me to call you, Mona. He told me you were having a difficult time today; that you needed to hear what I have to tell you. He wanted me to tell you that no matter how much you forsake Him, He will never forsake you. God loves you. Please remember that." And he hung up.

Stunned, I sat there staring at the phone. I was not a religious woman, never had been. I believed God existed mainly because it had been drilled into my head as a child, but I was convinced if He did exist, I wasn't one of His favorite people. I went to church occasionally, enjoyed the choir, took what I wanted from the minister's sermon, but I had no misconceptions about God embracing me. I never prayed, because as far as I was concerned, God wasn't listening.

I had met Reverend Raymond only one time, more than a year before at a Burger King when I dropped my son off for one of his meetings. At the time, Kalvin had recently been discharged from the Marine Corps and lived with me temporarily. The Reverend called once or twice to invite him to Bible study or to church on Sunday. I always said hello and passed the phone to my son. That was it. It was farfetched to think this man knew I was in agony, or had any inkling of my intentions to end my life. Still, it was strange that he called me. I soon dismissed it as some kind of cruel joke, another pile of woe to dump on top of my already overflowing soul. I cursed God again and decided the whole incident was happenstance.

I couldn't stop crying. I moaned like a wounded animal, thrashing back and forth across my bed. I could think of no instrument in my house I was brave enough to use for my demise. Hours passed. I decided to contact an acquaintance, a person I knew had the drugs that would take me out of my misery. I sucked up my tears and made the call.

"Yeah, baby. I got some Valium. I got whatever you want. But what you gon give me?"

"I've got money. How much is it?"

"Money? You know what I want. I've been trying to get wit you for a long time, you know that. A woman your age oughta be glad a 35-year-old brotha in good shape like me would even wanna do that. Any other young brother don't want nothing but to hit it a coupla times. I'm talking 'bout you and me starting something. And see, you'd be getting the whole package. When you need to freak, I'ma be there; when you need to chill, I'm the man for that, too."

I felt the tears welling back in my eyes. I didn't use drugs. I only knew to call him because he bragged about what he did. He was the cousin of a good friend, and every time he came around, he made a pass at me. He had given me a card for a carpet-cleaning business he operated, and I stuck it in my wallet. I hated myself for being so desperate. He was a detestable man, a man I wouldn't spit on in my right mind, but even that didn't stop his implications about my age and my worth from stinging me, sending me deeper into self-loathing and farther into my quest to quit living.

I grabbed my coat, wiped my face on my sleeve, and started out the door. I'd give him what he wanted and get what I needed; it was a way out. As I was closing the door, the phone rang again. I hesitated, but decided to answer it, thinking it might be him calling with a change of plans. I couldn't afford a mix-up. I couldn't face another day.

"Mona, this is Reverend Raymond. One more thing I need to tell you. God's not the only one who wants you...the devil is after you, too. Don't let him win. And remember, God will never forsake you, no matter what. Goodbye."

I have never talked to Reverend Raymond or heard from him since that day. And, needless to say, I didn't make my appointment with the devil. I cried long and hard after that last phone call, still not able to make sense of my life, but a miracle occurred that day. God heard me. After 47 years of believing He was deaf to my voice, I knew profoundly that God heard me.

No doubt, God's agenda is different from mine, and my prayers aren't always answered the way I hope, but from that day I have been convinced I am loved. The sun has seemed brighter. The flowers smell sweeter, and my children and grandchildren's laughter and joy has become my own. Five years have passed and many things are different, but I have not lamented one moment of my life since that day.

I'm still not a consistent churchgoer or an overly religious woman, but I've been changed. I accept my position in this universe. My power doesn't extend to a husband's cheating or an employer's lack of respect. I pull my own strings to the extent I can, and make the best of every situation I can influence, but now I know for a fact that God is here, in control, and He is good.

This is a true story. Names have been changed but that is all. I have never been able to locate God's angel. He moved from the address my son had for him, and his phone is no longer a working number. Nobody we've contacted seems to know where he is. I like to think he's somewhere out there delivering another message and saving another life.

I KNOW WHAT IT'S LIKE

I know what it's like to be a victim
Of devastation, humiliation, and shame;
I've been between the rock and the hard place
And in the clutches of Satan and his chain gang.

I know what it's like to be a nitwit
And people persist to scandalize your name;
They gossip your business all around town
'Til you sink deeper and deeper in guilt and shame.

I know what it's like to be lonely
And to cry all night long;
I know the taste of stale tears
When drowning sorrow in a song.

I know the feeling of full-fledged fear
That crucifies the crevices of the mind,
That constantly causes worry and despair
And yields sadness of the very worst kind.
I know what it's like to be deceived
Into thinking it was, when it wasn't;
I know the disappointment involved
When you do, but the other one doesn't.

I know what it's like to hate yourself
And to endlessly grieve on the inside,
Knowing that you are the one to blame
More so than those on whom you relied.

I know what it's like to fail
After you've rendered your very best;
I've swallowed some big chunks of pride
In trying to pass the worldly test.

I know what it's like to be converted
And to have God's grace extended to you;
I know the way from victim to victor
Because God has brought me through.

—Saundra Kay Mock

Chinese Kaleidoscope:
The Goat and Me

NORMA NG LAU

On January 5, three days after my 76th birthday, I retired. Freed from many years of structured time schedules for work and personal commitments, I found myself with "time on my hands." After several months of sleeping late, eating unwisely, spending many hours drifting in and out of stores, making unnecessary purchases, followed by watching reruns of *Matlock* and *Perry Mason* in the afternoons, I finally told myself, "Get a life."

That's when I took the library route and adopted the "hit or miss" approach in selecting my reading choices. I skimmed biographies, travel books, cooking books, how-to-grow-old and how-to-stay-young books, religions of the world, astrology books, and mysteries, to name a few. One day, I came across a writer's description of a factory's location, "...in a rocky field uptown in Manhattan...pastoral scene with the land sloping down toward the Hudson River and the only living creature being a goat."

This reference to a solitary goat reminded me of the old-time cartoons and comic strips in which there was usually a scene showing a goat munching on tin cans in a small, weed-infested backyard. As a child, I could never understand why the goat was always there, alone, quietly nibbling away, just minding his own business.

I came into the world on a cold January morning in the 1920s, having been delivered at home by a female Caucasian doctor, who was assisted by my tiny, non-English-speaking maternal grandma, Ah Paw. Not only was this an odd couple working together to deliver me, but also the doctor was married to a Chinese herbalist. So who could ask for more? If Western medicine couldn't handle a situation that might arise, then the ancient world of herbs would step in. But this was not to be. I turned out to be a scrawny, five-pound weakling. After four or five days, the doctor told my parents, "Love the baby as much as possible. She won't last much longer."

My parents despairingly asked, "Why? What's wrong? What can be done?"

It appeared that I had the so-called newborn "runs," which were not responding to treatment, neither Western nor ancient. The advice the doctor ultimately gave my parents was: "See if you can get hold of some goat's milk for her. That might help."

My parents knew of no goat in our neighborhood, nor of any goat in our town. However, my father persistently inquired here, there, and everywhere. Finally, he heard of a man with a goat who lived on the outskirts of town, about twelve miles away. So, early every morning, for several months, he drove to the outskirts of town in his Model T Ford and brought home a little bucket of goat's milk. By George! Or rather, by Goat! The goat's milk worked. My runs stopped. My life began anew.

After reading the astrology books, I was able to put two and two together. Those born between December 23 and January 20 belong to the Zodiac sign of Capricorn, the sign of the Goat. Astrologers say that the Goat leads a life of solitude and hardship. He survives only by being very careful as he leaps from crag to crag on the steep and treacherous mountainsides to forage for food.

"In appearance, the Goat is not a comely creature with his saturnine face, sturdy hooves, and a dull coat of shabby fur. Nor does he have a commanding presence like that of a lion or tiger. In disposition, he offers neither the affection nor the fellowship of a cat or dog. In spirit, he is careful and tenacious, and perseveres to overcome adversity and sustain survival."

The Goat's homely appearance and solemn attitude toward life matter little to me. What matters most is his sharing with me the spirit to "overcome adversity and sustain survival." This is evidenced by my success in overcoming a sickly childhood, raising a lovely family, and becoming a member of the septuagenarian group.

I offer these words of Agatha Christie as a tribute to the Goat, my lifelong benefactor, "While the light lasts, I shall remember you, and in the darkness, I shall not forget."

My Ancestors and Me

Long ago, flippant and comical sayings attributable to Confucius found their way into fortune cookies and joke books. As a child, I was introduced to the serious side of Confucius when we were trained at home and at Chinese school to respect one's elders and revere one's ancestors. The basic theme was family solidarity through ancestor worship.

The Chinese believe that after death, a person's soul resides in three places: home, burial site, and Heavenly Palace. To achieve the goal of eternal bonding of the past generations with living family members, the family needs to always perform certain rituals and observe given customs at each of the three places where the soul resides. And that is the crux of the concept of ancestor worship.

At Home

Family members show respect and reverence to their ancestors by burning incense and candles and by performing rituals of remembrance in front of ancestral plaques or tablets set up in the home.

As a child, I spent many happy hours being my grandma's little shadow. Every morning and evening, she lit three short joss sticks (incense) and placed them in a metal container, which was wrapped on the outside with red paper for good luck. This incense container was placed in a corner of her tiny back porch. I stood there quietly observing and wondering, but never questioning aloud. Somehow, deep inside of me, I felt that the incense-burning custom had something to do with the world of grown-ups, with life and its silent mysteries.

When I was home with my aunts, uncles, parents, and cousins, the incense-burning rituals were a little more elaborate. In the front room, the incense burners were on a shelf along with the ancestral plaques or tablets. Every morning and evening, my two aunts and mother took turns lighting little wicks, which floated in glasses filled with water, plus three tall joss sticks (nine inches in length) and three short joss sticks (six inches in length), and occasionally red candles, all placed like soldiers standing tall and straight in the handsome brass incense burners. Here, also, I quietly observed and wondered but never asked about the why or wherefore.

At the Burial Site

Family members are expected to visit the burial sites at least once a year on Spring Festival Day. It is usually a designated day in the third month of the lunar calendar. They call this day "Ching Ming," which means "Clear and Bright." On this visit, family members clear the sites of weeds and debris, bring offerings of food, and burn incense, candles, and memorial paper money for the ancestors to enjoy up in the Heavenly Palace. It is a happy outing. Often the children bring their colorful kites and fly them from the hilltop.

As a child, and later as an adult, I looked forward to these community visits to the cemetery. In the Bay Area, the Chinese cemetery is located in the city of Colma and is nestled in the hills adjacent to the Russian cemetery and a Catholic cemetery, among others.

The weather was invariably pleasant since Ching Ming usually falls some time in the month of May of the Gregorian calendar. Family associations chartered buses to transport the community members to the cemetery. There was a general feeling of good will, as the smoke from the incense and candles wafted upward to cloudless blue skies and eventually to the Heavenly Palace.

I can still recall my mother commenting that the fragrance from the incense and candles gave her such a wonderful feeling of peace and tranquility. Now that I am a grown-up little old lady and have developed a better understanding of life with its Yin and Yang aspects, I empathize with her simple, yet profound, comment.

The customary food offerings consisted of a poached chicken (uncut), a strip of roast pork, three cups of tea, three tiny cups of wine, and three oranges. After I grew up, I understood the significance of the number three. "Three" sounds the same as the word for life, which is a good omen.

The relatives then took turns standing in front of the grave site to show their respect by kowtowing, which is done by bowing three times from the waist, at the same time placing the palms of both hands together and making an up and down motion. The cups of tea and wine were then poured carefully over the site. The chicken, roast pork, and oranges were taken home for the evening meal.

On one occasion, as I trudged up the hill with my father, I noticed a cup of coffee, a donut, and a package of Lucky Strike cigarettes placed on a grave site instead of the usual food offerings. I pointed out the unusual offering to my father, who in his kind and understanding voice said, "That's nice. It's a special gesture of remembrance straight from someone's heart."

At the Temple (Heavenly Palace not being reachable)

The Chinese do not go to a temple on a regular basis to listen to delivered sermons. Instead, they visit the temple when they are moved by the spiritual urge, or on certain holidays. Family members go there to burn incense and candles as a means of sending prayers to their ancestors for help and protection. At times, they just sit there quietly to reflect upon their lives and renew their spirits.

When I was a child, my grandma occasionally took me to a temple in San Francisco's Chinatown. The interior of the temple was dark, with a mystical air. However, it wasn't scary, even to a timid soul like me who was afraid of spooky things and dark places. The walls and furniture were of red and black lacquer and were trimmed with gold. The ornate altar was impressive, with the incense burners filled with many joss sticks and beautifully decorated candles sending their fragrant smoke upward to the ceiling and onward to the Heavenly Palace. A priest tended the temple, and periodically during each hour he gently struck the gong, which sounded like a soulful call for peace and tranquility.

After more than seven decades of sunshine and rain, of living and coping, I feel that my childlike perception as a five-year-old shadow of my grandma was on target. The faithful burning of incense and candles, and visits to the burial sites and temple were all aimed at nurturing the "great human heart" of us all. Each culture, in its own way and manner, seeks the path to reach the universal goal, that of attaining understanding, kindness, and inner peace.

During the course of my reading, I came across these helpful words of Confucius, "A man should strive to be so full of joy that he forgets his worries, and does not notice that old age is coming on."

Thank you, Honorable Confucius, for reinforcing that philosophy. It will help to enhance the enjoyment of our many remaining years.

LOOKED BACK OVER MY LIFE YESTERDAY

Looked back over my life yesterday,
Looked at the girl, stared at the woman,
Smiled at her joy, lived again her pain.
Saw a crisis, stepped over it.
Her pain soothed by tears,
There were never enough.
Stop wasting time, she say to herself;
Got a man-child to raise.

Nowhere to turn, what do I do?
Hell, how will I do it? She moans again.
Saw that man-child reaching up,
Making his way with her,
Trust she gave him the right tools.
Don't know, she thinks,
Then, drinks just a little more.

Yeah, I looked back over my life yesterday,
Remembered the tears, the fears, the trials.
See she's grown rounder, and wiser
Don't know how, never stopped
To see it coming; had a man-child ta raise.
Rent ta pay, and demons to fight.
Child callin', job callin', man callin',
She drinks just a little more.

Looked back at my life yesterday,
Now, looking back's not so bad.
Can see the whole picture now.
See teachers, struggles,
Found hope out of prayer
Moved forward assured.
Climbed out of potholes, tamed fears,
Enemies slain, loves won,

No more man-child to raise;
For now he's a man.
Looked back at my life yesterday,
See me now, well worn, and fulfilled.
—Vicki Ward

EDITOR'S NOTE

Vicki's seasoned view of life stemmed in part from her ongoing interaction with women of different cultures and ages. These interactions continued to reaffirm the bond between her and women she met. She saw new lifestyles, blended families, and that the drive of Sistahs to achieve life's goals had replaced many of the nurturing rituals and supportive customs we engaged in long ago. *Life's Spices from Seasoned Sistahs* was born in her spirit, took hold, and grew into this collection of insights, truths, affirmations, and confirmations of life.

Actual life experiences by women sharing many of the same trials are what women want to hear. It is with a desire to reconnect with each other that this book has been compiled and edited so that Seasoned Sistahs of every culture, and our emerging young women, will find bits of seasoning and spice to use on their journey toward self-fulfillment, as they travel the same roads dotted with potholes, and fraught with danger, joy, and pain.

The resource directory included in this book provides a wealth of information on services across the country and in some U.S. territories. The online resources are a great start for you web-savvy women. Sistahs are encouraged not to isolate themselves, but to seek out other Sistahs and organizations that are making a difference, one woman at a time. Purchase this book for a Sistah in need. Determine today that you will become an active member of our great Sistahhood, helping to bring another woman of color to greater heights along with you.

Yes, Sistah, you can make it!

Appendix A

AUTHOR BIOS

JENNIFER BROWN BANKS

Jennifer Brown Banks is a feature writer for *Being Single* magazine and an award-winning poet. Her work has wowed local and national audiences in publications such as *Today's Black Woman* magazine, Simon and Schuster's "Chocolate" series, *Honey* magazine, and Writing for Dollars.com. She teaches in Illinois.

S. BRANDI BARNES

S. Brandi Barnes is a poet and journalist and is part of the African-American Writers Initiative at the Second City improv theater in Chicago. Her work has appeared in *Essence*, the *Chicago Reader* newspaper, and *Black Collegian*, *Afrique* newspaper, and *N'DIGO Magapaper*, and in literary anthologies such as *The Woman That I AM* (St. Martin's Press) and *NOMMO 2: A Literary Legacy of Black Chicago Writers* (OBAC-Press). Brandi is the author of the book *Blackberries in the China Cabinet* (Kar-Mel Publishers).

PATRICIA E. CANTERBURY

Patricia E. Canterbury is a mentor, political scientist (a former assistant executive officer for the California Board for Professional Engineers and Land Surveyors), wife, and author. She is the author of the *A Poplar Cove Mystery*, a trilogy for those 9 to 14 years of age, and the eight-volume *The Delta Mystery* series, for 6 to 9-year-olds. Pat is working on her first "boy" mystery trilogy, which will be part of the Popular Cove Mystery series.

JUANITA J. CARR

Juanita Carr, a native of East St. Louis, Illinois, has resided in California since 1955. She currently lives in Sacramento with her son and two sassy cats. Writing for pleasure and fun began at an early age when she crafted stories for her grammar school classmates. She has been a serious writer since 1997, when she joined an active and productive writing group. With one novel completed, she is diligently working on another. Inclusion in the *Seasoned Sistahs* anthology is her first published work.

LILLIAN COMAS-DIAZ

Lillian Comas-Diaz is a clinician, scholar, and activist, interested in reconciling liberation psychology, feminism, and multiculturalism. She has been a member of fact-finding delegations investigating human rights abuses in Chile, the former Soviet Union, South Africa, India, and Nepal. Lillian is the senior editor of two textbooks, *Clinical Guidelines in Cross Cultural Mental Health*, and *Women of Color: Integrating ethnic and gender identities in psychotherapy*. Additionally, she is the founding editor-in-chief of the American Psychological Association Division 45 official journal, *Cultural Diversity and Ethnic Minority Psychology*.

JOY COPELAND

Joy Copeland worked as an executive for a major corporation, one of many roles in a chain of careers until her recent retirement. Now Joy devotes her time to her passions: writing, traveling to the settings that serve as backdrops for her stories, and spending time with family. Joy writes both family stories and tales of fantasy. Her story "Hair Dreams" has been accepted for an upcoming anthology of African-American horror and suspense, which Kensington is scheduled to publish in 2004. She has just completed her first novel, a supernatural thriller entitled *Borrowed Destiny*, and is busy at work on a second novel, *Simon Says*.

J. M. CORNWELL

J. M. Cornwell is a professional editor, nationally syndicated freelance journalist, columnist, writer, and book reviewer who lives in the Rocky Mountains in Colorado.

LA RHONDA CROSBY-JOHNSON

La Rhonda Crosby-Johnson is a native of Oakland, California. Now beginning her tenth year as a self-employed health education consultant, she has spent the last 23 years working in the areas of health and education as a social worker and educator. She is the author of one published poem, "Who Told You," and is currently working on her first novel. She is a daughter, sister, niece, aunt, friend, mother, godmother, and grandmother, and she currently lives in San Leandro, California, with her husband.

DEIDRA SUWANEE DEES

Deidra Suwanee Dees was born into Muscogee Nation and is a doctoral candidate at Harvard University. Suwanee, named after her grandfather Suwanee Dees, is conducting research for her dissertation on cross-cultural education at Poarch Muscogee Nation in Alabama. She has worked as the director of education at Poarch Muscogee Nation, developing culturally appropriate educational curricula. Her research was published in a textbook for college literature courses, *Forced from the Garden* (Guild Press, 2003), a collection of scholarly literature by a diverse group of women writers. Her writings have also been published in a literature book, *Joining the Circle* (TA Publications, 2003), a component of the Writers Workshop of the annual Eastern Shawnee Pow Wow. Her first book has just been published and she is working on her second book, to be published later this year. Suwanee received two prestigious awards for excellence in journalism by the University of South Alabama. The People's Poet, in the United Kingdom, honored her for her creative verse. She also received the Mirrors International Tanka Award from AHA Books in Gualala, California.

JANET MICHELLE ELDER

Janet Elder is an RN and OB nurse manager for Wayne Memorial Hospital and is currently working on her master's degree in health care administration. Born and raised in rural Georgia, she is a single mother with one son, 4-year-old Jonathan, and is active in music ministry.

RENEE FAJARDO

Renee Fajardo is an attorney by training. After spending several years working with inner-city children and homeless families, she decided that her first love, writing, was a more effective way to use her skills. In 1996, as the mother of seven, she turned her passion for working with children and young adults into a career. Today, Renee writes for various publications in the Denver metro area and is the co-author of two multicultural children's books based on family foods, *Holy Mole Guacamole: And Other Tummy Tales* and *Pinch A Lotta Enchiladas: And Other Tummy Tales*. She is also a professional storyteller whose repertoire includes Inuit, Hispanic, Filipino, and Southwestern folk tales, along with creation myths. As a teacher of storytelling and creative writing workshops, her passion is to help young writers draw on their family and community ties to create a rich and vibrant world.

ESTELLE FARLEY

Estelle Farley is a member of the Carolina African-American Writers Collective. Her work is featured in the anthologies *Beyond the Frontier: African American Poetry in the 21st Century, Dark Eros: A Celebration of*

African American Eroticism, and *In the Company of Women*. She has also contributed to several literary journals. Estelle has shared her work at various venues around the country and currently resides in the San Francisco Bay Area.

LEVONNE GADDY

Levonne Gaddy was born and raised in rural Piedmont, North Carolina, during the 1950s and 1960s. She was the first in her family of origin and extended family to complete a college education. She majored in business education at North Carolina Central University and social work at University of California Los Angeles. Levonne has worked for the past twenty-five years in the human services field. Though her education has afforded her the ability to make a reasonable living, her heart has always lived in the world of words and in the practice of writing. Her story "A New Dancer" is part of her memoir in progress. Levonne lives in Tucson, Arizona, with her husband.

UMA GIRISH

Uma Girish is a writer based in Chennai, India. Covering a range of subjects such as parenting, health, fitness, culture, books, and authors, her work has appeared in the leisure pages of the *Economic Times*, in magazines like *Debonair* and *Gurlz*, and on sites like Einkwell, Seven Seas, Absolute Write, Writer's Ezine, and Write from Home. She has won awards for her fiction and non-fiction, for both adults and children, and has more work forthcoming in American and Canadian magazines.

JOYCE GITTOES

Joyce Gittoes is a 67-year-old retiree, living in Phoenix, Arizona. She was born and bred in New York City and also lived in Queens. She's a former high school English teacher and social worker, and is currently an actress in Phoenix.

EVE HALL

Eve Hall is an author and poet who resides in Atlanta, Georgia. She just released two new poetry books, *Enter Eve's Poetic Paradise* and *Dante's Poetic Playground*. Her work has received anywhere from first to fifth place in several writing contests, and it has also appeared in magazines such as *Purpose*, *Skyline Publications*, and *Threecupmorning*. One of her goals is to find an illustrator and a publisher for her children's books.

D.L. HARRIS

D.L. Harris is a poet and playwright living in Seattle, Washington. Her play *The Satin Sisters* was produced in Seattle and Atlanta, Georgia. She has her own company, BackBone Productions, and describes writing as her anchor.

JO ANN YOLANDA HERNÁNDEZ

Jo Ann Yolanda Hernández was born in Texas, raised her sons in Vermont, earned her master's in creative writing at the University of San Francisco, and now lives in Arizona. Her latest manuscript "The Throw Away Piece" won first place at the 2003 Latino/Chicano Literary Prize at the University of California, Irvine.

GILDA A. HERRERA

Gilda A. Herrera, a fifty-plus "sistah," is a freelance writer of non-fiction and fiction based in San Antonio, Texas, her hometown. She has written for newspapers and magazines and is thrilled that her first mystery novel, *Four Dogs with a Bone*, will be published this year.

CYNTHIA REGINA HOBSON

Cynthia Hobson was born on the Southside of Chicago, Illinois, where she attended the Art Institute of Chicago's Art Student Program. She and her family later moved to Elk Grove, California. Cynthia retired from a career executive assignment at the California Energy Commission in 1999 after 30 years' state service. She is continuing her love of art through painting and writing. She is the owner of Hobson's Corner.

BEATRICE M. HOGG

Beatrice Hogg lives in Sacramento, California. She has an MFA in creative writing from Antioch University Los Angeles and graduated in December 2004. Beatrice has been published in newspapers and magazines such as the *Sacramento Bee*, *Sacramento News & Review*, *Astronomy*, *Reminisce*, and *Whispers from Heaven*. She is working on a memoir about her hometown, a coal-mining town in western Pennsylvania.

GERI SPENCER HUNTER

Geri Spencer Hunter is a native of Marshalltown and a graduate of the University of Iowa's College of Nursing. She is the author of *Polkadots* (1998), a contemporary relationship novel. Her short story "Déjà Vu" has been included in Eleanor Taylor Bland's anthology *Shades of Black* (2004), a collection of short stories by black mystery writers. Her short story "A Woeful Tale" is included in Nan Mahon's anthology *Lily Love's Cafe*, a collection of short stories that were published as a fundraiser for Chicks in Crisis, a resource agency for pregnant teens. She is married with children and grandchildren and lives in Sacramento, California.

MARGARET HURLEY
Margaret Hurley lives in Northern California with her husband, and is a recent retiree from the U.S. Postal Service. Her love for animals led to her new business, breeding Brittany puppies, and creating scrumptious dog treats as M & M's Gourmet Dog Treats. Occasionally she also writes.

PAULA WHITE JACKSON
Paula White Jackson is an award-winning poet from Arvonia, Virginia. She is a member of the Carolina African American Writers Collective and has won two Emerging Artist Fellowships. The author of two poetry collections, *Saturday Morning Pancakes* and *Those Hands, Those Hands (A Mother's Life and Death)*, she has also placed work in the anthology *Catch the Fire*, as well as *Obsidian II*, the *Piedmont Literary Review*, and the *BMA Sonia Sanchez Literary Review*. Paula was a staff writer and columnist for the *Fluvanna Review*, *Scottsville Monthly*, and *More* magazine. In addition to poetry, she writes essays and children's picture books. Her non-fiction has appeared in FYAH and in *Women's World* magazine. She teaches workshops and enjoys performing readings of her work.

STRELLA JASPER
Strella Jasper is an expert in biblical Persian history. She is an international missionary who authors articles, songs, and poetry that reflect the human condition she experiences as she ministers in foreign lands. Ms. Jasper unwinds with her flower gardens in the shadow of the Rocky Mountains at her home in Denver, Colorado.

LARRAINE JOHNSON
Larraine Johnson exemplifies her credo, "Never Give Up on You." A prolific speaker and teacher, Larraine brings passion to any presentation. A recent graduate from Otterbein College, Larraine received her B. A. in Leadership and the Liberal Arts. She is presently attending the School of Social Work at Ohio State University to obtain her master's degree in social work. A retiree

from 25 years of public administration, Larraine is a proven professional and entrepreneur. Her website, www.EmberLightPress.com, is her personal statement for empowerment and the healing arts. She is the recipient of many community awards and has contributed three children to continue her personal legacy. She holds papers of Ministerial Fellowship with the Pentecostal Assemblies of the World. She resides in Columbus, Ohio, with her West Highland Terrier, Noel.

META JONES
Meta Jones is a 52-year-old retired contracting officer with three children and three grandchildren. Originally from Cincinnati, Ohio, she migrated to Atlanta after college and has lived there ever since. Recently, she decided to dust off her dreams and pursue a writing career. Her first story will be published in December in a new magazine, *What's Within You*, which will also publish one of her poems, "Whenever," in a future issue. She's currently working on a suspense novel.

SANDY KAY
Sandy Kay has written regularly all of her life, though it took a big push of support from a very close friend to help her see herself as a writer and not just as someone who writes. Given an opportunity to work with a published writer at the school she currently attends, she is reinventing herself in the middle of her life as a writer.

DONNA KINSLER
Donna Kinsler graduated cum laude from the University of New Haven in West Haven, Connecticut, and embarked upon a highly accelerated career path with AT&T. After a sabbatical, she traveled and lived in Barbados, Jamaica, Paris, and Stockholm. She returned to cofound Hi-Tek learning systems, a non-profit organization in Florida that prepared inner-city youth for high school equivalency exams with hours of aviation training. Donna is the former director of new business development at BlackPearl Entertainment (Warner Bros), where she assisted in producing the acclaimed television series *Judge Mathis*. She has held similar positions with Suzanne de Passe's, de Passe Entertainment, Bill Duke's Yagya Yagya Productions, Marla Gibbs Enterprises, and Stevie Wonder's Black Bull Music. She was the first operations manager for the NAACP Hollywood Bureau, which included administration of the prestigious NAACP Image Awards. Ms. Kinsler's current involvement is with PBS/KCET's daily children's bilingual television show,

A Place Of Our Own/Los Ninos En Su Casa. She resides in Los Angeles, California, and continues her God Inc. work with community, civic, and environmental programs, including Sparrow's Ministries, an AIDS hospice village in South Africa, through which she sponsors children afflicted with AIDS.

DEBBIE LA'SASSIER

Debbie La'Sassier resides in New York. In 2001, she self-published her first book, *Healing Through Poetry.* She's a member of the International Society of Poets, Black Writers United, ISP, Civil Rights Org., and Black World Newspaper. Debbie's poetry has appeared in several anthologies and is on various websites, including Poetry.com, Writerscrib, and A Mobius Pi. She has also recited and performed poetry at the Zen Den Coffee House in Babylon, New York.

NORMA NG LAU

Norma Ng Lau was born in Oakland in 1923. A Phi Beta Kappa graduate of University of California at Berkeley, she spent the 50s and 60s raising her two children and helping her parents run their small grocery on Oakland Avenue. She also studied to become certified as a state public accountant, internal auditor, and fraud examiner. At the age of 54, she began a 30-year political career. Elected five times as Oakland's city auditor, she exposed three major fraud scandals before retiring in 1998 to write a mystery novel. Deeply involved in professional, women's, and cultural organizations, she was named a "Woman of Achievement" by the Soroptimists in 1980 and "Woman of the Year" by the National Women's Political Caucus in 1982. She passed away in October 2004 at the age of 81.

ELAINE RUTH LEE

Elaine Lee is the author/editor of *Go Girl: The Black Woman's Book of Travel and Adventure* published by Eighth Mountain Press. She is a free-lance travel writer whose work has appeared in numerous national magazines and webzines. She cohosts a monthly travel radio show and has appeared on numerous local and national radio and TV shows. Elaine Lee is also a practicing attorney in the San Francisco Bay Area. Several years ago, she traveled solo around the world and continues to travel regularly. She has visited over 36 countries.

VIRGINIA K. LEE

Virginia Lee received a B.A. in sociology from California State University at Los Angeles and an M.S. degree in education from the City College of New York. She has been adjunct in early childhood education at the Borough of Manhattan Community College since 1988—She is also a member of the International Women's Writing Guild and a Cave Canem Fellows graduate. She is the poet laureate of Memorial Baptist Church in Harlem and an active member of Alpha Kappa Sorority, Inc.

JOAN MCCARTY

Joan McCarty is the author of the plays *A Time to Dance* and *Last Bus to Stateville*. She also wrote a collection of short stories entitled *Through My Windows*. She is a stage manager and a teacher at Spelman College in the Department of Drama and Dance, and currently resides with her husband Anthony, outside of Atlanta.

CAROLE MCDONNELL

Carole McDonnell's fiction and essays have appeared in print and online, in regional and national publications. Her story "Lingua Franca" is due to appear in Nalo Hopkinson's anthology, *So Long Been Dreaming*. Another story, "Black Is the Color of My True Love's Hair," is in *Fantastic Visions III*. Her devotionals appear in Christian online and print magazines and also on www.faithwriters.com. Her reviews are on www.compulsivereader.com, www.thefilmforum.com, and www.curledup.com. Her short story "Homecoming" won New Mass Media's Westchester Weekly annual fiction contest in September 1996 and received third place at the Annual Contemporary Western Fiction Contest. Published essays include "Oreo Blues," in W.W. Norton's *LIFENOTES: Personal Writings by Contemporary Black Women* and "That Smile" in the anthology *Then an Angel Came Along*. Carole lives in New York with her husband of twenty years and their two sons.

PAT MCLEAN-RASHINE

Pat McLean-RaShine is a 46-year-old mother of three. She has been writing short stories, essays, and particularly poetry for many years. She performs and teaches poetry throughout the Philadelphia, New Jersey, and Washington area. She is the author of two self-published books of poetry, *A Sister Speaks of....* and *Ain't Gonna Bite My Tongue No More*. She is the founder and a current member of an all-female poetry ensemble known as

In the Company of Poets. In addition to her regular 9 to 5, she teaches on a regular basis at area women's transitional homes.

CONSTANCE DIGGS MATTHEWS

Constance Matthews is president of Epiphany Management Inc., a San Diego-based marketing and PR firm with divisions serving the publishing and non-profit industries. The company's client roster includes such individuals and organizations as Manuelita Brown (artist), Jerry Hoover (author), Marlo Brooks (author/motivational speaker), California Southern Small Business Development Corporation, QBR: The Harlem Book Fair, Gordon "Specs" Powell, The Diamond Business Improvement District, The Jacobs Family Foundation, Market Creek Plaza, the University of California San Diego, the Chicken Soup For the African American Soul Empowerment Tour, and Hope in the City. Her written work has appeared in the *Amsterdam News, American Visions, Upscale*, and *Black Enterprise* magazines. She was recently named to the steering committee of the San Diego Commission for Arts and Culture Neighborhood Design Arts Project, where she is serving on the review committee for proposals submitted for the Commission's 2004 community public art project. When she's not consulting clients or writing, Constance enjoys antiquing, reading, and visiting galleries and museums. She lives in the community of Talmadge in San Diego, California, with her husband and business partner, Leon Matthews.

SAUNDRA KAY MOCK

Saundra Kay Mock is a freelance writer living in the Dallas, Texas, area, where she leads a quiet family life. She has been twice published with Standard Publishing.

CAROL NOWELL

Carol Nowell resides in the small town of Raeford, North Carolina. She has a daughter, son, and six grandchildren. Reading romance novels inspired her to start writing. Carol's first paid work appeared in the December 2003 issue of *True Story*. At the age of 44, she met her first true love, and they plan to be married in July of 2005 with her wearing her a red wedding dress.

SANDRA RAMOS O' BRIANT

Sandra Ramos O' Briant has been published both in print and online. An excerpt from her novel, *The Sandoval Chronicles: The Secret of Old Blood*, was published in *LA HERENCIA*. The novel is presently under consideration with an agent.

OKTAVI

Octavi has performed her spoken word in a variety of venues, including radio broadcasts throughout Los Angeles, California, and Raleigh/Durham North Carolina. A partial list of her published work includes *Fertile Ground*, Runnagate Press, Editors, Kalamu ya Salaam & Kysha N. Brown; *Dark Eros*, St Martins Press, editor Reginald Martin; *Catch the Fire*, Berkeley Publishing Co., editor, D. Knowledge; *Beyond the Frontier*, Black Classic Press, editor E. Ethelbert Miller; *bum rush the page*, Three Rivers Press, editors Tony Medina & Louis Reyes Rivera. She is an active member of the Carolina African-American Writer's Collective and participated in the California Arts Council, Artist-in-Communities Residency program. Oktavi was one of the founding members of the women's group Motley Cabal and founding editor of *Teen View*, a Los Angeles newsletter for young writers. Although her main focus is poetry, she has had short stories published. She currently resides in California.

ROBERTA ORONA-CORDOVA

Roberta Orona-Cordova was born in Albuquerque, New Mexico, and has an extensive career in writing, both as a writer and as an instructor. Roberta received her bachelor of arts degree in rhetoric from the University of California at Berkeley, her master of arts degree in speech and communication from San Francisco State University, and her master of fine arts in screenwriting from UCLA. She has written several screenplays, including *Viva la Vida: The Story of Frida Kahlo*; written and directed a narrative short film, *Rosie*; and written a collection of short stories, *Letter to My Daughter So I Can Sleep*.

KATHERINE A. PARKER

Katherine Parker is a member of a dynamic poetic duo in San Francisco, California, called "Sistahs Wid' Gaps" in celebration of being two very talented gap-toothed women. They have been performing around the Bay Area for at least 10 years and are currently involved in a CD project.

DORIS HOUSE RICE

Doris House Rice is the author of two self-published books and four gospel plays. Her plays have been performed at universities, colleges, civic centers, churches, and theaters. Her work is in *Kente Cloth*, *African*

American Writers In Texas (Center for Texas Studies University of North Texas); *Feminine Writes*; *Women*; *Wisdom & Writing* (National Association of Women Writers) and several anthologies. She is the president of the Officer Reginald R. R. House Scholarship Fund and Community Development, Inc., which she founded in memory of her son.

ELLA OROKI RICE

Ella Oroki Rice is the founder of Sisters on a Journey, an organization for women survivors of trauma. Oroki is an ordained minister, a writer and a former preschool and elementary school teacher. Her most current ministry uses her combined gifts to help women and children face life triumphantly. Oroki holds a bachelor of arts degree in applied behavioral sciences and is certified as a family development specialist. She has been trained extensively in the area of childhood sexual abuse. She also facilitates drumming and healing circles. The Sisters on a Journey Drumming and Healing Circle, is a group of women dedicated to keeping the ancient rituals of rhythm and body awareness alive in the healing process. Through the Circle many women have discovered the power of the drumbeat. They realize why the slave masters forbade Africans to gather and "make a joyful noise" by way of the drum.

ROCHELLE ROBINSON

Black feminist, writer, community activist, and global citizen, Rochelle Robinson lives and works in Oakland, California. She is currently participating in community-response project training, through Generation FIVE (San Francisco), around child sexual abuse. She has been active in the peace and solidarity movement and has been involved in numerous community-organizing projects. She holds a master's degree in women's studies from San Francisco State University and is co-founder of Sisters Solstice Writing Collective, a Black women's autobiography project.

ROSEMARIA SAGASTUME

Rosemaria Sagastume is a native of Guatemala and has lived in Boston for most of her life. She has written for many years of emotional experiences in her life. This is her first published work.

DEBRA SLEDGE

Debra Sledge is the co-founder and chief operating officer of the Sledge Group Inc., a non-profit organization founded by Mychal and Debra Sledge with a mission to empower at-risk youths by providing them with alternatives, strengthen families, and end the cycle of destruction. The organization provides one-on-one mentoring, group mentoring, tutoring, dance instruction, and parent/guardian support. Debra is a proud wife and mother of two beautiful daughters.

JANICE SMITH

Janice Smith is a native of Detroit, Michigan, and a 46-year-old mother of a 20-year-old son. A member of the Detroit Writer's Guild for approximately two years, she was recently selected as the first place winner of their 2003 short story contest. She also coordinates the Guild's Young Authors Program. She writes poetry and has been working on a first novel.

REGINA A. BRADFORD TARDY

A faithful child of God, Regina writes from a spiritual perspective with a voice of encouragement that speaks to the experiences of women of color. She is a playwright who enjoys spending precious moments with her wonderful husband and sons. ReGina is the author of *A Mustard Seed of Faith*, *Inner Strength For Inner Struggles*; *Resting On A Rainbow, Enlightening The Journey*, and *Onward & Upward, Elevating The Inner Woman*. She is founder of On A Positive Tip Productions, Inc. a theatrical ministry to bring the awareness of healing through acting, not acting out. She is the owner of Per-Fect Words Publishing Company.

DR. NORMA D. THOMAS

Dr. Norma Thomas is an associate professor and the assistant director of the Center for Social Work Education at Widener University in Chester, Pennsylvania. She is also president and CEO of the Center of Ethnic and Minority Aging, Inc., in Philadelphia. She received her bachelor of arts in social work from Penn State University, a master's in social work from the Temple University School of Social Administration, and her doctorate from the University of Pennsylvania School of Social Work. Norma is the vice president of the Tau Delta Omega chapter, Alpha Kappa Alpha Sorority, Inc., located in Chester, Pennsylvania. She has an extensive academic publication record and has also published poetry in a number of anthologies, including *Generations*. She is currently working on a book of poetry called *Home Remedies* and has self-published a book of poems titled *Sometimes I Hear Old Folks Singin* with her daughter Raina Leon.

LYNETTE VELASCO

Lynette Velasco is a children's book author and poet, and she is also president of Black Americans in Publishing.

FELISICIA WILLIAMS

Felisicia Williams resides in Chesapeake, Virginia, with her husband, Lamar. They have a combined family of two sons, one daughter, and four wonderful grandchildren. Felisicia loves to read and write. She was recently published in *Celebrations – Notes to My Mother*, an anthology of letters. Felisicia continues to pursue her love of writing and is presently working on a children's story. She is a certified juvenile and domestic relations mediator and juvenile probation officer.

RAMONA MORENO WINNER

Ramona Winner is an author of children's bilingual books. In 1996, she published her first book, *It's Okay to Be Different !Esta Bien Ser Differente¡*. She has since written several stories with multicultural themes. Her mission is to teach children to respect other cultures while embracing their own.

DIANTHA L. ZSCHOCHE

Diantha Zschoche is an African-American woman in her early 50s, married with two children in their 20s. Originally from Chicago, she has resided in Southern California since college. She and her husband have been involved in Christian ministry and community for 25 years. Her writing has mostly been used in the ministry, but in the last few years she has been submitting her work for publication.

Appendix B

Alabama

Governor's Office on
National & Community Service
PSA Union Building
Montgomery, AL 36130
Phone: 334-242-7110

Breast and Cervical Cancer
Early Detection Program
877-252-3324

Women, Infants, and Children (WIC)
Supplemental Nutrition Program
Division of WIC
Bureau of Family Health Services
Alabama Department of Public Health
RSA Tower, Suite 1300
P.P. Box 303017
Montgomery, AL 36130-3017
Phone: 334-206-5673 or
800-654-1385
Fax: 334-206-2914
www.adph.org/wic

Alabama Coalition
Against Domestic Violence
4518 Valleydale Road, Suite 201
Birmingham, AL 35242
Phone: 205-380-2395

Alabama Coalition Against Rape
P.O. Box 4091
Montgomery, AL 36102
Phone: 334-264-0128

Alabama Women's Initiative, Inc.
P.O. Box 59323
Birmingham, AL 35259-9323
Phone: 205-991-3221

Alaska

Division of Vocational Rehabilitation
Juneau Branch Office
10002 Glacier Highway, Suite 101
Juneau, AK 99801-8569
Phone: 907-465-3891

United Way of Anchorage
Phone: 907-263-3491

Breast and Cervical Cancer Early
Detection Program
800-478-2221 or 900-269-3491

Women, Infants, and Children (WIC)
Supplemental Nutrition Program
Division of Public Health
Nutrition Services – WIC
P.O. Box 110612
Juneau, AK 99811-0612
Phone: 907-465-3100
Fax: 907-465-3416
www.hss.stat.ak.us/dph/mcfh/
programs/WIC/wic.htm

AK Info: 800-478-2221 www.ak.org

Alaska Family Violence Prevention
(AFVPP) and Clearinghouse:
907-269-3400 or 800-799-7570
www.hss.state.ak.us/dph/mcfh/akfvpp/
descrip.htm

Statewide Women's Health
Partnership: 907-929-2722

American Samoa

American Samoa Disability
Resources: www.idonline.org/find-
ing_help.local.org/am_samoa.html
Medical Services Department

American Samoa Government
Territory of American Samoa
Pago, Pago AS 96799

Arizona

Points of Light Foundation Volunteer
Center: 800-865-8683

Breast and Cervical Cancer
Early Detection Program
888-257-8502

Women, Infants, and Children (WIC)
Supplemental Nutrition Program
Office of Nutrition Services
Department of Health Services
State Health Building
2927 North 35th Avenue, Suite 400
Phoenix, AZ 85017
Phone: 602-542-1886 or 800-252-5WIC
(800-252-59342)
Fax: 602-542-1886 or 1804
www.hs.state.az.us/cfhs/ons/wic.htm

Other State Resources For Women
State of Arizona Web Site: www.az.gov
Arizona Department of Health
Services: www.hs.state.az.us
Community Information and
Referral: 602-263-8856 or
800-352-3792

Arizona Child Care Resource
and Referral: 800-308-9000

Governor's Community Policy Office
1700 West Washington, Suite 101
Phoenix, AZ 85007
Phone: 602-542-4043
www.governor.state.az.us

Arkansas

Department of Human Services
Division of Aging and Adult Services
P.O. Box 1437, Slot S530

700 South Main Street, Fifth Floor
Little Rock, AR 72203-1437
Phone: 501-682-2441
www.state3.ar.us/dhs/aging

Division of Volunteerism
P.O. Box 1437, Slot S530
700 South Main Street, Second Floor
Little Rock, AR 72203-1437
Phone: 501-682-7540

Breast and Cervical Cancer
Early Detection Program
BreastCare: 877-670-Care
(877-670-2273)

Women, Infants, and Children (WIC)
Supplemental Nutrition Program
WIC
Arkansas Department of Health
5800 West 10th Street
Little Rock, AR 72204
Phone: 501-661-2473 or
800-235-0002
Fax: 501-661-2004

Breastfeeding Information:
800-445-6175

California

California State Department
of Rehabilitation:
• Assistive Technology: 916-263-8687
or 916-263-8685(TTY);
Email: atinfo@dor.ca.gov
• Blind Services: 916-263-8953;
Email: blindinfo@dor.ca.gov
• Client Assistance Program: 916-263-7367 or 800-598-3273 (TTY);
Email: capinfor@dor.ca.gov
• Deaf and Hard of Hearing Services:
916-263-8936 or 916-263-7481
(TTY); Email: dhhs@dor.ca.gov
• Independent Living: 916-263-8944;
Email: ilinfo@dor.ca.gov

California Federation of Women's Clubs
3350 Shelby Street, Suite 200
Ontario, CA 91764
Phone: 909-944-2522

Breast and Cervical Cancer
Early Detection Program
Every Woman Counts: 800-511-2300

Women, Infants, and Children (WIC)
Supplemental Nutrition Program
Supplemental Nutrition Branch
Department of Health Services
3901 Lennane Drive
Sacramento, CA 95834
Phone: 916-928-8806 or 888-WIC-
WORKS (888-942-9675)
FAX: 916-928-0706
www.wicworks.ca.gov

MediCal: 800-427-1295

Colorado

Breast and Cervical Cancer Early
Detection Program
303-692-2600

Women, Infants, and Children (WIC)
Supplemental Nutrition Program
Nutrition Services
Colorado Department of Health
FCHD-NS-A4
4300 Cherry Creek Drive
South Denver, CO 80246-1530
Phone: 303-692-2400
Fax: 303-756-9926
www.chdphe.state.co.us/ps/ns/wic/wic
hom.asp

Elderly Abuse Prevention Program
1905 Sherman Street, Suite 920
Denver, CO 80203
Phone: 303-831-4043

Denver Indian Center
4407 Morrison Road

Denver, CO 80219
Phone: 303-936-2688

Colorado Housing Assistance
Corporation
670 Santa Fe Drive
Denver, CO 80204
Phone: 303-572-9445

Colorado Division of Employment
and Training
1515 Arapahoe Street
Tower 2, Suite 400
Denver, CO 80202
Phone: 303-318-8800

Connecticut

Office of Protection and Advocacy for
Persons with Disabilities: 800-842-7303
(Voice and TTY) or 860-297-4300

Breast and Cervical Cancer
Early Detection Program
800-203-1234 or 860-509-7804

Women, Infants, and Children (WIC)
Supplemental Nutrition Program
State WIC Program
Department of Public Health
410 Capitol Avenue MS #11WIC
P.O. Box 340308
Hartford, CT 06134-0308
Phone: 860-509-8084 or 800-741-2142
Fax: 860-509-8391

Office of Health Care Access:
800-797-9688

Department of Children and Families:
860-418-7001 or 800-842-2288

Capital Region Mental Center, Mental
Health and Addiction Services: 860-
297-0800

Delaware

Services for Aging and Adults with
Physical Disabilities
1901 North DuPont Highway
Herman Holloway Campus
New Castle DE 19720
Phone: 302-577-4791

Division of State Services Centers
Office of Volunteerism
1901 North Dupont Highway,
Debnam Building
New Castle, DE 19720
Phone: 302-255-9748 or 800-815-5465

Delaware Treatment Access Center:
302-577-2711

Breast and Cervical Cancer
Early Detection Program
800-464-4357 or 800-273-9500

Women, Infants, and Children (WIC)
Supplemental Nutrition Program
Delaware Health and Social Services
Division of Public Health
WIC Program
Blue hen Corporate Center
655 Bay Road, Suite 4-B
Dover, DE 19901
Phone: 302-739-3970, 302-739-3671,
or 800-222-2189
Fax: 302-739-3970

Delaware Helpline: 800-464-HELP
(800-464-4357) or 800-273-9500

Healthy Mothers, Healthy Babies
Coalition
Perinatal Association of Delaware
Phone: 302-654-1088 or 302-984-
BABY
www.healthybabies.org

District of Columbia

Greater DC Cares
1411 K Street, NW, Suite 1200
Washington, DC 20005
Phone: 202-289-7378
Fax: 202-289-4108
ww.dc-cares.org

Breast and Cervical Cancer Early
Detection Program
Phone: 888-833-9474 or
877-672-7368 (TDD)

Women, Infants, and Children (WIC)
Supplemental Nutrition Program
WIC State Agency
2100 Martin Luther King J. Avenue,
SE, Suite 409
Washington, DC 20020
Phone: 202-645-5662 or 800-345-
1WIC (800-345-1942)
Fax: 202-645-0516
www.dchealth.com/wic/welcome.htm

Immunization Program: 202-576-7130

Tobacco Control Program:
202-442-5433,
Email: TobaccoControl@dchealth.com

Baby Healthline: 800-MOM-BABY

Drug Abuse Hotline: 888-294-3572

Domestic Violence Intake Center:
202-294-0152

Florida

Developmental Services
Department of Children and Families
1317 Winewood Boulevard
Building 3, Room 325
Tallahassee, FL 32399
Phone: 850-488-4257

Breast and Cervical Cancer
Early Detection Program
888-538-7788

Women, Infants, and Children (WIC)
Supplemental Nutrition Program
Bureau of WIC and Nutrition
Services
Florida Department of Health
Bin #A-16, HSFW
4052 Bald Cypress Way
800-342-3556
Fax: 850-922-3936
www9.myflorida.com/family/wic/defa
ult.html

Family Healthline: 800-451-2229

Florida Council Against Sexual
Violence: 888-956-1273

Florida Domestic Violence Hotline:
800-500-1119

Florida AIDS Hotline: 800-FLA-AIDS
(800-352-2437)

Georgia

Division of Aging Services:
404-657-5258

Breast and Cervical Cancer
Early Detection Program
800-477-9774

Women, Infants, and Children (WIC)
Supplemental Nutrition Program
State WIC Office
Division of Public Health
Georgia Department of Human
Resources
Two Peachtree Street, NW, 10th
Floor, Suite 476
Atlanta, GA 30303
Phone: 404-657-2910

www.ph.dhr.state.ga.us/programs/wic/
index.shtml

Women's Health Powerline:
800-822-2539

Tobacco Use Prevention Program:
404-657-3143

Violence Against Women:
404-657-3143

Division of Family and
Children Services: 404-657-7660

Guam

Guam Disability Resources:
www.idonline.org/finding_help/local_
org/guam.html

Breast and Cervical Cancer Early
Detection Program
850-245-4455, 617-735-7174,
617-735-7168

Women, Infants, and Children (WIC)
Supplemental Nutrition Program
Nutrition Health Services/
Guam WIC Program
Department of Public Health
and Social Services
Government of Guam
P.O. Box 2816
Hagatna, GU 96932
Phone: 671-475-0287
Fax: 671-477-7945
www.admin.gov.gu/pubhealth/index.html

Women's Health Powerline:
800-822-2539

Department of Public Health
and Social Services
123 Chalan Kareta, Route 10
Mangilao, Guam 96923

Phone: 671-735-3999
Fax: 671-734-5910

Hawaii

Disability and Communication
Access Board
919 Ala Moana Boulevard, Room 101
Honolulu, HI 96814
Phone: 808-586-8121 (Voice or TDD)
Fax: 808-586-8129
Email: accesshi@aloha.net

Breast and Cervical Cancer
Early Detection Program
808-692-7460

Women, Infants, and Children (WIC)
Supplemental Nutrition Program
WIC Services Branch
Department of Health
235 South Beretania Street, Suite 701
Honolulu, HI 96813
Phone: 808-586-8175, 888-820-6425,
or 808-586-8175 (TDD)
Fax: 808-586-8189
Mano.icsd.Hawaii.gov/doh/resource/fa
mily/wic/index.html

Hawaii Immunization Program:
808-586-8300

Diabetes Control Program:
808-692-7462; 808-692-7461 (Fax)

Child Health Services Section:
808-733-9044

Healthy Start Program: 808-733-9033

Idaho

Idaho Council on Developmental
Disabilities
802 West Bannock Street, Suite 308
Boise, ID 83702-5840
Phone: 800-544-2433 or 208-334-2178

United Way of Southeastern Idaho
Email: wecare@unitedwayscid.org
www.idaho.unitedway.org

Breast and Cervical Cancer
Early Detection Program
800-926-2588

Women, Infants, and Children (WIC)
Supplemental Nutrition Program
Idaho WIC Program
Division of Health (6230-94)
Department of Health and Welfare
P.O. Box 83720
Boise, ID 83720-0036
Phone: 800-962-2588
www2.state.id.us/dhw/wic/index.html

Illinois

Health Resource Center
for Women with Disabilities
Rehabilitation Institute of Chicago
RIC Room 106
345 East Superior
Chicago, IL 60611
Phone: 312-238-8003
Email: HRCWD@rehabchicago.com

Breast and Cervical Cancer Early
Detection Program
888-522-1282

Women, Infants, and Children (WIC)
Supplemental Nutrition Program
Bureau of Family Nutrition
Office of Family Health
Illinois Department of Human Services
535 West Jefferson Street
Springfield, IL 62702
Phone: 217-785-5247
www.statil.us/agency/dhs/wicnp.html

Women's Health Line: 888-522-1282

Illinois Coalition Against
Domestic Violence: 217-789-2830

Illinois Department of Public Health,
Sexually Transmitted Disease Hotline:
800-243-2437

Illinois Department of Human
Services, Women and Infant Care:
800-323-FGROW (800-323-4769)

Indiana

Disability, Aging and
Rehabilitation Services
402 West Washington Street
P.O. Box 7083
Indianapolis, IN 46207-7083
Phone: 317-233-3828

Indiana Commission for Community
Service and Volunteerism
302 West Washington Street, E220
Indianapolis, IN 46204

Breast and Cervical Cancer
Early Detection Program
Indiana Family Helpline: 800-433-0746

Women, Infants, and Children (WIC)
Supplemental Nutrition Program
WIC Program
Indiana State Department of Health
2 North Meridian Street, Suite 25
Indianapolis, IN 46204
Phone: 317-233-5610
Fax: 317-233-5609

State Information Center
402 West Washington Street, W160A
Indianapolis, IN 46204
Phone: 800-457-8283
or 317-233-0800
www.in.gov/sic

Maternal and Child Health Hotline:
800-433-0746

Iowa

Division of Persons with Disabilities
Phone: 888-219-0471 (Voice and TTY)
Email: dhr.disabilities@dhr.state.ia.us

Elderly In-Home Health Program:
515-242-6021

Iowa Commission
on Volunteer Service
200 East Grand Avenue
Des Moines, IA 50309
Phone: 515-242-4799 or 800-308-5987
Fax: 515-242-4809
Email: icus@ided.state.ia.us
www.volunteeringiowa.org

Breast and Cervical Cancer
Early Detection Program
800-369-2229

Women, Infants, and Children (WIC)
Supplemental Nutrition Program
Bureau of Nutrition and WIC
Iowa Department of Public Health
Lucas State Office Building
Des Moines, IA 50319-0075
Phone: 515-281-3713 or 800-532-1579
Fax: 515-281-4913
idph.stat.ia.us/fch/n-wic.htm

Iowa Healthy Families Line: 800-369-
2299 or 800-735-2942

Iowa Substance Abuse
Information Center:
866-242-4111; www.drugfreeinfo.org

Kansas

Disability Resource
Department on Aging: 800-432-3535

Kansas Commission on Disability
Concerns: 800-295-5232 or
785-296-1722 (in Topeka)

Breast and Cervical Cancer Early
Detection Program
877-277-1368

Women, Infants, and Children (WIC)
Supplemental Nutrition Program
Nutrition and WIC Services
Kansas Department of Health and
Environment
Charles Curtis Office Building
1000 Southwest Jackson, Suite 220
Topeka, KS 66612-1274
Phone: 785-296-1320 or 800-332-6262
Fax: 785-296-1326
www.kdhe.state.ks.us/nws-wic/index.htm

Kansas Department of Health and
Environment: 785-296-5591

Alcohol Abuse Line: 800-432-3535

Kentucky

Kentucky Council Developmental
Disabilities: 877-367-5332

Kentucky Department of Vocational
Rehabilitation: 800-372-7172

Kentucky Commission on Women
312 West Main Street
Frankfort, KY 40601
Phone: 502-564-6643
Fax: 502-564-2315

Breast and Cervical Cancer
Early Detection Program
Kentucky Women's Cancer Screening
Program: 800-462-6122

Gynecologist Cancer Screening,
University of Kentucky:
800-766-8279 or 859-323-4687

Women, Infants, and Children (WIC)
Supplemental Nutrition Program
Nutrition Services Branch

Division of Maternal and Child Health
Kentucky Department of Public Health
Cabinet for Health Services
275 East Main Street
Frankfort, KY 40621
Phone: 502-564-8389 or 800-462-6122
Fax: 502-564-8389
www.publicheath.state.ky.us/wic-program.htm

Kentucky HIV/AIDS Program:
800-420-7431

Kentucky Parent Information
Network: 800-327-5196

Kentucky State Health Insurance
Information and Assistance Program:
877-293-7447

Louisiana

Vocational and Rehabilitative Services
Office for Citizens with
Developmental Disabilities
P.O. Box 3117
Baton Rouge, LA 70821-3117
Phone: 225-342-0095
Fax: 225-342-8823

Independent Living
8225 Florida Blvd
Baton Rouge, LA 70806
Phone: 225-925-4184
www.dss.state.la.us/offlrs/html/independent_living.html

Breast and Cervical Cancer
Early Detection Program
Women's Preventive Health Program:
888-599-1073

Women, Infants, and Children (WIC)
Supplemental Nutrition Program
Louisiana department of Health and
Hospitals Nutrition Services
325 Loyola Avenue, Room 406

New Orleans, LA 70160
Phone: 504-568-3065
Fax: 504-568-3065
www.oph.dhh.state.la.us/nutrition/wic
/index.htm

Domestic Violence Hotline: 504-411-1333

Family Planning Hotline: 504-568-5330

Maine

Bureau of Elder and Adult Services:
800-262-2232

Maine Mentoring Partnership
PO Box 406
Augusta, ME 04338-0406
Phone: 888-387-8755
www.mainementoring.org/resourcegui
de.html

Breast and Cervical Cancer Early
Detection Program
800-350-5180 or 207-287-8015
(TDD)

Women, Infants, and Children (WIC)
Supplemental Nutrition Program
Maine WIC Nutrition Program
Division of Maternal and Family Health
Department of Human Services
11 SHS
Key Bank Plaza, 8th Floor
Augusta, ME 04333
Phone: 207-287-3991 or
800-437-9300
Fax: 207-287-3993

Partnership for a Tobacco Free Maine:
800-207-1230
(Tobacco Quit-Line), 877-PTM-
4YOU (877-786-4986)

MaineCare: 877-KIDS NOW
(877-543-7669)

Republic of the Marshall Islands

Resources for Women
Program for Children with
Special Needs: 692-525-6941

Women's Reproductive Health
Service, Family Planning Clinic:
692-625-5569/7588

Maryland

Disability Resource
Developmental Disabilities
Administrations:
Central Maryland: 410-902-4500
Eastern Shore: 410-334-6920 or
888-219-0478
Southern Maryland: 301-362-5100,
888-207-2479, or 301-362-5131
(TDD)
Western Maryland: 301-791-4670 or
888-791-0193

Volunteer Resource
Volunteer Maryland
100 Community Place
Crownsville, MD 21032
Phone: 410-514-7270 or 771 TTY
(through Maryland relay)
Fax: 410-514-7277

Breast and Cervical Cancer Early
Detection Program
800-477-9774

Women, Infants, and Children (WIC)
Supplemental Nutrition Program
WIC Administration
Maryland Department of Health and
Mental Hygiene
201 West Preston Street
P.O. Box 13528
Baltimore, MD 21203-3528
Phone: 410-767-5242, 800-242-4WIC

(800-242-4942), OR 800-735-2258 (TDD)
Fax: 410-333-5243
www.mdwic.org

Maryland Center for Immunization: 410-767-6679

Massachusetts

Massachusetts Office on Disability
One Ashburton Place
Boston, MA 02108
Phone: 617-727-7440 or
800-322-2020

Retired and Senior Volunteer
Program: 508-755-2216

Incarcerated Women Resource
Education and Advocacy
Massachusetts Public Health
Association
305 South Street, Room 131
Jamaica Plain, MA 02130
Phone: 617-524-6696
www.phaweb.org

Breast and Cervical Cancer Early
Detection Program
877-414-4447 or 617-624-5992
(TDD)

Women, Infants, and Children (WIC)
Supplemental Nutrition Program
Massachusetts WIC Program
Massachusetts Department of Public
Health
250 Washington Street, 6th Floor
Boston, MA 02108-4619
Phone: 617-624-6100 or 800-WIC-
1007 (800-942-1007)
Fax: 617-624-6179
www.state.ma.us/dph/wic.htm

Domestic Violence SafeLink: 877-
785-2020 or 877-521-2601 (TDD)

Women's Health Network:
877-414-4447

Massachusetts Substance Abuse
Information and Education Health:
800-327-5050

Michigan

Michigan Department of Civil Rights
110 West Michigan Street, Suite 802
Lansing, MI 48933
Phone: 517-335-3164 or 313-961-
1522 (TDD)
Fax: 517-241-0546

Breast and Cervical Cancer Early
Detection Program
800-9220MAMM (800-922-6266)

Women, Infants, and Children (WIC)
Supplemental Nutrition Program
WIC Division
Michigan Department of
Community Health
2150 Apollo Drive
P.O. Box 30195
Lansing, MI 48906
Phone: 517-335-8951 or 800-942-1636
Fax: 517-355-8835
www.mdch.state.mi.us/dch/clcf/wic.asp

Michigan Office of Financial and
Insurance Services: 877-999-6442

MIChild, Health Care for Children:
888-988-6300 or 888-263-5897
(TDD)

Micronesia, Federated States of

Family Village Community Center:
www.familyvillage.wisc.edu/territo-
ries/micronesia.html

Department of Health, Federated
States of Micronesia Government:
691-320-2619

Minnesota

Minnesota State Council on Disability
121 East 7th Place, Suite 107
St. Paul, MN 55101
Phone: 651-296-6785 or
800-945-8913 (Voice and TDD)
Fax: 651-296-5935
Email: cdisability@sate.mn.us
www.disability.state.mn.us

Breast and Cervical Cancer Early
Detection Program
888-643-2584

Women, Infants and Children (WIC)
Supplemental Nutrition Program
Minnesota Department of Health
85 East Seventh Place
P.O. Box 64882
St. Paul, MN 55101
Phone: 651-215-8957 or
800-WIC-4030 (800-942-4030)
Fax: 651-215-8951
www.health.state.mn.us/divs/fh/wic/wic.htm

Family Planning/Sexually Transmitted
Disease Hotline: 800-78-FACTS
(800-783-2287)

Minnesota Children
with Special Health Needs:
800-728-5420 (Voice and TDD) or
651-215-8956, or 612-623-5150
(in the Twin Cities)

Immunization Hotline: 800-657-3970

Mississippi

Coalition for Citizens with Disabilities
754 North President Street
Jackson, MS 39202
Phone: 601-969-0601

Mississippi Commission
for Volunteer Service
Jackson, MS 39211
Phone: 601-432-779
Fax: 601-432-6790
www.mcus.org

Breast and Cervical Cancer Early
Detection Program
800-721-7222

Women, Infants, and Children (WIC)
Supplemental Nutrition Program
WIC Program
Bureau of Health Services
State Department of Health
570 East Woodrow Wilson
Jackson, MS 39216
Phone: 601-576-7100 or 800-721-7222
Fax: 601-576-7070

Mississippi State Department of
Health, Bureau of Women's Health:
800-721-7222

Missouri

Governor's Council on Disability:
800-877-8249
Breast and Cervical Cancer Early
Detection Program
800-4-CANCER (800-422-6237) or
573-522-2845

Women, Infants and Children (WIC)
Supplemental Nutrition Program
Missouri Department of Health and
Senior Services
920 Wildwood, P.O. Box 570
Jefferson City, MO 65102-0570
Phone: 573-751-6204, 800-392-8209,
or 800-TEL-LINK (800-835-5465)
for clinics

Missouri Department of Health
and Senior Services
Section of STD/HIV, P.O. Box 570

930 Wildwood Drive
Jefferson City, MO 65102-0570
Phone: 573-751-6439 or 800-392-0272
Fax: 573-751-6447

Montana

Disability Services Division
111 North Sanders
P.O. Box 4210
Helena, MT 59604-4210
Phone: 406-444-3054 or
406-444-2590 (TDD)
Fax: 406-444-3632

Breast and Cervical Cancer Early
Detection Program
888-803-9343

Women, Infants, and Children (WIC)
Supplemental Nutrition Program
Human Services
Department of Public Health and
Human Services
Cogswell Building
1400 Broadway Avenue
Helena, MT 59620-2951
Phone: 406-444-5533 or 800-433-4298
Fax: 406-444-0239
www.dphhs.state.mt.us/hpsd/index.htm

Title X Family Planning Programs:
800-965-1137

Nebraska

Breast and Cervical Cancer Early
Detection Program
Every Woman Matters
301 Centennial Mall South, 3rd Floor
P.O. Box 94817
Lincoln, NE 69509-4817
Phone: 402-471-0929, 800-532-2227,
or 800-833-7352 (TDD)
Fax: 402-471-0913

Women, Infants, and Children (WIC)
Supplemental Nutrition Program
WIC
Family Health Division
Nebraska Dept. of Health and
Human Services
P.O. Box 95044
301 Centennial Mall South
Lincoln, NE 68509-5044
Phone: 402-471-2781 or 800-942-1171
Fax: 402-471-7049
www.hhs.state.ne.us/nut/Wic01.htm

Nevada

Nevada Rehabilitation Division
Office of Community Based Services
711 South Stewart Street
Carson City, NV 89701
Phone: 775-687-4452

Volunteer Center of Southern Nevada
1660 East Flamingo Street
Las Vegas, NV 89119
Phone: 702-892-2321
Email: volunteernevada@yahoo.com

Breast and Cervical Cancer Early
Detection Program
Women's Health Connection: 888-
463-8942 or 775-684-5936

Women, Infants, and Children (WIC)
Supplemental Nutrition Program
Nevada WIC Program
Health Division
505 East King Street, Room 204
Carson City, NV 89701-4799
Phone: 775-684-5942 or 800-8-NEV-
WIC (800-863-8942)
Fax: 775-684-4246
www.health2k.state.nv.us/wic/index.htm

Early Prenatal Care, Baby Your Baby
Campaign: 800-429-2669

Senior Prescription Program:
800-243-3638

Financial Help for Prenatal Care,
Maternal and Child Health Prenatal
Program: 775-684-4285

Domestic Violence Prevention
Hotline: 800-500-1556

New Hampshire

New Hampshire Developmental
Disabilities Service System
105 Pleasant Street
Concord, NH 03301
Phone: 603-271-5034, 603-271-5166,
800-852-3345 or 800-852-2964 (TDD)
Fax: 800-852-3345

Breast and Cervical Cancer Early
Detection Program
800-852-3345, option 1, extension
4931 or 603-271-4931

Women, Infants and Children (WIC)
Supplemental Nutrition Program
Bureau of WIC Nutrition Services
Officer Community and Public Health
6 Hazen Drive
Concord, NH 03301
Phone: 603-271-4546 or 800-WIC-
4321 (800-9421-4321)
Fax: 603-271-4779
Email: wicprogram@dhhs.state.nh.us

Tobacco Prevention: 603-271-6891 or
800-852-3345, extension 6891

Alcohol and Drug Abuse Prevention
Program: 603-271-6100 or
800-804-0909

Celebrate Wellness: 603-271-6887 or
800-852-3345, extension 6887

New Jersey

Division of Disability Services
Information and Referral Hotline:
888-285-3036 or 609-292-7800

Good Neighbors, Community Living
for People with Disabilities:
877-DHS-Line (877-347-5463)

New Jersey Commission on National
and Community Services, New Jersey
Department of Education
PO Box 500
100 Riverview Plaza
Trenton, NJ 0888625-0500
609-633-9627

Breast and Cervical Cancer Early
Detection Program
800-328-3838

Women, Infants, and Children (WIC)
Supplemental Nutrition Program
New Jersey State WIC Program
Department of Health, CN 364eeee
Trenton, NJ 08625-0364
Phone: 609-292-9560 or 800-328-3838
Fax: 609-292-3580 or 9288
www.state.nj.us/health/fhs/wichome.htm

Child Care Hotline: 800-332-9227

Domestic Violence Hotline:
800-572-7233

Teen Pregnancy Hotline:
800-THE-KIDS (800-843-5437)

New Mexico

Project Succeed: 505-954-8523 or
800-318-1469;
Fax: 505-954-8562

Commission for the Blind:
888-513-7968

Breast and Cervical Cancer
Early Detection Program
877-852-2585

Women, Infants and Children (WIC)
Supplemental Nutrition Program
New Mexico Department of Health,
Family, Food and Nutrition
2040 South Pacheco Street
Santa Fe, NM 87505
Phone: 505-476-8801
Fax: 505-476-8512
www.home.sprynet.com/~jtpierce/wic.htm

Human Services Department: 505-
827-7750 or 800-609-4833 (TDD)

Children, Youth and Family:
505-827-4690

Office of African American Affairs:
866-747-6935 or 505-841-4835; Fax:
505-841-4865

Agency on Aging: 800-432-2080

Veteran Services Commission: 505-
827-6300

New York

New York State Office of Advocate for
Persons with Disabilities
1 Empire State Plaza, Suite 1001
Albany, NY 12223
Phone: 800-522-4369 (Voice, Spanish
and TDD)

New York State Commission on
National and Community Service
Capital View Office Park
52 Washington Street
Rensselaer, NY 12144-2796
Email: volunteernewyork@dfa.state.ny.us

The Retired and Senior Volunteer
Program
www.agingwell.state.ny.us/ccenter/vol-
unteer/rsvp.htm

Breast and Cervical Cancer
Early Detection Program
800-4-CANCER (800-426-6237) or
800-ACS-2345 (800-227-2345)

Women, Infants and Children (WIC)
Supplemental Nutrition Program
Bureau of Supplemental Food
Programs Division of Nutrition
New York State Department of Health
150 Broadway, Floor 6
West Albany, NY 12204-2719
Phone: 518-402-7093 or 800-522-5006
Fax: 518-402-7348
Email: NYSWIC@health.state.ny.us

Ovarian Cancer Information:
800-682-7426

Smoker's Quitline: 888-609-6292

North Carolina

Council on Development Disabilities
1001 Navaho Drive, Suite GL-103
Raleigh, NC 27609
Phone: 919-850-2833
Fax: 919-850-2895
www.nc.ddc.org

North Carolina Commission on
Volunteerism and Community Service
Office of the Governor
0312 Mail Service Center
116 West Jones Street
Governor's Administrative Bldg
Raleigh, NC 27560
Phone: 919-715-3470 or
800-820-4483
Fax: 919-715-8677
Email: volcommission@ncmail.net

Breast and Cervical Cancer Early
Detection Program
800-4-CANCER (800-426-6237) or
919-715-0111

Women, Infants and Children (WIC)
Supplemental Nutrition Program
Nutrition Services Branch
North Carolina Division
of Public Health
Department of Health
and Human Services
1914 Mail Service Center
Raleigh, NC 27699-1914
www.nutritionc.com/wic/
Phone: 919-733-2973 or 800-FOR
BABY (800-367-2229)
Fax: 919-733-1384

CARE-LINE, Health Information &
Referrals: 919-733-4261, 800-662-
7030 (English and Spanish),
919-733-4851 (TDD), or
877-452-2514 (TDD)

North Dakota

North Dakota Association
for the Disabled
1913 South Washington Street
Grand Folks, ND 58201
Phone: 800-532-NDAD
(800-532-6323)
www.ndad.org

Breast and Cervical Cancer Early
Detection Program
Women's Way: 800-44- WOMEN
(800-449-6636) or 701- 328-2333

Women, Infants and Children (WIC)
Supplemental Nutrition Program
WIC
Maternal and Child Health
North Dakota State
Department of Health
600 East Boulevard Avenue

Bismarck, ND 58505-0200
Phone: 701-328-2493 or 800-472-2286
Fax: 701-328-1412
www.health.stats.nd.us/ndhd/pre-
vent/mch/wic

Maternal and Child Health:
800-472-2286

Northern Mariana Islands, Commonwealth of

Northern Marianas Protection and
Advocacy System
P.O. Box 3529 C.K.
MP 96950
Phone: 670-235-7274 or 7273
Fax: 670-235-7275

Commonwealth Health Center
Lower Navy Hill, Garapan
(Middle Road)
Saipan, MP 96950
Phone: 670-234-8950
Fax: 670-236-8600

Ohio

FirstLink: 614-221-2255 or
614-341-2272 (TDD)
www.firstlink.org

Breast and Cervical Cancer Early
Detection Program
For local programs call:
Cancer Information Service:
800-4-CANCER (800-422-6237)

Ohio Department of Health
Health Promotion
and Risk Reduction
Breast and Cervical Cancer Project
246 North High Street
P.O. Box 118
Columbus, OH 43216-0118
Phone: 614-644-8700
Fax: 614-644-7740

263

Women, Infants and Children (WIC)
Supplemental Nutrition Program
Bureau of Women,
Infants and Children
Ohio Department of Health
246 North High Street
P.O. Box 118
Columbus, OH 43216-0118
Phone: 614-644-8006 or
800-755-GROW
Fax: 614-728-2881

Ohio Women's Information Line:
800-282-3040

Aging: 800-728-1206

Office of Women's Health Initiatives:
614-644-1105
www.odh.state.oh.us/ODHPrograms/
WOM_IMI/wom_ini1htm

Oklahoma

Oklahoma ABLE: 800-257-1705 or
888-885-5588 (TDD)

Oklahoma Department of Human
Services, Developmental Disabilities
Services Division: 405-521-6267

Aging Services: 405-521-2327 (for
volunteer opportunities with the
aging)

Breast and Cervical Cancer Early
Detection Program
Take Charge!: 888-669-5934

Breast and Cervical Cancer Program,
Kaw Nation of Oklahoma:
580-362-1039

Cherokee Nation of Oklahoma:
918-458-4491

Women, Infants and Children (WIC)
Supplemental Nutrition Program
Oklahoma State Department
of Health
WIC Services
2520 Villa Prom Street
Oklahoma City, OK 73107-2419
Phone: 405-271-4676 or
888-655-2942
Fax: 405-271-5763
www.health.state.ok.us/program/wic

Aging Services: 800-211-2116
Fax: 405-521-2086

Family Support Services:
866-411-1877 or 405-521-3076

Oregon

Breast and Cervical Cancer Early
Detection Program
503-731-4273

Women, Infants and Children (WIC)
Supplemental Nutrition Program
Oregon WIC Program
Oregon Health Division, Suite 865
800 Northeast Oregon Street
Portland, OR 97232-2162
Phone: 503-731-4022 or 800-
SAFENET (TDD) (800-723-3638)
Fax: 503-731-3477
www.ohd.hr.state.or.us/wic/welcome.htm

Oregon Health Services
800 Northeast Oregon Street, #825
Portland, OR 97232

Palau, Republic of

Palau Interagency Project:
680-488-4804 or 680-488-1757

Breast and Cervical Cancer
Early Detection Program
680-488-2552

Family Planning Hotline:
680-488-1756

Pennsylvania

Breast and Cervical
Early Detection Program
HealthyWoman Project:
717-783-1457

Women, Infants and Children (WIC)
Supplemental Nutrition Program
Pennsylvania Department of Health
Division of WIC
Health and Welfare Building, Room 604
P.O. Box 90
Harrisburg, PA 17108-0090
Phone: 717-783-1289 or 800-
WICWINS (800-942-9467)
Fax: 717-705-0462
www.health.state.pa.us/php/wic

Puerto Rico

Programa de Assistencia Médica
787-250-7429 or 787-765-1230

Breast and Cervical Cancer
Early Detection Program
787-274-6861 or 787-274-5640

Women, Infants and Children (WIC)
Supplemental Nutrition Program
WIC Program
Puerto Rico Department of Health
Pinero Hato Rey
198 Calle Trinidad
P.O. Box 25220
San Juan, PR 00928
Phone: 787-766-2805
Fax: 787-763-1444

Proyecto Especial de Violencia
Doméstica
P.O. Box 194735

San Juan, PR 00919-4735
Teléfono: 787-764-0524
Facsîmil: 787-764-0524

Rhode Island

Governor's Commission on Disabilities
401 Cherrydale Court
Cranston, RI 02920
Phone: 401-462-0100
Email: disabilities@gcd.state.ri.us

Volunteer Center of Rhode Island
55 Brandford Street, Suite 302
Providence, RI 02903
Phone: 401-421-6547

Incarcerated Women Resource
Women in Transition, Inc.
Pinel Building
B28 Wilma Schesler Lane
Cranston, RI 02920
Phone: 401-462-1767
Email: womentransition@msn.com

Breast and Cervical Cancer Early
Detection Program
Women's Cancer Screening Program:
401-222-4324

Women, Infants and Children (WIC)
Supplemental Nutrition Program
WIC Program
Department of Health
Cannon Building
3 Capitol Hill, Room 302
Providence, RI 02908-5097
Phone: 401-222-1442, 800-942-7434,
or 800-745-5555 (TDD)
Fax: 401-222-1442
www.health.state.ri.us

Health for her: 800-942-7434

Domestic Violence Hotline:
800-494-8100

Rhode Island Commission on
Women: 800-494-8100

South Carolina

South Carolina Department of
Disabilities and Special Needs
Phone: 803-898-9600 (Voice and TTY)
or 888-DSN-INFO (888-376-4636)
Fax: 803-898-9653

Breast and Cervical Cancer Early
Detection Program
803-896-0000

Women, Infants and Children (WIC)
Supplemental Nutrition Program
Division of Preventive and
Personal Health
South Carolina Dept. of Health
and Environmental Control
Mills/Jarrett Complex
P.O. Box 101106
1751 Calhoun Street
Columbia, SC 29201-2911
Phone: 803-898-0743 or
800-868-0404
Fax: 803-898-0383
www.scdhec.net/hs/mch/wic/index.htm

Department of Health and Human
Services: 803-898-2500

South Dakota

Department of Human Services
C/o 500 East Capitol
East Highway 34
Hillsview Plaza
Pierre, SD 57501
Phone: 605-773-5483
Fax: 605-773-5483

Breast and Cervical Cancer Early
Detection Program
All Women Count!: 800-738-2301

Women, Infants and Children (WIC)
Supplemental Nutrition Program
Nutrition Services
Division of Health Services
South Dakota Department of Health
615 East 4th Capitol
Pierre, SD 57501-5070
Phone: 605-773-3737 or
800-738-2301
Fax: 605-773-5509
www.state.sd.us/doh/Famhlth/wic.htm

All Women Count!: WISEWOMAN
Chronic Disease Screening Program:
605-773-3622 or 800-738-2301

Family Planning Program:
800-738-2301

Bright Start: 800-305-3064

South Dakota Domestic Abuse
Hotline: 800-430-SAFE
(800-430-7233)

McKennan Hospital Statewide Suicide
Hotline: 800-691-4336

Tennessee

Tennessee Disabilities Information
and Referral Office: 800-640-INFO
(800-640-4636)

Volunteer Tennessee:
www.volunteertennessee.org

Breast and Cervical Cancer Early
Detection Program
Tennessee Department of Health
Cordell Hull Building, Fourth Floor
425 Fifth Avenue,
North Nashville, TN 37247
Phone: 877-969-6636

Women, Infants and Children (WIC)
Supplemental Nutrition Program

Supplemental Food Programs
Nutrition Services Section
Tennessee Department of Health
Cordell Hull Building, 5th Floor
435 Fifth Avenue, North Nashville,
TN 37247-4501
Phone: 615-741-7218 or 800-DIAL-
WIC (800-342-5942)
Fax: 615-532-7189
www.state.tn.us/health/wic/index.htm

BABY Line: 800-428-2229

Parenting & Domestic Violence
Help Line: 800-356-6767

Child Care Resource & Referral
Hotline: 800-462-8261

Osteoporosis Hotline:
888-734-BONE

HIV/AIDS Hotline: 800-525-AIDS

Texas

Breast and Cervical Cancer
Early Detection Program
800-452-1955 or 512-458-7644

Women, Infants and Children (WIC)
Supplemental Nutrition Program
Bureau of Nutrition Services Texas
Department of Health
1100 West 49th Street
Austin, TX 78756-3199
Phone: 512-458-7444 or 800-WIC-
FOR-U (800-942-3678)
Fax: 512-458-7446
www.tdh.state.tx.us/wichd

Domestic Violence Hotline:
800-799-7233

Family Health Information and
Referral Hotline: 800-422-2956

Bureau of Women's Health:
www.tdh.state.tx.us/women

Utah

Children with Disabilities:
health.utah.gov/cfhs/cshcn/index.html

Breast and Cervical Cancer Early
Detection Warning
Division of Family Health Services
Utah State Department of Health
288 North 1460 West
P.O. Box 141013
Salt Lake City, UT 84114-1013
Phone: 801-538-6960 or 877-WIC-
KIDS (877-942-5437)
Fax: 801-538-6729
www.health.utah.gov/wic

Cardiovascular Program
P.O. Box 142107
Salt Lake City, UT 84114-6142

Division of Community
and Family Health Services
288 North 1460 West
P.O. Box 142107
Salt Lake City, UT 84114-2107
Phone: 801-538-6261 or
888-222-2542
Fax: 801-538-9495

Utah Diabetes Control Program:
801-538-6141; 801-538-9495 (Fax)

Substance Abuse Prevention Center:
www.hsdsa.utah.gov/Prevent_Provider
s.htm

Vermont

Disability Determination Services:
802-864-2463

Make A Wish Foundation of
Vermont: 802-864-9393

Breast and Cervical Cancer
Early Detection Program
Ladies First: 802-865-7758 or
800-508-2222

Women, Infants and Children (WIC)
Supplemental Nutrition Program
Vermont WIC Program
Division of Community Public
Health
Department of Health
P.O. Box 70
108 Cherry Street
Burlington, VT 05402-0070
Phone: 802-863-7333 or 800-464-
4343, extension 7333
Fax: 802-863-7229
www.healthyvermonters.info/cph/nutr
ition/wic.shtml

AIDS Hotline: 802-863-7245 or 800-
882-AIDS (800-882-2437)

Smoker's Toll-Free Quit Line: 877-
YES-QUIT (877-937-7848)

Poison Hotline: 800-222-1222

Healthy Babies, Kids and Families:
800-649-HELP (00-649-4357)

Virginia

Virginia Board for People with
Disabilities
202 North 9th Street, 9th Floor
Richmond, VA 23219
Phone: 800-846-4464 (Voice & TDD)

Breast and Cervical Cancer Early
Detection Program
800-ACS-2345 (800-227-2345)
or 804-786-5916

Women, Infants and Children (WIC)
Supplemental Nutrition Program
Division of Chronic Disease

Prevention and Nutrition
Department of Health
1500 East Main Street, Room 132
Richmond, VA 23219
Phone: 804-786-5420, 888-WIC-
FOOD (888-942-3663), or
800-828-1120 (TDD)
Fax: 804-371-6162
www.vahealth.org/wic

Comprehensive Family Services:
800-468-8894

Virgin Islands

Virgin Islands Advocacy Agency
74 Whim Street, Suite 2
Frederiksted, VI 00840
Phone: 340-772-1200, 340-776-4303,
or 340-772-4641 (TDD)

Breast and Cervical Cancer Early
Detection Program
Ever Woman at Heart: 800-ACS-2345
(800-227-2345), 340-773-2676, or
340-774-9000

Women, Infants and Children (WIC)
Supplemental Nutrition Program
Virgin Islands WIC Program
Department of Health
Charles Harwood Complex
3500 Estate Richmond
Christiansted, VI 99821
Phone: 340-773-9157 (St. Croix)
Fax: 340-773-6495 (St. Croix), 340-
774-5820 (St. Thomas)

Special Health Care Needs Program,
Department of Health, Maternal and
Child Health: 809-773-1311

Washington

Division of Vocational Rehabilitation
State Office/Lacey
P.O. Box 45340

Olympia, WA 98504
Phone: 800-637-5627

Breast and Cervical Cancer Early
Detection Program
888-438-2247

Women, Infants and Children (WIC)
Supplemental Nutrition Program
WIC Program
Office Community Wellness and
Prevention
P.O. Box 47886
Olympia, WA 98504-7886
Phone: 360-236-3688, 800-841-1410,
or 800-833-6388 (TDD)
Fax: 3600-586-3890

Healthy Mothers, Healthy Babies:
800-322-2588

Tobacco Quitline: 877-270-7867

Family Planning Hotline: 800-770-4334

West Virginia

State Developmental Disabilities
Council
110 Stockton Street
Charleston, WV 25312
Phone: 304-558-2376

Breast and Cervical Cancer Early
Detection Program
800-642-8522 or 800-422-6237

Women, Infants and Children (WIC)
Supplemental Nutrition Program
West Virginia WIC Program
350 Capitol Street, Room 519
Charleston, WV 25301-3717
Phone: 304-558-0030 or 888-WV-
FAMILY (888-983-2645)
Fax: 304-558-1541
www.wvdhhr.org/ons

West Virginia Office of Maternal,
Child and Family Health: 800-642-8522

West Virginia Women's Commission:
304-558-0070

West Virginia Coalition Against
Domestic Violence: 304-965-3552

West Virginia Family Planning
Program: 800-642-8522

Wisconsin

Wisconsin Council on
Developmental Disabilities
600 Williamson Street,
P.O. Box 7851
Madison, WI 53701-7851
Phone: 608-266-7826

www.wcdd.org
Breast and Cervical Cancer
Early Detection Program
Women's Health Hotline: 800-218-8408

Women, Infants and Children (WIC)
Supplemental Nutrition Program
Wisconsin WIC Program
Wisconsin Department of Health
and Family Services
1 West Wilson Street, P.O. Box 2659
Phone: 608-266-9824 or 800-722-2295
Fax: 608-266-3125

www.dhfs.state.wi.us/wic
Wisconsin Women's Health Hotline:
800-218-8408

BadgerCare: 800-362-3002
(TTY and translation services available)

Wyoming

Developmental Disabilities Division
122 West 25th Street
Cheyenne, WY 82002
Phone: 307-777-7115

Wyoming Commission for National
and Community Service: 307-777-6006

Women, Infants and Children (WIC)
Supplemental Nutrition Program
WIC Program
Division of Public Health
Department of Health
456 Hathaway Building
Cheyenne, WY 82002-0050
Phone: 307-777-7494 or 800-994-4769
Fax: 307-777-5643
wdhfs.state.wy.us/WDH/wic.htm

Maternal and Child Health
4020 House Avenue
Cheyenne, WY 82002
Phone: 307-777-6921

Diabetes Control Program: 307-777-3579

Appendix C

ONLINE RESOURCES FOR WOMEN

Faith
www.womenoffaith.com/
www.lifeway.com
www.askmoses.com
www.faithstreams.com
www.faith.com
www.catholic.org
www.crosswalk.com
www.islam101.com
www.islam.com
www.religioustolerance.org

Arts
www.nmwa.org
www.womanarts.org
www.womensstudiocenter.org

Misc.
www.africancraft.com
African American Web Ring
www.halcon.com/halcon/1ring.html
National Women's Health Information Center
http://www.4women.gov/pub/steps

Grants
www.thewritersplace.com/writestuff/
www.ssisters.org (sisters supporting sisters, Inc.)

Women
www.mydaughterskeeper.org/pages
www.sistapower.com/
www.sisterfriends.com/
www.sistasearch.com/
www.blackwomeninc.com/
www.members.aol.com/aawon1/welcome

Women's Health
www.blackwomenshealth.com/
www.healthquestmag.com/healthq/default.asp?
www.nwmaf.org

Life's Spices from Seasoned Sistahs:
A Collection of Life Stories from Mature Women of Color

ORDER FOR YOUR FAMILY AND FRIENDS!

ITEM	PRICE	SHIPPING	TOTAL
Seasoned Sistahs Books	$14.95	$3.85	$18.80
Seasoned Sistahs T-Shirts	$14.95	$2.00	$16.95
Seasoned Sistahs Full-Color Posters	$14.95	$2.00	$16.95

Send this form and your check or money order, plus shipping charges payable to:
[T-Shirt Sizes: SMALL to XXXL. Shipping for each additional item $1.00]

Nubian Images Publishing
P.O. Box 1332
El Cerrito, California 94530
www.nubianimagespublishing.com

Subtotal _____

8.5% tax (CA delivery only) _____

Foreign Delivery
add to regular shipping charge _____

TOTAL amount _____

ITEM	QUANTITY	DESCRIPTION	SIZE/COLOR	PRICE	TOTAL

Please print your billing address:

First name _____ Middle initial _____ Last name _____

Street address _____ Apt or suite _____

City _____ State _____ Zip code _____

E-mail address _____

If different from above, please ship to:

First name _____ Middle initial _____ Last name _____

Street address _____ Apt. or suite _____

City _____ State _____ Zip code _____

ONLINE: Log on to order@nubianimagespublishing.com *Please allow 5-7 days for delivery.*
❑ Check here to receive a press kit. Consider having the editor, Vicki Ward, as a speaker or workshop presenter at your next event. Contact her at: *www.nubianimagespublishing.com*

Life's Spices from Seasoned Sistahs:
A Collection of Life Stories from Mature Women of Color

ORDER FOR YOUR FAMILY AND FRIENDS!

ITEM	PRICE	SHIPPING	TOTAL
Seasoned Sistahs Books	$14.95	$3.85	$18.80
Seasoned Sistahs T-Shirts	$14.95	$2.00	$16.95
Seasoned Sistahs Full-Color Posters	$14.95	$2.00	$16.95

Send this form and your check or money order, plus shipping charges payable to:
[T-Shirt Sizes: SMALL to XXXL. Shipping for each additional item $1.00]

Nubian Images Publishing
P.O. Box 1332
El Cerrito, California 94530
www.nubianimagespublishing.com

Subtotal _____

8.5% tax (CA delivery only) _____

Foreign Delivery
add to regular shipping charge _____

TOTAL amount _____

ITEM	QUANTITY	DESCRIPTION	SIZE/COLOR	PRICE	TOTAL

Please print your billing address:

First name _____ Middle initial _____ Last name _____

Street address _____ Apt or suite _____

City _____ State _____ Zip code _____

E-mail address _____

If different from above, please ship to:

First name _____ Middle initial _____ Last name _____

Street address _____ Apt. or suite _____

City _____ State _____ Zip code _____

ONLINE: Log on to order@nubianimagespublishing.com *Please allow 5-7 days for delivery.*
❑ Check here to receive a press kit. Consider having the editor, Vicki Ward, as a speaker or workshop presenter at your next event. Contact her at: *www.nubianimagespublishing.com*